How Economists Model the World into Numbers

The practice of economic science is dominated by model building. In order to comprehend economic practices, it is important to understand how models function in economic research. This book examines the reliability of mathematical models and how they are applied to empirical research, particularly those used in macroeconomics and econometrics.

By exploring a variety of economic research practices and studying the solutions offered by prominent economists including Irving Fisher, Milton Friedman, Trygve Haavelmo, Robert Lucas and Jan Tinbergen, this book allows the reader to gain a greater understanding of what economists achieve by building models.

This informative book will be essential for students and researchers of economic methodology and the philosophy and history of science.

Marcel Boumans is Associate Professor of Philosophy and History of Economics at the University of Amsterdam.

Routledge INEM Advances in Economic Methodology
Series Edited by D. Wade Hands
Professor of Economics, University of Puget Sound, Tacoma, USA

The field of economic methodology has expanded rapidly during the last few decades. This expansion has occurred in part because of changes within the discipline of economics, in part because of changes in the prevailing philosophical conception of scientific knowledge, and also because of various transformations within the wider society. Research in economic methodology now reflects not only the developments in contemporary economic theory, the history of economic thought, and the philosophy of science, but it also reflects developments in science studies, historical epistemology, and social theorising more generally. The field of economic methodology still includes the search for rules for the proper conduct of economic science, but it also covers a vast array of other subjects and accommodates a variety of different approaches to those subjects.

The objective of this series is to provide a forum for the publication of significant works in the growing field of economic methodology. Since the series defines methodology quite broadly, it will publish books on a wide range of different methodological subjects. The series is also open to a variety of different types of works: original research monographs, edited collections, as well as republication of significant earlier contributions to the methodological literature. The International Network for Economic Methodology (INEM) is proud to sponsor this important series of contributions to the methodological literature.

How Economists Model the World into Numbers

Marcel Boumans

Taylor & Francis Group

LONDON AND NEW YORK

First published 2005
by Routledge
2 Park Square, Milton Park, Abingdon, Oxon OX14 4RN

Simultaneously published in the USA and Canada
by Routledge
270 Madison Ave, New York, NY 10016

Routledge is an imprint of the Taylor & Francis Group

© 2005 Marcel Boumans

Typeset in Times by
HWA Text and Data Management, Tunbridge Wells
Printed and bound in Great Britain by
Antony Rowe Ltd, Chippenham, Wiltshire

British Library Cataloguing in Publication Data
A catalogue record for this book is available from the British Library

Library of Congress Cataloging in Publication Data
Boumans, Marcel.
   How economists model the world into numbers / Marcel Boumans.
      p.   cm.
   Includes bibliographical references and indexes.
  1. Economics, Mathematical. 2. Economics–Mathematical models.
3. Econometrics. 4. Economics–Methodology–History–20th century.
5. Economics, Mathematical–History–20th century. I. Title

   HB135.B68 2005
   330′.01′5195–dc22   2004012725

ISBN 0–415–34621–5

To Emma, Fien and Nathan

Contents

Illustrations

Figures

Tables

Acknowledgements

This book is the result of working for many years with the members of the Amsterdam Research Group in History and Methodology of Economics. The Amsterdam Research Group was successfully linked to research projects at the Centre for Philosophy of Natural and Social Science of the London School of Economics and Political Science. The first project, from 1993 to 1996, was on modelling in physics and economics and was directed by Nancy Cartwright, Mary Morgan and Margaret Morrison. I am very grateful to all three for the encouraging support they gave to my work on modelling and measurement. The second research project, 'Measurement in Physics and Economics', launched in 1996 and concluded in 2001, was directed at the LSE by Nancy Cartwright, Hasok Chang, Carl Hoefer and Mary Morgan. Their ideas on measurement were very helpful and influential in shaping mine. Both projects at the Amsterdam Research Group were inspiringly and successfully led by Mary Morgan. I am very privileged to have worked closely with her for all these years. I would particularly like to thank Harro Maas. What a luxury to have a colleague with whom you can discuss ideas on a daily basis. The material in this book was gathered and explored in the period in which Neil de Marchi, Mary Morgan and Mark Blaug consecutively chaired the Amsterdam Research Group. My thanks to Neil for giving me a start in the right direction, to Mary for helping me on the bumpy road, and to Mark for making me worldly wise. And there are, of course, my other former and current Amsterdam colleagues with whom it always was and is a pleasure to work: Hsiang-Ke Chao, Joshua Cohen, Arnold Heertje, Edith Kuiper, Geert Reuten, Peter Rodenburg, Adrienne van den Bogaard and Robert Went. I am also grateful to the members of the LSE research groups who made every visit to the Centre a stimulating and fruitful experience: Marco Del Seta, Philip Epstein, Francesco Guala, Makiko Ito, Sabina Leonelli, Julian Reiss, Mauricio Suárez and Sang Wook Yi. I benefited a lot from the contributions of scholars who were involved in one or both projects: Bert Balk, Frank den Butter, C.K. Folkertsma, Stephan Hartmann, R.I.G. Hughes, Jan Magnus, Freeke Mulder, Bernard van Praag, Jan van Tongeren, Roy Weintraub and Mike Williams. I would especially like to thank Kevin Hoover who has always been a great support to my research and who helped me a lot in improving the arguments of this book.

The book itself was compiled in the year 2001–2 when I was a fellow at the Netherlands Institute for Advanced Study in the Humanities and Social Sciences. This institute provided all the necessary ingredients to finish a manuscript: the company of experts in fields ranging from Biography to Theoretical Sociology, efficient facilities and the peaceful environment of the Wassenaar dunes. In particular, I would like to thank Petry Kievit-Tyson. She not only corrected my English but also forced me to express my sometimes-vague ideas more clearly and explicitly.

I thank the following societies and publishers for their permission to reprint diagrams and other materials used in this book: Cambridge University Press for Figure 1.1 (Figure 4.1 on p. 69 of M.S. Morgan and M. Morrison (eds) (1999), *Models as Mediators*); MIT Press Journal for Figure 2.2 (Figure 'Bimonthly averages of cycles of groups A, B, and C' on p. 112 of W.M. Persons, 'An index of general business conditions', *The Review of Economic Statistics*, 1:2 (April 1919), pp. 111–205); Institute of Measurement and Control for Figure 5.2 (Figure 1 'Diagrammatic representation of the set-theoretical definition of measurement' on p. 105 (T17) of L. Finkelstein, 'Fundamental concepts of measurement: definitions and scales', *Measurement and Control*, 8, pp. 105–10); The American Physiological Society for Figure 6.2 (Figure 22 on p. 430 of I. Fisher, 'A new method for indicating food values', *American Journal of Physiology*, 15 (1906), pp. 417–32). I also thank the grandson of Irving Fisher, George W. Fisher, Professor of Geology at Johns Hopkins University for permission to reprint Figure 6.1 (Figure showing triangles in three different spaces on p. 527 of A.W. Phillips and I. Fisher (1896) *Elements of Geometry*, New York: American Book Company), Figure 6.3 (Figure 2 on p. 21 and Figure 3 on p. 22 of I. Fisher [1911] (1963) *The Purchasing Power of Money*, 2nd rev. edn, New York: Kelley), Figure 6.4 (Chart 52 on p. 286 of I. Fisher [1922] (1967) *The Making of Index Numbers*, 3rd rev. edn, New York: Kelley) and Figure 6.5 (Figure 4 and Figure 5 on p. 10 of I. Fisher and O.M. Miller (1944) *World Maps and Globes*, New York: Essential Books).

The author acknowledges permission to use previously published material in this monograph:

Chapter 1. Parts from M. Boumans, 'Built-in Justification', in M.S. Morgan and M. Morrison (eds), *Models as Mediators*, 1999, Cambridge University Press.

Chapter 4. Parts from M. Boumans, 'Lucas and Artificial Worlds', in *History of Political Economy*, 1997 annual supplement to Volume 29, 'New Economics and Its History', ed. J.B. Davis, 1998, 63–88. Parts from M. Boumans, 'A Macroeconomic Approach to Complexity', in A. Zellner, H.A. Keuzenkamp, M. McAleer (eds), *Simplicity, Inference and Modelling, Keeping it Sophisticatedly Simple*, 2002, Cambridge University Press. Parts from M. Boumans, 'How to Design Galilean Fall Experiments in Economics', *Philosophy of Science* 70 (2003): 308–29, published by University of Chicago Press. © 2003 by the Philosophy of Science Association. All rights reserved.

Chapter 5. Parts from M. Boumans, 'Representation and Stability in Testing and Measuring Rational Expectations', *The Journal of Economic Methodology* 6.3 (1999): 381–401, http://www.tandf.co.uk. Parts from M. Boumans, 'Calibration of Models in Experiments', in L. Magnani and N.J. Nersessian (eds) *Model-Based Reasoning; Science, Technology, Values*, 2002, 75–93.

Chapter 6. From M. Boumans, 'Fisher's Instrumental Approach to Index Numbers', in *History of Political Economy*, 2001 annual supplement to Volume 33, 'The Age of Economic Measurement', eds J.L. Klein and M.S. Morgan, 2001, 313–44.

1 Introduction

Only a further development of the engineering skill of econometrics will help in this respect.

(Tinbergen [1936] 1959: 84)

But technique is interesting to technicians (which is what we are, if we are to be of any use to anyone)

(Lucas 1987a: 35)

A separate methodology of models

The practice of economic science is dominated by model building. Therefore, to understand economic practice we must try to apprehend how models function in economic research. The kinds of models discussed in this monograph are the mathematical models built and applied in empirical economic research, particularly in macroeconomics and econometrics. These models are meant as quantitative representations of our world. Their function is to generate numbers to inform us about economic aspects of the world. The central problem of this monograph is the assessment of the reliability of these bodies of knowledge.

In modern economics, it is taken for granted that quantitative expressions of our world are useful and that mathematical representations constitute – even better – knowledge about economic phenomena. This latter belief was explicitly voiced by Irving Fisher (1867–1947), one of the founders of modern economics:

The effort of the economist is to *see*, to picture the interplay of economic elements. The more clearly cut these elements appear in his vision, the better; the more elements he can grasp and hold in mind at once, the better. The economic world is a misty region. The first explorers used unaided vision. Mathematics is the lantern by which what before was dimly visible now looms up in firm, bold outlines. The old phantasmagoria disappear. We see better. We see also further.

(Fisher [1892] 1925: 119)

This statement was made in the very last section of Fisher's PhD thesis *Mathematical Investigations in the Theory of Value and Prices*, written in the last decade of the nineteenth century. When Fisher wrote his PhD, the belief that economic phenomena could be better understood through mathematics was not widely held. His work marked the beginning of a new era in which, bit by bit, economics became mathematicised. This process of mathematisation took not place by means of translating verbally expressed theories, one by one, into mathematical language, but through the emergence of a new practice of economic research characterised by mathematical modelling.[1]

To understand their specific function in economic research, models should be distinguished from economic theories. As will be shown, they are not theories about the world but instruments through which we can see the world and so gain some understanding of it. As mathematical representations, models should also be distinguished from pure formal objects. They should be seen, as the quote above says, as 'lanterns', as devices that help us to see the phenomena more clearly. Models are the economist's instruments of investigation, just as the microscope and the telescope are tools of the biologist and the astronomer. In a textbook on optical instruments, we find the following description that can easily be projected on models:

> The primary function of a lens or lens system will usually be that of making a pictorial representation or record of some object or other, and this record will usually be much more suitable for the purpose for which it is required than the original object.
>
> (Bracey 1960: 15)

In the same way, models can be used to function as instruments to perform a particular kind of observation, namely measurement. Measurement is a specific kind of observation; it generates a numerical representation of the phenomenon under investigation, which is often the kind of information needed for the purpose of policy deliberations.

Although mathematical models are not material, they are used as though they are physical instruments. Therefore, standard economic methodology, traditionally focused on theories, is not suitable.[2] Standard accounts define models in terms of their logical or semantic connections with theories,[3] and methodology is traditionally seen as a way to appraise theories. Instruments (models) are not theories and therefore should be assessed differently. A methodology needs to be developed that is able to assess how mathematical models function. The aim of this monograph is to construct and refine such a methodology. To do this we investigate a variety of economic research practices in the twentieth century, an epoch that has seen the emergence of macroeconomics, econometrics, and the combination, macro-econometrics. In this way, we hope to gain better understanding of what economists achieve by building models and applying these instruments.

We elaborate on Margaret Morrison and Mary S. Morgan's (1999) account of models. According to their account, models must be considered as one of the critical instruments of modern science. Morrison and Morgan demonstrated that models function as instruments of investigation helping us to learn more about theories and the real world, because they are autonomous agents: that is to say, they are partially independent of both theories and the real world. We can learn from models because they can represent either some aspect of the world, or some aspect of a theory. The intended elaboration is limited to empirical models, that is, those models that inform us about the world.

Despite the fact that models function as physical instruments in economics, they cannot be assessed as such. One usually associates the word instrument with a physical device, such as a thermometer, microscope or telescope. However, the instruments of economics – models – are not material objects, they are mathematical objects. The absence of materiality means that the physical methods used to test material instruments, such as control and insulation, cannot be applied to models.[4] This means that we cannot easily borrow from the philosophy of technology, which is geared to physical objects. Models, being 'quasi-material' objects belonging to a world in between the immaterial world of theoretical ideas and the material world of physical objects, require an alternative methodology.

In several accounts of what models are and how they function, a specific view dominates. This view contains the following characteristics. Firstly, there is a clear-cut distinction between theories, models and data, and secondly, empirical assessment takes place after the model is built. In other words, the contexts of discovery and justification are disconnected. An exemplary account can be found in Hausman's *The Inexact and Separate Science of Economics* (1992). In his view, models are definitions of kinds of systems, and they make no empirical claims. Although he pays special attention to the practice of working with a model – i.e. conceptual exploration – he claims that even then no empirical assessment takes place. 'Insofar as one is only working with a model, one's efforts are purely conceptual or mathematical. One is only developing a complicated concept or definition' (Hausman 1992: 79). In Hausman's view, only theories make empirical claims and can be tested. Above that, he doesn't make clear where models, concepts and definitions come from. Even in Morgan's account 'Finding a satisfactory empirical model' (1988), which comes closest to mine and will be dealt with below, she mentions a 'fund' of empirical models of which the most satisfactory model can be selected.

This view in which discovery and justification are disconnected is not in accordance with several practices of mathematical model building. What these practices show is that models have to meet implicit criteria of adequacy, such as satisfying theoretical, mathematical and statistical requirements, and be useful for policy. So in order to be adequate, models have to integrate enough items to satisfy such criteria. These items include besides theoretical notions, policy views, mathematical concepts and techniques, analogies and metaphors and also empirical data and facts. So, the point of departure for a methodology of models is that the context of discovery is the successful integration of those items that satisfy the criteria of adequacy. Because certain items are empirical data and facts, justification can be built in.

The process of model building

Models are built by fitting together elements from disparate sources. To clarify the integration process, it is very helpful to compare model building with baking a cake without having a recipe. If you want to bake a cake and you do not have a recipe, how do you take the matter up? Of course you do not start blank, you have some knowledge about, for example, preparing pancakes and you know the main ingredients: flour, butter, raising agent and sugar. You also know what a cake should look like and how it should taste. You start a trial-and-error process till the result is what you would like to call a cake: the colour and taste are satisfactory.

Model building is like baking a cake without a recipe. A comparable view is expressed by Clive Granger on model building in his study, *Empirical Modeling in Economics*:

> I think of a modeler as starting with some disparate pieces – some wood, a few bricks, some nails, and so forth – and attempting to build an object for which he (or she) has only a very inadequate plan, or theory. The modeler can look at related constructs and can use institutional information and will eventually arrive at an approximation of the object that they are trying to represent, perhaps after several attempts.
>
> (Granger 1999: 6–7)

Others (e.g. Stehling 1993) compared model building with 'basteln' – tinkering – to denote the 'art' of model building. The reason that I prefer the analogy of baking is that one of its characteristics is that in the end product you can no longer distinguish the separate ingredients; they become blended and homogeneous.

In a model, the ingredients are theoretical ideas, policy views, mathematical concepts and techniques, metaphors and analogies, stylised facts and empirical data. Integration takes place by translating the ingredients into a mathematical form and merging them into one framework. This idea of mathematics as homogeniser and harmoniser can be clarified by enlarging on the metaphor Morrison and Morgan (1999) use for the function of models, namely as mediator. The mathematical forms that are entered in a model are the result of painstaking negotiations. One could see it as a meeting at which various parties need to come to an agreement. They have little in common and are characterised more by their differences than their similarities, so they are highly suspicious of each other. An impartial mediator is needed to bring the parties involved closer together, step by step, carefully formalising each result in the negotiations. The development and selection of appropriate formulations is part and parcel of the process and it cannot be determined beforehand.

To help elucidate the role of mathematics in modelling, let us take a closer look at how models are built. We are going to look first at two cases of model building. The first case is a business-cycle model, which is considered to be the first mathematical business-cycle model in the history of economics.[5] The second case is one of the rare exemplars of a material model in economics, namely Phillips' hydraulic machine (discussed in Morgan and Boumans, 2004).

Case 1: Kalecki's business-cycle model

Michal Kalecki's (1899–1970) mathematical business-cycle model first appeared as 'Proba teorii koniunktury' in 1933.[6] This Polish essay was read in French as 'Essai d'une théorie des mouvements cycliques construite à l'aide de la mathématique supérieure' at the Econometric Society in Leiden in 1933. Its essential part was translated into English as 'Macrodynamic theory of business cycles', and was published in *Econometrica* in 1935. A less mathematical French version was published in *Revue d'Economique Politique*, also in 1935. The English paper was discussed in Tinbergen's survey of quantitative business-cycle theories (1935b), appearing in the same issue of *Econometrica*. The model ingredients are summarised in Figure 1.1.

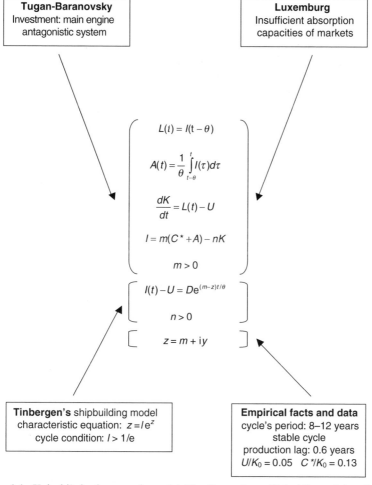

Figure 1.1 Kalecki's business-cycle model. The figure shows Kalecki's model as the integration of different ingredients.

The model

Kalecki's model contained four equations describing 'the functioning of the economic system as a whole', using Frisch's term 'macrodynamic' to denote this ambition. Three relations described capitalistic production:

$$L(t) = I(t - \theta) \tag{1.1}$$

$$A(t) = \frac{1}{\theta} \int_{t-\theta}^{t} I(\tau) d\tau \tag{1.2}$$

$$\frac{dK(t)}{dt} = L(t) - U \tag{1.3}$$

where I denotes total of investment orders; A, total production of capital goods; L, volume of deliveries of industrial equipment; and K, volume of existing industrial equipment. U denotes demand for restoration of equipment used up and was assumed to be constant. θ denotes the average production lag. The fourth relation resulted from the interdependence between investment and yield of existing enterprises (see below):

$$I = m(C^* + A) - nK \tag{1.4}$$

where C^* denotes autonomous consumption, m and n are positive.

Kalecki arrived at this latter equation in the following way. B, total real income of capitalists is equal to the sum of their consumption, C, and production of capital goods, A:

$$B = C + A$$

Consumption, C, is composed of an autonomous part, C^*, and a part proportional to income, B:

$$C = C^* + \lambda B$$

From this we get:

$$B = \frac{1}{1-\lambda}(C^* + A)$$

The ratio of volume of investment orders, I, to the volume of existing industrial equipment, K, is an increasing function of the gross yield, B/K:

$$\frac{I}{K} = f\left(\frac{B}{K}\right)$$

We already saw that B is proportional to $C^* + A$, we thus obtain:

$$\frac{I}{K} = \phi\left(\frac{C^* + A}{K}\right)$$

Kalecki assumed ϕ to be linear, i.e.

$$\frac{I}{K} = m\frac{C^* + A}{K} - n \tag{1.5}$$

where the constant m is positive. Normally, n is not restricted to any range of values, but it will be shown below that to get the main cycle Kalecki had to assume n to be positive too.

The ingredients

Kalecki's essay was not inspired by the contemporary mainstream of orthodox economics but first and foremost by Marxist economics, whose theorists of crises were Mikhail Tugan-Baranovsky and Rosa Luxemburg. Tugan-Baranovsky's ideas were developed at the beginning of the twentieth century by, among others, Albert Aftalion. Kalecki's model was one of the first attempts at a mathematisation of verbal theories of the business cycle.

Tugan-Baranovsky

The role of investment as the main factor of reproduction in capitalism was an element of Kalecki's theory that he owed to Tugan-Baranovsky. Many years later, in 1967, Kalecki wrote that he regarded Tugan-Baranovsky's argument on problems of realisation in capitalism as his lasting contribution to the analysis of how capitalism functions in its various phases (Osiatynski 1990: 439). Tugan-Baranovsky was possibly the first interpreter of Marx's schemes of reproduction to stress investments as the main engine of capitalistic economic development in Marx's theory. Tugan-Baranovsky believed that capitalism was not a 'harmonious' but an 'antagonistic' system. In an antagonistic system consumption is neither the ultimate goal nor the criterion of economic activity. Production that only serves further production is entirely justified, provided that it is profitable. Hence he did not regard as absurd the assumption that capitalism is based on investments that serve only further investment and so, with the appropriate inter-industry proportions, the development of capitalism did not depend on sales outlets.

Luxemburg

The fact that Kalecki did not aim at an equilibrium model was inspired by the contemporary debates about the theory of capital accumulation put forward by Luxemburg. She emphasised the difficulties of realising production because of the insufficient absorption capacity of markets, which she believed was a barrier to expanded reproduction under capitalism. Kalecki himself several times pointed to his ties with Luxemburg's theory and, through it, with the Marxist school of thought (Osiatynski 1990: 439).

Tinbergen's shipbuilding model

To mould the above Marxist views into a mathematical model of a cycle, Kalecki used Tinbergen's shipbuilding paper (1931). Tinbergen's shipbuilding model, in itself an example of a very important investment cycle, provided the idea of how to construct a mathematical model of the cycle and also the mathematical techniques used for that purpose.

In an empirical study, Tinbergen found that the increase in tonnage, $f'(t)$, the time derivative of f, is an inverse function of total tonnage two years earlier, $f(t-\theta)$, i.e.

$$f'(t) = -af(t-\theta)$$

where $a > 0$, $\theta \approx 2$ years. This equation was analysed by Tinbergen by solving the characteristic equation

$$z = a\theta e^z \tag{1.6}$$

where z is a complex number, $z = x + iy$.

As a result, the general solution is a sum of trigonometric functions:

$$f(t) = \sum_{k=1}^{\infty} D_k e^{-x_k t} \sin(y_k t + \omega_k) \tag{1.7}$$

where the amplitudes D_k and the phases ω_k are determined by the shape of the movement in an initial period. It followed from Tinbergen's analysis that only one sine function had a period longer than the delay, θ, and that this cycle only exists when $a\theta > e^{-1}$. According to Tinbergen, this cycle was the only cycle with an economic meaning, because the other sine functions had a period shorter than the delay θ. The parameter a had a value somewhere between ½ and 1, so that

$$a\theta > e^{-1} (= 0.37)$$

and thus the main cycle existed and had a period of about eight years.

Empirical facts and data

The observed business cycle was a rather stable cycle: 'In reality we do not observe a clear *regular* progression or digression in the amplitude of fluctuations' (Kalecki 1990: 87, see also Kalecki 1935: 336). By 'statistical evidence' the cycle's period was given to be between eight and twelve years. The average production lag was determined on the basis of data of the German Institut für Konjunkturforschung. The lag between the beginning and termination of building schemes was eight months; the lag between orders and deliveries in the machinery-making industry was six months. So, Kalecki assumed the average duration of θ to be 0.6 years.

Two other important empirical values (see below) were U/K_0 and C^*/K_0, where K_0 is the average value of K. The 'rate of amortisation' U/K_0, determined on the basis of combined German and American data, was about 0.05. For the evaluation of C^*/K_0, Kalecki used only American data, and fixed on 0.13.

Clearly Kalecki did not use Polish data, although he worked at the Polish Institute for Economic Research, which affiliation was printed at the bottom of his *Econometrica* paper. The most probable reason for using German and American data, and not Polish data, was that one of his model assumptions was that total volume of stocks remains constant all through the cycle. This assumption was justified by existing 'totally or approximately isolated' economic systems like that of the USA.

Integration

The integration of the ingredients (discussed above) had to be done in such a way that mathematisation of the Marxist views resulted in a reduced form equation which resembled Tinbergen's cycle equation and fulfilled its cycle criterion. Beyond that, the cycle which resulted from that equation should meet the generic empirical facts. How far one is able to reconstruct the integration process that actually took place is, of course, very difficult but with the aid of Kalecki's published works one can lift a tip of the veil. Namely, one part of mathematical moulding is calibration: the values of certain parameters have to be chosen in such a way as to make the integration successful.

From Kalecki's four-equation model (equations (1.1) to (1.4)) one can derive an equation in one variable, the so-called reduced form equation. The reduced form equation of this four-equation model is a mixed differential-difference equation of both differential order and difference order one:

$$(m + \theta n) J (t - \theta) = m J (t) - \theta J' (t) \tag{1.8}$$

where $J(t)$ is the deviation of $I(t)$ from U, $J(t) = I(t) - U$. To use Tinbergen's shipbuilding results to discuss his own macro-model, Kalecki transformed this equation into the equation Tinbergen analysed in his shipbuilding paper (cf. equation (1.6)), by assuming that $J(t) = De^{(m-z)t/\theta}$:

$$z = le^z \tag{1.9}$$

where $l = e^{-m}(m + \theta n)$. One result is that the main cycle only exists when the following inequality is satisfied:

$$l > e^{-1}$$

which is equivalent to

$$m + \theta n > e^{m-1}$$

The parameter m is already assumed to be positive (see equation (1.5)). It can be shown that the above inequality is satisfied only when n is also positive. In other words the main cycle exists only when n is positive.

In the original Polish version of 1933, Kalecki tried to prove that n must be positive. This proof was questioned by Rajchman (Kalecki 1990: 471), who in conclusion, rightly, accepted the condition $n > 0$ as an additional assumption by Kalecki. In his 'Macrodynamic theory' Kalecki (1935) asserts only that the constant m is positive, but adds that a necessary condition for a cyclical solution is the positive value also of the coefficient n.

As in Tinbergen's case, z is a complex number: $x + iy$. The general solution of the reduced form equation (1.8) was:

$$J(t) = ae^{\frac{(m-x)t}{\theta}} \sin\frac{yt}{\theta}$$

where a is a constant. Kalecki also chose x to be equal to m, so that the amplitude of the main cyclical solution became constant, which was in accordance with reality: 'This case is especially important because it corresponds roughly to the real course of the business cycle' (Kalecki 1990: 87, see also Kalecki 1935: 336). Then:

$$J(t) = a\sin\frac{yt}{\theta}$$

By taking into consideration this 'condition of a constant amplitude' ($x = m$), Kalecki derived from equation (1.9) the following equations:

$$\cos y = \frac{m}{m + \theta n}$$

and

$$\frac{y}{\tan y} = m$$

Between *m* and *n* there was another dependency for they are both coefficients in equation (1.4). That equation must also hold true for the one-cycle-averages of *I* and *A* equal to *U*, and for the average value of *K* equal to K_0:

$$U = m(C^* + U) - nK_0$$

Hence:

$$n = (m-1)\frac{U}{K_0} + m\frac{C^*}{K_0}$$

Using his empirical values for θ, U/K_0 and C^*/K_0, the result was that the model generated a cycle with a period of ten years, which was in accordance with the empirical business cycle period, ranging from eight to twelve years, so 'the conclusions from our theory do not differ very much from reality' (Kalecki 1990: 91, see also Kalecki 1935: 340).

By building his business-cycle model, Kalecki was able to integrate a list of ingredients: Marxist's theoretical ideas on the role of investment and reproduction in capitalistic economies, Tinbergen's mathematical model of an investment cycle and generic data of the business cycle. To make the integration of these ingredients satisfactory, two parameters, *n* and *m*, had played a crucial but controversial role. The choice of *n* to be positive was not suggested by economic or by empirical considerations but was only justified by the motive of integration: it made the model fulfill Tinbergen's cycle condition. The choice of the real part *x* of the complex number *z* to be equal to *m*, enabled Kalecki to integrate into the model the fact that the cycle is rather stable. This choice was not suggested by economic theory or by Tinbergen's cycle model. Thanks to the integration of the cycle condition and the characteristic of a stable cycle, the ingredients could be combined together to make a model with a resulting cycle period of ten years. This was seen by Kalecki as an empirical justification of the model and thus as a justification of both choices of *n* and *x*. Kalecki's case shows that integration and justification are both sides of the same coin.

Case 2: the Phillips machine

In the 1940s, macroeconomics in Britain was based on the ideas found in John Maynard Keynes' *General Theory* (1936). It was a very complex book to read.[7] To clarify the meaning of Keynes' system, small abstract graphic or algebraic models were built, but these were not sufficient to represent fully the ideas and conceptions of his theory. While the verbal Keynesian approach tended to see the economy as a dynamic system, these mathematical models were static. Proposals to create dynamic mathematical models by introducing both lags and differential terms into the model equations only led to new problems of clarity, namely to difficulties of solving these systems of equations and to questions of interpretation (see below).

Another source of confusion was that contemporary arguments about how the macro-economy worked often involved reference to both stocks and flows. Although such notions were well worked out in the context of monetary theory before the 1940s, Keynesian theory dealt in terms of the aggregate national income and these notions were not well represented in the mathematical models. Moreover, the macroeconomic breakthrough of Keynesian economics involved the principle of effective demand operating in a continuous circular flow of macroeconomic activity. However, this, also, was not easily represented in the small-sized mathematical models.

To get a hold on macroeconomic thinking, and to resolve the gaps in his own understanding, A.W.H. Phillips (1914–75) used his engineering skills to create the hydraulic machine.[8] It seems fairly clear, from descriptions of the machine building process, that Phillips did not simply translate and apply the extant mathematical models. He tried to resolve the problems indicated above by linking the economic ideas directly to hydraulic principles. This was in part an iterative process in which Phillips began to learn about and understand the macroeconomic system, and he embedded this understanding in his representations of the machine.

This process also involved Phillips in incorporating elements from various other publications. One of these was a study by Richard Goodwin (1948) in which the dynamics of the economic process were represented by differential equations not by difference equations, in other words, not by discrete steps but as a continuous process. Phillips designed the machine's governing relations to incorporate Goodwin's formulations. Similarly, Phillips was inspired by Kenneth Boulding's study, *Economic Analysis* (1948) to represent the stock-flow conceptualisation of the machine. Boulding used the image of a hydraulic-mechanical device to represent economic stocks and flows in an attempt to clarify how prices regulate production and consumption. Phillips borrows this analogy in his own representation of a machine.

These two ingredients, namely Goodwin's dynamics and Boulding's hydraulic design, and ideas about economics that Phillips acquired from Walter Newlyn and James Meade, were integrated to construct the machine. Consequently, the machine was able to represent the circular flow of national income, the relationships between elements in the economy, and stocks and flows in terms of the tanks of hydraulic fluid with in- and out-flows and governing valves. The machine thus represented the aggregate economy and could be utilised to model Keynesian ideas and alternative theses about the economy.

In a joint study (Morgan and Boumans 2004) we argue that moving from a metaphor to a model on paper, and from a model on paper to a working machine means that you have to make an increasing number of commitments about exactly what you mean in detail at every step. Phillips was required to specify the economic elements and relations of the macro-economy in terms of the following physical elements:

a   the flows and stocks in the system
b   the size, shape and relative positions of the tanks (containing the stocks)

c   how the flows go between different stocks including feedback loops

d   the nature of the connections between flows and stocks: valves, sluices, plugs, springs

e   the motive power(s) and their positions in the system

f   the viscosity of the fluid

g   the shape of the outflow slots in the tanks

h   the devices to maintain a constant head of water over the valves

i   measuring devices so that flows can be monitored (for which they are transformed into stocks) to regulate the valves via floats or servo-mechanisms.

All the hydraulic elements in the list need to be fully specified, for if the machine does not work successfully as a hydraulic system, it cannot function as a mode of understanding. There were various ways to design the hydraulic machine. This points to implicit assumptions or decisions about the details of the economic equivalences, for the choices can be made to represent one or another interpretation of the relations thought to occur in the economy. Thus, the machine that Phillips built was constrained not only by the laws of hydraulics but also by the modeller's commitments to his account of the economic world being modelled. However, it should be noted that, although all the parts put into the machine must be set out in detail, not all aspects of the economy have to be specified. Phillips constructed his model to represent a set of elements and their economic relations, along with a set of controls and regulators, all built in line with economic theories of the day; he did not build his model to be a complete representation of everything in the economy. Besides, not every part of the machine will necessarily have an economic meaning. Choosing to model the economy as a hydraulic machine entails dealing with the physical constraints of the materials being used as well as commitment about which aspect of the economy is to be physically represented. These problems are inextricably linked: each modelling decision is affected by both physical constraints and economic commitment.

Phillips' belief about the ability of his machine to enlighten and to produce understanding out of confusion proved correct. The machine as a large physical 'inscription' could create 'optical consistency'. Latour put forward this notion in his account of visualisations (1986: 7–8). He said that all the theoretical elements and institutional arrangements were made homogeneous in space in such a way 'that allows you to change scale, to make them presentable, and to combine them at will'. Although not two-dimensional, the Phillips machine functions in the same overlapping domains of visualisation and cognition that Latour (1986) ascribes to maps, diagrams and so forth.

Mathematical moulding

Mathematics is the stuff that non-material models are made of. It fulfills the role that Perspex, water, cords and pulleys do in Phillips' hydraulic machine. The selection of mathematical forms must be such that the disparate ingredients can be harmonised and homogenised into one effective model. Modelling is a process of committing oneself to how aspects of the economy should mathematically be represented and at the same time being constrained by the selected mathematical forms. Moreover, as in the case of the Phillips machine, not every element in the mathematical model necessarily has an economic meaning. To make the model workable, sometimes, elements of convenience or fiction have to be introduced.[9]

An important element in the modelling process is mathematical moulding. Mathematical moulding is shaping the ingredients in such a mathematical form that integration is possible, and contains two dominant elements. The first element is moulding the mathematical formalism ingredient in such a way that it allows the other elements to be integrated. The second element is calibration, the choice of the parameter values, again for the purpose of integrating all the ingredients.

As a result, the choice of the mathematical formalism ingredient is important. It determines the possibilities of the mathematical modelling. However, which formalism should be chosen is not obvious. It is often assumed that mathematics is an efficient and transparent language. One of the most well-known supporters of this view is Paul Samuelson (1952). He considers mathematics to be a transparent mode of communication and that it is this transparency that will stop people making the wrong deductive inferences. We will see in this monograph different examples that show that mathematics is not always transparent (neither, some would say, is language) and it does not necessarily function as a language.

As 'quasi-matter',[10] mathematical objects are, in certain respects, parts of Popper's third world (see Popper 1968) and, therefore, not always transparent. This is shown by the fact that formalisms can be interpreted in different ways. More examples will be given in later chapters, but a first glance at this kind of problem, already mentioned above, is the assumption held by people such as Jan Tinbergen, Ragnar Frisch and Michal Kalecki, that mixed difference-differential equations are the most suitable formalism for business-cycle models (see Case 1 above). In general, it is difficult to solve mixed differential-difference equations. Moreover, in the 1930s, at the time Tinbergen, Kalecki and Frisch were studying them, there were hardly any systematic accounts available. Systematic overviews on mixed differential-difference equations did not appear until the early 1950s.[11] As a consequence, they were studied as if they were the same as the more familiar differential equations. The general solution of this latter kind of equation is a finite weighted sum of trigonometric and exponential functions, so that their periodic behaviour can easily be analysed. In contrast, the general solution of a mixed difference-differential equation is an infinite weighted sum of harmonic functions, cf. equation (1.7). This is not necessarily a periodic movement if the weights are not further specified. In a more recent study, Zambelli's (1992) 'The wooden horse that wouldn't rock', Frisch's system of four mixed difference–differential equations was analysed and worked out using computer simulations. It appeared that Frisch's system was not a cycle model because when it is subjected to an external shock it evolves back to the equilibrium in a non-cyclical manner.

Two related accounts

The role of mathematics as homogenising and harmonising material implies that the model-building process is the integration of several ingredients in such a way that the result – the model – meets certain *a priori* criteria of quality. And because empirical data and stylised facts belong to the set of ingredients that are integrated, justification is built in. Models built in this way are not appraised by *ex post* empirical testing. Such models are assessed by whether they satisfy their purpose, and, because in the model-building process one works towards this goal, integration and justification are two sides of the same coin. A well-known saying tells us that 'the proof of the pudding is in the eating', but if one prepares a pudding, tasting is an essential part of cooking.

This account of assessment is closely related to Mary Morgan's (1988) observation that econometricians of the 1930s were primarily concerned with finding 'satisfactory' empirical models. Assessing whether the models were satisfactory depended on the purpose of the models. Morgan presents five statements that cover the aims and criteria of the early econometricians:

1   To measure theoretical laws: Models must satisfy certain theoretical requirements (economic criteria).
2   To explain (or describe) the observed data: Models must fit observed data (statistical or historical criteria).
3   To be useful for policy: Models must allow the exploration of policy options or make predictions about future values.
4   To explore or develop theory: Models must expose unsuspected relationships or develop the detail of relationships.
5   To verify or reject theory: Models must be satisfactory or not over a range of economic, statistical, and other criteria.

(Morgan 1988: 205)

Morgan (see also Kim *et al.* 1995) presents these criteria of assessment as a form of quality control. If an empirical model exhibited a basic set of qualities, that is, satisfied some of the criteria listed above, it was considered satisfactory. Several practices in econometrics and macroeconomics show that Morgan's observations can be summarised as: the integration of the various theoretical and empirical ingredients is deemed satisfactory when it meets a number of *a priori* criteria.

The second related view is Nancy Cartwright's simulacrum account of models in her *How the Laws of Physics Lie* (1983). Her account deals with the problem of bridging the gap between theory and phenomena in physics. Her aim is to argue against the facticity of fundamental laws, they do not picture the phenomena in an accurate way. For this we need models: 'To explain a phenomenon is to find a model that fits it into the basic framework of the theory and thus allows us to derive analogues for the messy and complicated phenomenological laws which are true of it' (Cartwright 1983: 152). The striving for too much realism in the models may be an obstacle to explaining the relevant phenomenon. For that reason she introduces an 'anti-realistic' account of models: models are simulacra, that is, 'the success of the model depends on how much and how precisely it can replicate what goes on' (Cartwright 1983: 153).

To fulfill this bridge function, Cartwright argues that models consist partly of genuine properties of the objects modelled, but others will be merely properties of convenience or fiction. The properties of convenience are introduced into the model to bring the objects modelled into the range of the theory. These latter properties play an important role in her argument that fundamental explanatory laws cannot be interpreted realistically. To bridge the gaps on the route from phenomena to models to theory, properties of convenience or fiction have to be introduced.

The main difference between the view of this book and Morgan and Cartwright's accounts is that they conceive models as instruments to bridge the gap between theory and data (Figure 1.2).

This view is too one-dimensional; here the view is maintained that models integrate a broader range of ingredients, than only theory and data (Figure 1.3).

Cartwright's account is on how models are built to fit theory to data. Her conception of models is a sub-case of the view developed here. In the first place because it is one-dimensional (see above). In her view, the theory is true of the

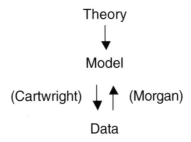

Figure 1.2 Comparison of Cartwright's and Morgan's model accounts

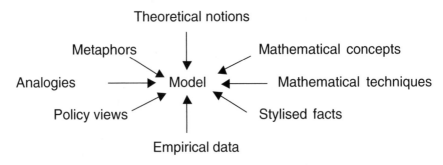

Figure 1.3 Model as the result of integrating a broad range of ingredients

objects of the model and the model is true of the objects in reality (Cartwright 1983: 4). In my account a broader range of ingredients are integrated and the truth relation has a different direction (see the arrows in Figures 1.2 and 1.3): the model is true for all of these ingredients. Secondly, when Cartwright talks about theories, these already provide a mathematical framework, in contradiction to the usually verbal theories used in economics. The mathematical formalism is often one of the ingredients that should be integrated. But more importantly, the introduction of properties of convenience in the model is a special case of mathematical moulding. Of course, Cartwright's account is designed to clarify her position in a realism debate, so she does not go further into the meaning of the concept of convenience.

The emphasis in Morgan's account of satisfactory empirical models is on what good models are: models are matched with both theory and data to satisfy certain criteria. She compares this way of satisfying with quality control testing. Her story is about econometric models of the 1930s, but her conception of quality control testing can be extrapolated to mathematical models in general. Morgan's account of satisfactoriness is for that matter more clarifying and broader. Models not only have to meet theoretical requirements but also other 'qualities'. The success of model-building processes depends on the fulfillment of a broader range of requirements than only the theoretical.

How economists model the world into numbers

The title of this monograph, *How Economists Model the World into Numbers*, encapsulates our main aim. Let me explain the title word by word.

How ...

By using the interrogative pronoun 'how', the subject is confined to heuristics: the methodological appraisal of economists' solutions to modelling (in particular measuring) problems. The word 'how' is used in the sense akin to its meaning in the title of Polya's (1957) work *How To Solve It*:

> Studying the methods of solving problems, we perceive another face of mathematics. Yes, mathematics has two faces; it is the rigorous science of Euclid but it is also something else. Mathematics presented in the Euclidean way appears as a systematic, deductive science; but mathematics in the making appears as an experimental, inductive science.
>
> (Polya 1957: vii)[12]

The pronoun 'how' is not used to answer historical questions about twentieth-century economics and econometrics. These questions are addressed in excellent accounts by Klein (forthcoming), Morgan (1990, 2003a), Qin (1993), and Weintraub (2002). These works give the historical context of the problems discussed in this monograph and are referred to if necessary.

... economists ...

The heuristic problems described above were typical for twentieth-century economics as is illustrated by the birth, during that century, of two new branches: econometrics and macroeconomics. Discussion of the problems of modelling and measurement was most productive at the point where these two branches overlap and interact. It is at these intersections that solutions to these problems were worked out intellectually and in practical terms. Irving Fisher, Ragnar Frisch, Jan Tinbergen, Trygve Haavelmo, Milton Friedman, Tjalling Koopmans, Herbert Simon, Robert Lucas and Edward Prescott, are some of the economists who have dealt with these problems explicitly in their work.

... model ...

As said before, we only discuss mathematical models as quantitative representations of the world and do not concentrate on theories.

... the world ...

The world represented in the models is a world of economic aggregates that cannot be observed without the aid of models. The models are not representations of individual commodities, prices or behaviour.

... into numbers

This kind of modelling is mapping the world into numbers. The aim of the modelling practices discussed in this monograph is to express properties in the world of economic aggregates through numbers. To ensure that these numbers will produce reliable data about the economic world, the correspondence between these properties and the numbers should be such that there is an analogy of the relations between the property manifestations with relations between their images in the number set. To make sure that the analogy is satisfactory, it must satisfy specific criteria. What kind of criteria these should be is a central theme of this monograph. As will be shown, there is a close connection between these criteria and the conditions for measurement found in the representational theory of measurement. This theory defines measurement as a homo-morphic mapping of an empirical relational system into a numerical relation system (see Finkelstein 1982). Broadly spoken, quantitative empirical modelling is considered here as mapping aspects of the economic world into numbers.

Outline of the argument

To conclude this chapter, an outline of this monograph's argument will be unfolded. The first time the term 'model' was used in the sense of a mathematical output of empirical economic research was in 1935 by the Dutch economist Jan Tinbergen. It was the result of a new type of economic research practice. Chapter 2 traces the origins of this modelling practice in James Clark Maxwell's use of formal analogies and his views on their function in science. Heinrich Hertz interpreted these analogies – 'images' – as a specific kind of idealisations: they should be logically consistent, empirically correct, appropriate and simple. The requirement of appropriateness entailed that the idealisation should contain essential character-istics. What these essential characteristics are depends on the purpose of the model. Ludwig Boltzmann followed Hertz's interpretation, with the essential distinction that unlike Hertz he did not believe it necessary that the analogies should be based on logic but they must represent experience. Tinbergen exploited this heuristic of using formal analogies to construct schemes of business-cycle mechanisms. These schemes had to fulfill three requirements of theoretical, statistical and mathematical significance. Theoretical significance was achieved by basing the choice of the explanatory variables on economic theory. The theories used did not have to agree with each other. The significance of the variables also depended on statistical verification – they should be empirically correct. The third, but certainly not the least important, requirement was that the behaviour of the output of the scheme should have similar characteristics to the phenomenon being investigated. In other words, the scheme should be appropriate. Appropriateness was achieved by making sure that the estimated parameters are mathematically significant, a requirement that can be fulfilled by calibration. In case of business-cycle models, calibration boils down to 'tuning', that is the parameter values should be such that the resulting cyclical behaviour is of the same wavelength as the business cycle.

To attain a full list of causal factors all three requirements of significance are important. Chapter 3 shows that task of detecting all relevant factors is, in fact, an essential part of the so-called problem of autonomy. In particular, it is important, but difficult, to detect factors that have remained dormant for a long time but can become active at any time and so cause what seems to be a structural break. However, in the probabilistic revolution that followed Tinbergen's innovative work in econometrics, the requirement that there should be feedback from the phenomena to assess the significance of the causal factors was ignored. This resulted in a loss of the requirement of mathematical significance. The main reason was that one never could be sure whether to consider phenomena, like business cycles, as permanent. Cut off from this kind of empirical input, one has to lean heavily on theory to acquire a full list of causal factors. Because of this strong *apriorist* position, the Cowles Commission approach became one not of testing or of discovery but of measurement.

The economic world we try to understand is complex and unstable. To build reliable models involves idealisations to sieve the invariant properties – structural features – of the economic world out of the inflow of data from that world. Different strategies of appropriate idealisations are discussed in Chapter 4.

Models that function as measuring instruments provide quantitative facts about phenomena, facts that are contained in, but not immediately visible in observable data. Chapter 5 discusses several different ways of assessing these instruments. Which way is most appropriate depends on how many facts are already known about the phenomenon in question. These are, in order of decreasing availability of information on the (stylised and stable) facts about the phenomenon: characteristic testing, tuning, gauging and standardisation. These different ways of assessment, all included under the heading 'calibration', share the requirement that models, on the whole, have to be based on autonomous relationships. A lack of appropriateness undermines the reliability of the instrument. These different kinds of assessments are explored in two case study appendixes: 'Output–Inflation Tradeoffs' and 'Filters'.

When there are no empirical facts yet available to verify the model, because the instrument is a first-generation model of the phenomenon, the model has to be assessed by standardisation, that is by determining if the model has been constructed in line with set criteria and according to sound rules. In other words, reliability is then achieved through rigour. However, Chapter 6 shows that rigour does not necessarily imply logical consistency. The model is a compromise of relevant but, on occasion, incompatible qualities built according to certain set standards.

A separate methodology of models that does justice to the idea that models function as autonomous instruments of investigation has to reconsider and consequently redefine central methodological concepts; to see how models acquire reliability, testing of models has to be re-evaluated in terms of calibration; and explanatory lawful relationships have to be redefined in terms of autonomous relationships. While theoretical principles, or axioms if you like, have to form a consistent system, instruments are built on the basis of a compromise of often incompatible theoretical and empirical requirements. Theories should be true, or at least not false, but models have only to fulfill their goal satisfactorily.

2 A new practice

In general, I believe that one who claims to understand the principles of flight can reasonably be expected to be able to make a flying machine, and that understanding business cycles means the ability to make them too, in roughly the same sense.

(Lucas 1981: 8)

Introduction

At the fifth European meeting of the Econometric Society held in Namur, Belgium, 1935, Jan Tinbergen (1903–94) read a paper on 'A mathematical theory of business cycle policy'. As usual, a report of this meeting appeared in *Econometrica*, the society's journal. This time the report was written by Hans Staehle and published in 1937. The report noted that Tinbergen's paper consisted of three parts:

(1) the presentation of a simplified business cycle 'mechanism',
(2) an analysis of its various 'influencing coefficients' (*Beeinflussings-koeffizienten*), with a view to discovering those which might be modified by policy, and
(3) an analysis of the conditions which would have to be satisfied in order to achieve the aims set by various types of policy.

(Staehle 1937: 87)

The paper appeared as part of Tinbergen's article 'Quantitative Fragen der Konjunkturpolitik' in *Weltwirtschaftliches Archiv*, published in 1935. At the end of the article, there were summaries in three different languages, English, French and Spanish. Instead of 'mechanism', now the terms 'scheme', 'schéma' and 'esquema' were used. However, in the article itself, Tinbergen used the term 'Modell'. It was the first time an economist used the term 'model' to denote a specific mathematical product of one's empirical research. This cautious name-giving marked the beginning of a new practice in economics, today loosely called modelling.[1]

Up until then, the term 'model' had been used to mean a substantive analogy, as distinct from a formal analogy that was denoted by the term 'scheme' (see for this distinction Nagel 1961: 110). In substantive analogies, a system of elements possessing certain already familiar properties assumed to be related in known ways, is taken as a recipe for the construction of a theory for some second system. In formal analogies, the system that serves as the recipe is some familiar structure of mathematical relations. For example, in 1931 during the meeting of the Econometric Society at Lausanne, Ragnar Frisch used the term 'modèles mécaniques de "cycles"' (Staehle 1933: 83) to indicate that the pendulum is used as a substantive analogy to the business cycle. In the final section of his essay in the Cassel volume (Frisch 1933b), this model was explicated and designated as a 'mechanical analogy'. Frisch visualised the business cycle as a pendulum above which a receptacle filled with water is suspended. Water accumulating in the receptacle above the pendulum was seen as analogous to Schumpeterian innovations (Frisch 1933b: 203–5).

To see what the new practice of 'modelling' involved, let first have a closer look at Tinbergen's article (1935a). The 'model' was meant as a macro-dynamic *Darstellung*[2] of reality and was 'constructed' to investigate problems of business-cycle explanations and problems of business-cycle policy (Tinbergen 1935a: 370–1). The model was seen as a simplified representation of reality. The problem was to find the right degree of simplification in order to balance between approximating reality as close as possible while keeping the model manageable. Tinbergen recommended investigating a wide range of different models as the model discussed in the article could only provide incomplete answers.

The model consisted of 18 equations connecting 18 variables. Eight of these equations represented definitions, some of which were clarified by a scheme of economic circulation. The other ten equations expressed 'reactions' (Staehle 1937: 87) of some variables to others. Although these reaction equations were suggested by actual statistical enquiries, they were still abstract expressions. The parameter values were not yet measured but represented by symbols. The model was not yet a representation of a real economy, it was a blueprint for the model he presented the year after to the Dutch Society of Economics and Statistics, namely a model of the Dutch economy consisting of 24 equations (Tinbergen 1936a). This 1936 model was the very first macroeconometric model in the history of economics.[3]

Halfway through the 1930s, a new practice was born that was based on instruments called 'models'. In mathematics and physics, the term 'model' originally specifically referred to material objects. In other words, 'a representation in three dimensions of some projected or existing structure, or of some material object artificial or natural, showing the proportions and arrangement of its component parts', or 'an object or figure in clay, wax, or the like, and intended to be reproduced in a more durable material' (OED 1933). Ludwig Boltzmann's entry for 'Model' in the *Encyclopaedia Britannica* [1902a] (1974) also indicates its material roots: 'a tangible representation, whether the size be equal, or greater, or smaller, of an object which is either in actual existence, or has to be constructed in fact or thought' (p. 213). To Boltzmann, models could only be material, a view that can also be found in his contribution to the *Katalog Mathematischer und Mathematisch-physikalischer Modelle, Apparate und Instrumente* [1892] (1974).

At the beginning of the twentieth century, the term 'mathematical model' referred to a physical three-dimensional representation of a mathematical entity.[4] Usually the term 'scheme' was used to denote a non-material, mathematical representation. As will be shown in the subsequent sections, this shift in terminology from 'scheme' to 'model' gave name to a new practice of 'explicit mathematising as technique' which matched with an empiric-oriented alternative to the logical view on mathematics (see also Alberts 1998: 134–5).

Before we discuss the tradition that led to the use of the concept of mathematical model in economics, it is worth mentioning two early instances where the term 'model' was used in mathematics to designate a non-material object. However, this usage was not followed at that time (Alberts 1998: 107–13). The first mathematician who used the term model in this non-material sense was Philip E.B. Jourdain (1879–1921) in his article 'The nature of mathematics' [1912] (1988).

> The end of very much mathematics – and of the work of many eminent men – is *the simple and, as far as may be, accurate description* of things in the world around us, of which we become conscious through our senses. … Our ideal in natural science is to build up a working model of the universe out of the sort of ideas that all people carry about with them everywhere 'in their heads', as we say, and to which ideas we appeal when we try to teach mathematics. These ideas are those of *number, order*, the numerical measures of *times* and *distances*, and so on. … Indeed, the 'world' with which we have to deal in theoretical or mathematical mechanics is but a mathematical scheme, the function of which it is to imitate, by logical consequences of the properties assigned to it by definition, certain processes of nature as closely as possible. Thus our 'dynamical world' may be called a model of reality, and must not be confused with the reality itself.
>
> (Jourdain [1912] 1988: 41)

His view on mathematics was that it 'is based on logic, and on logic alone', so a model was 'constructed solely out of logical conceptions' (p. 41). However, the mathematics and physics community did not adopt his concept of a model.

The second mathematician to use the term model to designate non-material aspects was Émile Borel (1871–1956) in an account that was not based on logic. In a paper discussing the relations between the mathematical sciences and the physical sciences, he refers to the term 'model' as a 'form of thought':

> There is evidently nothing mysterious in the fact that mathematical theories constructed on the model of certain phenomena should have been capable of being developed and of providing a model for another phenomena; … if new physical phenomena suggest new mathematical models, mathematicians will have to study these new models and their generalisations, with the legitimate hope that the new mathematical theories thus evolved will prove fruitful in their turn in providing the physicists with useful forms of thought.
>
> (Borel 1915: 165)

Although Borel's usage of the term 'model' was similar to Tinbergen's later application, the term itself became only accepted as a non-material mathematical object after 1935.

From material objects to physical analogies

The tradition that led to Tinbergen's use of the concept of mathematical model is rooted in work by James Clark Maxwell (1831–79).[5] Tinbergen studied physics at the University of Leiden where Paul Ehrenfest (1880–1933) had a major influence on his early scientific development. Ehrenfest in his turn was initiated into both the substance and the spirit of theoretical physics by Ludwig Boltzmann (1844–1906).

> Ehrenfest's life had been tied to Boltzmann's since he entered the university, closely tied during the last few years, in which he worked on his dissertation under Boltzmann's direction and then continued to participate in Boltzmann's seminar even after receiving his degree. Boltzmann, more than anyone else, by his teaching and by his example, helped set the direction of Ehrenfest's scientific interests and helped form his intellectual style.
>
> (Klein 1970: 75–6)

Throughout his scientific career, Boltzmann admired, developed, and expounded Maxwell's ideas. In Maxwell's work, a heuristic shift took place that was to lead to the new method of modern physics. It was this method that Tinbergen applied in economics.[6]

In his first paper on electromagnetism, 'On Faraday's lines of force' [1855] (1965a) (see Boltzmann [1892] 1974; Klein 1970: 56), Maxwell set out the method he intended to use. He suggested that to effectively study the considerable body of results from previous investigations, these results have to be simplified and reduced to 'a form in which the mind can grasp them'. They could take the form of 'a purely mathematical formula', but then one would 'entirely lose sight of the phenomena to be explained' (Maxwell [1855] 1965a: 155). On the other hand, if they take the form of a 'physical hypothesis', that is, an assumption as to the real nature of the phenomena to be explained, this would mean that 'we see the phenomena only through a medium', making us 'liable to that blindness to facts and rashness in assumption which a partial explanation encourages' (pp. 155–6).

> We must therefore discover some method of investigation which allows the mind at every step to lay hold of a clear physical conception, without being committed to any theory founded on the physical science from which that conception is borrowed, so that it is neither drawn aside from the subject in pursuit of analytical subtleties, nor carried beyond the truth by a favourite hypothesis.
>
> (Maxwell [1855] 1965a: 156)

To obtain physical ideas without adopting a physical theory we have to exploit 'physical analogies', 'that partial similarity between the laws of one science and those of another which makes each of them illustrate to other' (p. 156). In other words, to the extent that two physical systems obey laws with the same mathematical form, the behaviour of one system can be understood by studying the behaviour of the other, better known, system. Moreover, this can be done without making any hypothesis about the real nature of the system under investigation. However, Maxwell stated clearly that a physical analogy, valuable as it might be, was not a substitute for 'a mature theory, in which physical facts will be physically explained' (p. 159).

In a second paper, 'On physical lines of force' [1861] (1965b), he went further still and constructed a mechanism based on fluid vortices and friction rollers moving inside cells with elastic walls that served as a mechanical model for electromagnetism. It was the analysis of this mechanical model that brought Maxwell to the first formulation of the electromagnetic theory of light. It was not until his 'Dynamical theory of the electromagnetic field' [1865] (1965c), that the formulae become more detached from the mechanical models. Maxwell still used mechanical analogies, but he no longer specified them in detail. Instead, he looked for the general mechanical assumptions that are most suitable to lead to phenomena that are analogous to that of electromagnetism. In a letter written to Peter Guthrie Tait, Maxwell contrasted his vortex and particle model with the later, more schematic, dynamical analogy.

> The former is built up to show that the phenomena (of electromagnetism) are such as can be explained by mechanism. The nature of the mechanism is to the true mechanism what an orrery is to the Solar System. The latter is built on Lagrange's Dynamical Equations and is not wise about vortices.
>
> (quoted in Klein 1970: 57)

In a later paper, 'On the mathematical classification of physical quantities' [1871] (1965d), Maxwell drew a distinction between a 'physical analogy' and a 'mathematical or formal analogy'. In the case of a formal analogy,

> we learn that a certain system of quantities in a new science stand to one another in the same mathematical relations as a certain other system in an old science, which has already been reduced to a mathematical form, and its problems solved by mathematicians.
>
> (Maxwell [1871] 1965d: 257–8)

We can speak of a physical analogy when, in addition to a mathematical analogy between two physical systems, we can identify the entities or properties of both systems. To avoid confusion about the shift in the meaning of the concept 'physical analogy', we follow Nagel (see above) by referring to this later interpretation of physical analogy as 'substantive analogy'.

Maxwell's success with a theory based on dynamical analogies stimulated a variety of reactions among his contemporaries. Some only saw the dynamical analogy as a mechanical model. Maxwell's method, involving both formal and substantive analogies, was based on William Thomson's (Lord Kelvin, 1824–1907) analogy between heat flow and electrostatic action. Thomson, who had an 'immense admiration for Maxwell's mechanical model of electromagnetic induction', stated that: 'It seems to me that the test of "Do we or do we not understand a particular subject in physics?" is, "Can we make a mechanical model of it?"' (Thomson [1884] 1987: 111).

Others physicists recognised the value of the concept of formal analogy in trying to understand the essential features of the natural world. Heinrich Hertz (1857–94) was one of these. As Janik and Toulmin (1973) wrote about Hertz:

> Hertz had been trying to determine the precise nature of Maxwell's theory, by considering the several different sets of equations used by Maxwell to express his theory, and thus to discern what sorts of things Maxwell was asserting about the deeper nature of electromagnetic phenomena. It occurred to Hertz that, in actual fact, Maxwell was saying nothing at all about the physical nature of these phenomena. His equations were logical formulas which enabled him to deal with the phenomena and to understand how they operated.
>
> (Janik and Toulmin 1973: 142)

Or as Hertz himself put it more succinctly: 'To the question, "What is Maxwell's theory?" I know of no shorter or more definite answer than the following: – Maxwell's theory is Maxwell's system of equations' (Hertz [1893] 1962: 21).

For Hertz, representations of mechanical phenomena could only be understood in the sense of Maxwell's dynamical analogies, which is obvious in the section 'Dynamical models' of his last work, *The Principles of Mechanics Presented in a New Form* [1899] (1956). First he gave a definition of a 'dynamical model':

> A material system is said to be a dynamical model of a second system when the connections of the first can be expressed by such coordinates as to satisfy the following conditions:
> (1) That the number of coordinates of the first system is equal to the number of the second.
> (2) That with a suitable arrangement of the coordinates for both systems the same equations of condition exist.
> (3) That by this arrangement of the coordinates the expression for the magnitude of a displacement agrees in both systems.
>
> (Hertz [1899] 1956: 175)

From this definition, Hertz inferred that 'In order to determine beforehand the course of the natural motion of a material system, it is sufficient to have a model of that system. The model may be much simpler than the system whose motion it represents' (p. 176). However, it is impossible to carry our knowledge of the connections of the natural systems further than is involved in specifying models of the actual systems. We can then, in fact, have no knowledge as to whether the systems which we consider in mechanics agree in any other respect with the actual systems of nature which we intend to consider, than in this alone, – that the one set of systems are models of the other.

(Hertz [1899] 1956: 177)

While the 'model' was still considered as something material, its relation to the system of inquiry was on a par with the images (*Bilder*) that are formed of a system.[7]

The relation of a dynamical model to the system of which it is regarded as the model, is precisely the same as the relation of the images which our mind forms of things to the things themselves. For if we regard the condition of the model as the representation of the condition of the system, then the consequents of this representation, which according to the laws of this representation must appear, are also the representation of the consequents which must proceed from the original object according to the laws of this original object. The agreement between mind and nature may therefore be likened to the agreement between two systems which are models of one another, and we can even account for this agreement by assuming that the mind is capable of making actual dynamical models of things, and of working with them.

(Hertz [1899] 1956: 177)

Right in the beginning of the introduction of his *Principles of Mechanics*, Hertz formulated the three requirements that an image should fulfill:

The images which we may form of things are not determined without ambiguity by the requirement that the consequents of the images must be the images of the consequents. Various images of the same objects are possible, and these images may differ in various respects. We should at once denote as inadmissible all images which implicitly contradict the laws of our thought. Hence we postulate in the first place that all our images shall be logically permissible – or, briefly, that they shall be permissible. We shall denote as incorrect any permissible images, if their essential relations contradict the relations of external things, *i.e.* if they do not satisfy our first fundamental requirement. Hence we postulate in the second place that our images shall be correct. But two permissible and correct images of the same external objects may yet differ in respect of appropriateness. Of two images of the same object that is the more appropriate which pictures more of the essential relations of the object, – the one which we may call the more distinct. Of two images of equal distinctness the more appropriate is the one which contains, in addition to the essential characteristics, the smaller number of superfluous or empty relations, – the simpler of the two. Empty relations cannot be altogether avoided: they enter into the images because they are simply images, – images produced by our mind and necessarily affected by the characteristics of its mode of portrayal.

(Hertz [1899] 1956: 2)

In short, the three requirements that an image of a phenomenon should fulfill are: (1) 'logically permissible', that is logical consistency; (2) 'correctness', that there is correspondence between the relations of the representation and those of the phenomenon; and (3) 'appropriateness', that it contains the essential characteristics of the phenomenon (distinctness) as simply as possible. It is fairly straightforward to determine whether an image satisfies the first two require- ments, but 'we cannot decide without ambiguity whether an image is appropriate or not; as to this differences of opinion may arise. One image may be more suitable for one purpose, another for another; only by gradually testing many images can we finally succeed in obtaining the most appropriate' (p. 3). Appro- priateness will appear as the crucial requirement for any satisfactorily model building process. Every model is necessarily a simplified picture of a phenom- enon under investigation, but this simplification should be such that the picture remains appropriate.

Ludwig Boltzmann placed great importance on Maxwell's concept of analogies, describing Maxwell as having been 'as much of a pioneer in epistemology as in theoretical physics' (Boltzmann 1912: 100 trans).[8] The dynamical analogies were particular appealing to him. According to the historian Martin Klein, 'Boltzmann himself found the concept of a theory as an analogy or metaphor of reality a particular liberating one' (Klein 1970: 63).

> Most surprising and far-reaching analogies revealed themselves between apparently quite disparate natural processes. It seemed that nature had built the most various things on exactly the same pattern; or, in the dry words of the analyst, the same differential equations hold for the most various phenomena.
>
> (Boltzmann [1892] 1974: 9)

According to Boltzmann [1902b] (1974: 149), 'It is the ubiquitous task of science to explain the more complex in terms of the simpler; or, if preferred, to represent the complex by means of clear pictures borrowed from the sphere of the simpler phenomena'. Boltzmann's standpoint towards the role of '*Bilder*' in scientific explanation was explicitly expressed in an essay 'On the development of the methods of theoretical physics' [1899a] (1974). Boltzmann, referring to Hertz 'programme', stated that:

> [N]o theory can be objective, actually coinciding with nature, but rather that each theory is only a mental picture of phenomena, related to them as *sign* is to *designatum*. From this it follows that it cannot be our task to find an absolutely correct theory but rather a picture that is, as simple as possible and

that represents phenomena as accurately as possible. One might even conceive of two quite different theories both equally simple and equally congruent with phenomena, which therefore in spite of their difference are equally correct.

(Boltzmann [1899a] 1974: 90–1)

Although Boltzmann frequently referred to Hertz when discussing '*Bilder*' there is an important difference between the two men (for other references see De Regt 1999: 116). Boltzmann rejected Hertz's demand that the pictures we construct must obey laws of thought considered as 'indubitably correct': 'the sole and final decision as to whether the pictures are appropriate lies in the circumstance that they represent experience simply and appropriately throughout so that this in turn provides precisely the test for the correctness of those laws' (Boltzmann [1899b] 1974: 105).

In physics, Boltzmann is better known as the man who founded 'statistical mechanics'.[9] Boltzmann developed his ideas on statistical mechanics in a series of long memoirs written over a number of years. His ideas provoked intense discussion and sharp controversy. There was much confusion about what he meant and how much of it had, or had not been, properly underpinned.[10] What was needed was an analysis and critique of the foundations of this matter. Ehrenfest was asked to provide such analysis and critique for the German *Encyclopedia of Mathematical Sciences* (*Encyklopädie der Mathematischen Wissenschaften*, 1912). The resulting review article 'The conceptual foundations of the statistical approach in mechanics' [1912] (1990), was prepared in collaboration with his wife Tatiana Ehrenfest-Afanassjewa.

In this article, Ehrenfest described what was understood by explanation in Boltzmann's 'older' and 'modern' formulations of statistical mechanics. The older formulation was a 'kineto-statistics of the molecule' and thus characterised by its use of the distribution function for a single molecule.

Older works on the kinetic theory of gases quite uniformly show the following attitude toward the application of probability theory: The goal is the 'explanation' of the observable aerodynamic processes on the basis of two groups of 'assumptions'. These are:

1. Assumptions about the mechanical structure. Each gas quantum is a mechanical system, consisting of an enormous number of identical molecules of strictly specified structure.
2. The so-called 'probability assumptions'. In the motion of molecules, which is too complicated to be observed, certain regularities are described in terms of statements about the relative frequency of various configurations and motions of the molecules.

(Ehrenfest and Ehrenfest [1912] 1990: 1)

The term 'probability' appealed 'explicitly to a certain feeling of estimation which is expected to be able to fill in gaps in the observations and calculations' (p. 43).

The modern formulation was a 'kineto-statistics of the gas model', meaning a kinetic-statistical theory of the gas as a whole (Klein 1970: 123). It was assumed that the gas consisted of N identical molecules, each having r degrees of freedom. The phase of the gas was defined by the 'generalised coordinates' q_i^j and the 'generalised momenta' p_i^j ($i = 1, \ldots, r; j = 1, \ldots, N$). The phase of the gas model can now be characterised as a point in a space of $2rN$ dimensions, whose coordinates are the q_i^j and p_i^j. The totality of theoretical 'points' in the resulting multidimensional coordinate system gave one a representation of the ensemble of possible phases of the physical system in question. The general problem for statistical mechanics was then to discover mathematical relations governing the frequencies with which the actual phases of a physical system would be distributed among all possible phases. In this way, the relative probabilities of finding the system, in actual fact, in one overall physical phase than another could be computed.

> The kinetic interpretation of an aerodynamic process, just as any other 'explanation' of a physical phenomenon, consists of the representation of the observed sequence of states by a purely conceptual scheme. A special feature of kinetic interpretations, however, is the statistical character of these schemes.
>
> (Ehrenfest and Ehrenfest [1912] 1990: 36)

The third part of the Ehrenfest's review was a discussion of J. Willard Gibbs's *Elementary Principles in Statistical Mechanics* ([1902] 1960). Gibbs (1839–1903) was more sceptical about the relation between the hypotheses and reality:

> Difficulties of this kind have deterred the author from attempting to explain the mysteries of nature, and have forced him to be contended with the more modest aim of deducing some of the more obvious propositions relating to the statistical branch of mechanics. Here, there can be no mistake in regard to the agreement of the hypotheses with the facts of nature, for nothing is assumed in that respect.
>
> (Gibbs [1902] 1960: x)

This was a position Ehrenfest would not defend.

> The kinetic 'explanations' become representations or mappings of some conceptual scheme … , and correspondingly the two groups of hypotheses become more or less arbitrary assertions about the structure of this conceptual scheme. These assertions will be –
>
> 1   About the structure of the gas model.
> 2   About the selection of the group of motions.
>
> Freedom in the choice of these assertions seems to be restricted essentially by only one requirement: the scheme has to be self-consistent.
>
> (Ehrenfest and Ehrenfest [1912] 1990: 43–4)

To Ehrenfest, the requirement of self-consistency was insufficient; he believed that statistical mechanics was 'in some sense, a "real" theory and no mere analogy' (Klein 1970: 136). If he had to choose between the requirements of 'logically permissible' and 'appropriateness', Ehrenfest would no doubt choose the latter.

From physical analogies to economic schemes

Tinbergen studied physics at the University of Leiden from 1922 to 1926 and was Ehrenfest's assistant from 1923 until 1925. On 22 March 1929, he received his doctorate for the thesis 'Minimumproblemen in de natuurkunde en ekonomie' ('Minimum problems in physics and economics', 1929a). The doctoral thesis served to ease Tinbergen's transition from theoretical physics to mathematical economics. He was interested in economics because of his concern for the unemployed. He was a member of the Socialist Party and felt that he could be more useful as an economist than as a physicist (Magnus and Morgan 1987: 118–19).

'The subject of this thesis was specially chosen because of the probable analogy between the physical problems treated and certain economic problems' (Tinbergen 1929a: 1 trans). Ehrenfest himself had been occupied with it ten years earlier. At the time, he had been struck by the possibility of developing an analogy between thermodynamics and economics and tried to formulate economic concepts as parallels of thermodynamic concepts, with the concept of equilibrium occupying the central position in both theories. His notebooks covering the period from October 1917 to May 1918 contained numerous entries on 'Öko-dynamik' – a contraction of 'Ökonomie' and 'Thermodynamik'. He hoped to be able to use the formalism of thermodynamics to gain new insight into economic problems. Ehrenfest never published any of his work on economics (Klein 1970: 305–6).

In mechanics, motion is described using Hamilton's equations or Lagrange's equations. Both kinds of equations are obtained by setting the differential of a relevant integral equal to zero. This variational problem is known as Hamilton's Principle, and the whole approach is called the Calculus of Variations. The problem is to find that specific relevant integral or Hamiltonian. When one is able to define the integral belonging to a certain phenomenon, then the phenomenon is considered explained. In other words, the aim was to formalise each problem as the solution of a 'minimum problem'. This is what Hamilton's formalism manages so well for mechanics. In his thesis, Tinbergen elaborated a more general formalism and could thus classify different fields in physics. Economic problems were discussed in an appendix. This economic part was also published in the *Archiv für Sozialwissenschaft und Sozialpolitik* (1929b). He did not pretend to be exhaustive, only problems in which one 'ophelimity function'[11] appears were discussed. So, he did not address exchange. In the problems treated, he postulated a striving to optimal ophelimity.

Tinbergen's main interest in economics has always been that of economic policy. This can already be seen from the kind of problems he treated in his thesis and particularly in the *Archiv* paper. These problems were discussed in terms of optimal policy. Especially he discussed the question whether stabilisation is the optimal business cycle policy. 'Is it in the interest of the labour class to strive for stabilisation or not?' (Tinbergen 1929a: 56 trans). This question was reformulated as: 'which movement of prices maximises the purchasing power of total earnings over the whole business cycle period?' (p. 57 trans). The answer deduced from this approach was that stabilisation provided the optimal path.

In a lecture held at the University of Amsterdam in 1933, Tinbergen (1933a) expounded the method he used in these investigations. His aim was 'to know the implications of certain changes in the social mechanism or in the conditions under which that mechanism works' (pp. 66–7 trans). To gain this understanding, observation was not enough. One should, in addition, make use of 'reasoning'. Tinbergen distinguished two types of reasoning: 'deductive' and 'inductive'. He equated inductive reasoning with statistical analysis. Deductive reasoning was the 'economic part of the reasoning', namely the deduction of propositions from one central principle, the economic motive, that is, the pursuit of maximum satisfaction. Conceived in this way, economic problems were maximisation problems and the mechanism should be described by Lagrange's equations.

Tinbergen was able to deduce four schemes from the central principle. These schemes were derived from the optimal problem to maximise profit, and each took into account specific conditions: 'static competition', 'static monopoly', 'limited competition under static conditions' ('Cournot's scheme'), and 'dynamic competition'.[12] Statistical analysis had to determine which scheme would be able to provide the best explanation of the available empirical data. The relation between Hamilton's principle, schemes and statistics is shown in Figure 2.1.

After finishing his thesis, Tinbergen worked at the Dutch Central Bureau of Statistics (CBS). His early research at the CBS consisted of applying these four schemes to his investigation of the structure of various supply industries: the potato flour industry (Tinbergen 1930), the coffee market (Tinbergen and Van Luytelaer 1932), and the cotton, wheat and sugar markets (Tinbergen 1932, 1933b). He was

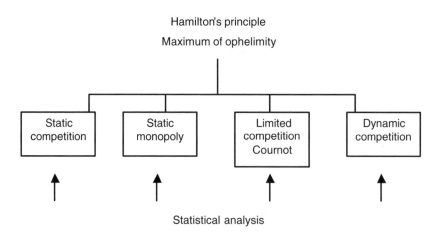

Figure 2.1 Tinbergen's schemes as explanations of the supply curve

interested in the supply side of the market because of the influence of supply regulation on price. The empirical data he had at his disposal at the CBS were used to identify the schemes as possible mathematical descriptions of the structure of the supply markets. Tinbergen found that the dynamic scheme could best explain the supply policy of the cartel-dominated coffee market, while Cournot's scheme produced the best explanation for the supply curve of the potato flour market.

From business-cycle schemes to macrodynamic models

Tinbergen always considered the problem of economic policy as being about determining the optimum policy. To deal with this, one had to dispose of some collective ophelimity function and calculate which policy would optimise this function. Although Tinbergen admitted that determining such a function was an almost impossible task, he always remained optimistic that in the future this problem would be solved (Tinbergen 1935b: 306).

In the calculus, the business cycle can only considered to be explained if it forms the optimal path of an economic relevant Hamiltonian. However, one of the conclusions of Tinbergen's thesis was that with respect to purchasing power, which was the relevant Hamiltonian to be optimised, the business cycle was not the optimal path. So, Tinbergen was not able to derive a scheme from Hamilton's principle to 'explain' the business cycle. Within the framework of the calculus, price fluctuations could only be explained by exogenous (with respect to the mechanism) influences, which was also the case for his dynamic scheme of the supply markets. To Tinbergen, no explanatory mechanism meant no control of the phenomenon. As a result, Hamilton's principle could not provide the tools to regulate or control the cycle. For economic policy reasons, Tinbergen was interested in how a mechanism could generate fluctuations itself, but he understood that he would have to find such a mechanism in another way; applying Hamilton's principle did not help him in this direction.

Critique of empirical business-cycle research

The kind of empirical business-cycle research he came across at the CBS did not help him either in finding a mechanism. The CBS took its methods from the Harvard Committee on Economic Research (run by Charles J. Bullock, Warren M. Persons and William L. Crum) and the Berlin Institut für Konjunkturforschung (run by Ernst Wagemann). Business-cycle research at these institutes consisted of constructing so-called 'barometers' to forecast business cycles. That is to say, their research focused on investigating whether certain economic time-series were correlated. If there is a lag between correlated time-series then it is possible to forecast the course of one time-series with the aid of another time-series.

The Harvard Committee on Economic Research owed its international fame to such a 'barometer' based on three indices of the business cycle, the so-called A–B–C curves, see Figure 2.2. These three indices represented 'speculation' (A), 'business' (B), and 'money' (C), and were lag-correlated. B lagged about six months

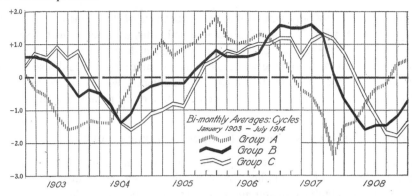

Figure 2.2   Harvard *A–B–C* barometer. Picture shows curves of bimonthly averages of
groups *A*, *B*, and *C*. Group *A* (index of speculation) consists of yield of ten
railroad bonds, price of industrial stocks, price of 20 railroad stocks, and New
York clearings. Group *B* (index of physical productivity and commodity prices
combined) consists of pig-iron production, outside clearings, Bradstreet's prices,
Bureau of Labor prices, and reserves of New York banks. Group *C* (index of
financial situation in New York) consists of rate on 4–6 months paper, rate on
60–90 day paper, loans of New York banks, and deposits of New York banks.
Source: Persons (1919: 112).

behind *A*, and *C* lagged about four months behind *B*. Therefore, *A* could forecast
B and both *A* and *B* could forecast *C*.

Tinbergen opposed the non-theoretical character of the Harvard barometer. His
very first scientific publication, 'Over de mathematies-statistiese methoden voor
konjunktuuronderzoek' ('On mathematical-statistical methods of business-cycle
research', 1927), was a review of this kind of business-cycle research. In it he
criticised the Harvard approach for not being based on any kind of causal theory.
Moreover, Bullock, Persons and Crum (1927: 79) had admitted that their method
was not based on any theory whatsoever; on the contrary, the curves were 'derived
solely from observation of the facts': 'Causal relations have, indeed, received
increasing attention from us; but no theory of causation or of time relation between
cause and effect ever entered into the construction of the index' (p. 79). In addition,
they observed 'how foreign to actual experience are fixed mechanical, or exact
mathematical, relationships in the economic world' (p. 79).

Tinbergen (1927) claimed that the aim of correlation analysis should ultimately
be the recovery of causal connections, as Karl G. Karsten's 'theory of quadrature'
had suggested. Karsten (1926), who had touched 'not without merit' on the problem
of causal relations, had shown the existence of cumulative relations between the
three Harvard barometer indices, which he interpreted as causal relationships. In
the first place, he found by correlation analysis that the cumulative values of the
Harvard *B*-index parallel those of the Harvard *A*-index, with a lag of three months:

$$\sum_{i=1}^{t} B_i = A_{t+3} \qquad\qquad (2.1)$$

Second, he found the empirical relationship that the C-index was a cumulative of both the A and B indices:

$$\sum_{i=1}^{t} \left(\tfrac{1}{4} A_i + \tfrac{3}{4} B_i \right) = C_t \tag{2.2}$$

Thus, according to Karsten (1926: 417), the B-index was the 'generating force' of the three; the other two indices depended upon, and were derived from, changes in the business index.

Equations (2.1) and (2.2) express cumulative relations of discrete processes. For continuous processes, cumulative relations can be expressed by means of integrals:[13]

$$\int_0^t B(\tau)d\tau = A(t+3)$$

$$\int_0^t \left[\tfrac{1}{4} A(\tau) + \tfrac{3}{4} B(\tau) \right] d\tau = C(t)$$

or by differentials, for example:

$$B(t) = \frac{dA(t+3)}{dt} = \dot{A}(t+3) \tag{2.3}$$

In classical mechanics, there is a close connection between the calculus of variations and relationships describing the interaction of forces. It is because of this connection that Karsten wanted to apply the 'theory of quadrature' to investigate the kind of relations that exists between economic quantities. When a cause-and-effect relation exists between two phenomena, then according to the quadrature theory one phenomena is expected to be cumulatively affected by the other:

> In the calculus such relations are familiar in the form of integrals and derivatives, and although these functions are purely mathematical, they are useful to describe the behavior of related forces in the physical sciences. It is the quadrature theory that economic data or statistics betray the same relationships when similarly treated, and that when this is the case, the economic forces or phenomena measured by statistics may be said to be in quadrature and a real [causal] relation is strongly suggested.
>
> (Karsten 1924: 14)

Tinbergen found these cumulative relations exemplary for the kind of causal relation one could expect in business-cycle research. It was the application of this

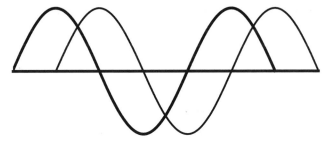

Figure 2.3 One cycle is the cumulation of the other cycle

connection between calculus and causal relationships that made Karsten's approach so appealing to Tinbergen.

Apart from the fact that cumulative relations could be considered as indications of causal connections, they also had the advantage that they could explain the existence of variable lags. 'The quadrature theory is that *the time-lags between the cycles of various economic phenomena are constant functions of the periods of the cycles*' (Karsten 1924: 16).

As above, the cumulative relation between two quantities, X and Y, can also be represented by a differential equation:

$$\int_0^t X(\tau)d\tau = Y(t) \implies X(t) = \dot{Y}(t)$$

The equation on the right side of the arrow shows that the maxima and minima of one cycle $\left(\dot{Y}(t) = \dfrac{dY}{dt} = 0 \right)$ coincide with the zero points of the other ($X(t) = 0$). Therefore, one can say that one cycle lags a quarter-period behind the other, see Figure 2.3. If the period of one cycle is not constant then neither is the lag.

Critique of economic theory

Tinbergen was looking for causal explanations of business cycles but economic theory did not provide the appropriate mechanisms. On the one hand, business cycles were explained by exogenous influences; on the other hand, each cycle was examined and explained individually or, worse still, each phase of a cycle was explained separately. However, Albert Aftalion's (1874–1956) 'Theory of economic cycles based on the capitalistic technique of production' (1927) was an exception, as Tinbergen said about Aftalion's theory:

> An economic dynamics could be constructed based on the [lag] relation between economic quantities, which results in the derivation of perfect cyclic oscillations of an economic system. This is the mathematical interpretation of Aftalion's crisis theory.

I mention this theory in particular because it explains most clearly how the relations considered here can happen, in that every cycle already contains the seed for the next cycle and thus real periodicity occurs.

(Tinbergen 1927: 715 trans)

Aftalion's thesis was 'that the chief responsibility for cyclical fluctuations should be assigned to one of the characteristics of modern industrial technique, namely, the long period required for the production of fixed capital' (Aftalion 1927: 165). For producers, the value of a product depends on the price it is expected to fetch; that is to say, their value depends on the forecast of future prices. Aftalion assumed that the expectations of those directing production are, alternately, either too optimistic or too pessimistic.

In other words, the rhythm is a consequence of the long delay which often separates the moment when the production of goods is decided upon and a forecast is made from the moment when the manufacture is terminated, and the forecast is replaced by reality.

(Aftalion 1927: 165)

Producers forecast future prices on the basis of present prices and the present state of demand.

That is the source of their errors. In modern capitalistic technique the actual state of demand and prices is a bad index of future demand and prices, because of the long interval which separates the moment when new constructions are undertaken from that when they satisfy the demand.

(Aftalion 1927: 166)

In a paper, 'Opmerkingen over ruilteorie' ('Observations on exchange theory') published in 1928, Tinbergen constructed a numerical example demonstrating how a delayed adjustment of supply to price would generate fluctuations about equilibrium over time. Shortly after this he stumbled across an empirical example of this numerical construction in a pork market study by Arthur Hanau (1928) (Tinbergen 1928: 548n; see also Magnus and Morgan 1987: 120). Hanau was a researcher at the Berlin Institut für Konjunkturforschung. According to Tinbergen, this scheme of delayed supply adjustment to price could be extended by taking into account expectations based on observed past fluctuations, or by attributing a delay to demand. 'All these assumptions lead to the same kind of results, of which the essence … consists in the explanation of cyclic motion by the economic mechanism itself' (Tinbergen 1928: 546 trans).

Early business-cycle schemes

At the first European meeting of the Econometric Society in 1931, Tinbergen (1933c) had a number of mathematical formalisations of an endogenous business-cycle mechanism to offer for consideration. Hanau's (1928, 1930) research into the pork market, 'le cas le plus simple', served as point of departure:

Scheme I

Supply: $A_0 + A_1 p(t - \theta)$

Demand: $B_0 - B_1 p(t)$

where A_0, A_1, B_0 and B_1 are positive constants and $p(t)$ the deviation from the equilibrium price P at time t. θ was the time needed to produce the relevant commodity. The mechanism represented by this scheme generated a cycle with a period equal to 2θ. This scheme, known as the cobweb mechanism because of the likeness between its graphical representation and a cobweb, was the simplest explanation of an economic cycle and a mathematical generalisation of Tinbergen's earlier numerical example.

However, the aim was to find mechanisms that could explain the so-called Juglars. These were business cycles with a cycle period of about six to ten years. Scheme I (see above) that implied a production time of three to five years is unrealistic for most production processes. To arrive at a more realistic representation of business cycles, Tinbergen examined more complicated schemes to see what influence each 'complication', which is introduced, could have on the length of the cycle period.

In a second scheme, he introduced 'demande spéculative'. There was some empirical evidence that demand could also be influenced by price changes, for example, as was seen in the wholesale lumber trade, or corn speculation.

Scheme II

Supply: $A_0 + A_1 p(t - \theta)$

Demand: $B_0 - B_1 p(t) + B_2 \dot{p}(t)$

where B_2 is positive and $\dot{p}(t)$ denotes the time differential of price p, $dp(t)/dt$, indicating price changes. In the above Scheme II, the period of the solution (T) lies between: $\frac{3}{4}\theta < T < 2\theta$. So, the introduction of a differential shortens the period of the business cycle with respect to the production lag. In other words, if Scheme II is considered as a possible explanation for the Juglar, it assumes an even longer production time.

Another way of complicating the scheme was to introduce purchasing power into the demand function. First, Tinbergen considered constant purchasing power, C.

Scheme III

Supply: $A_0 + A_1 p(t - \theta)$

Demand: $\dfrac{C}{P + p(t)}$

The solution of this scheme had a period length equal to 2θ. So, constant purchasing power did not influence the cycle's period. Next, he assumed that purchasing power was dependent on economic activity, which he defined as the numbers of workers employed during the production process:

$$N(t) = \alpha \int_{t-\theta}^{t} \left[A_0 + A_1 p(\tau) \right] d\tau$$

If wages are constant and equal to S, then total purchasing power equals SN, and the scheme becomes:

Scheme IV

Supply: $A_0 + A_1 p(t - \theta)$

Demand: $\dfrac{S\alpha \int_{t-\theta}^{t} \left[A_0 + A_1 p(\tau) d\tau \right]}{P + p(t)}$

The cycle's period was equal to 2.7θ. Thus, by assuming that purchasing power is dependent on economic activity, Tinbergen was able to extend the period compared with the production lag, and thus arrived at a more realistic business-cycle mechanism.

In this period Tinbergen (1931) found another empirical example of an endogenous cycle: the shipbuilding cycle. Moreover, a mathematical representation of its mechanism showed how a lag of two years could generate a cycle of eight years. The shipbuilding market mechanism was a combined lag and cumulative relation (cf. equation (2.3)):

$$\dot{X}(t) = -aX(t - \theta) \tag{2.4}$$

where X represents world tonnage, and θ the average needed time to build a ship, approximately two years. The parameter a has a constant value between ½ and 1. The cycle generated by this mechanism has a period equal to $4\theta = 8$ years.[14]

Synthetic economics

With the above theoretical and empirical results in mind, Tinbergen gradually developed a larger programme for business-cycle research to deal with the central question: 'is it possible for an economic community to display a swinging movement without the external non-economic factors, on which this is based, having such a movement?'

(Tinbergen 1933d: 8 trans). The first time he outlined such a programme in public was at his inaugural lecture, 'Statistiek en wiskunde in dienst van het konjunktuuronderzoek' ('Statistics and mathematics of use to business-cycle research', 1933d) on his appointment as professor at the Rotterdam School of Economics. This lecture offered a survey of the business-cycle research that had already taken place as well as a kind of programme, or work proposal, for what needed to be done. Other schemes than the four business-cycle schemes above were candidates for movement-generating mechanisms, on the condition that they were dynamic. A scheme was called dynamic when at least one of its equations was dynamic, that is, a relation between variables that relates to different moments of time. Dynamic relations were obtained by introducing lag terms, differentials or integrals.

However, these mathematical considerations were only part of the proposed programme. Each scheme put forward, even each separate equation, had to be statistically verified by regression analysis. Any regression equation thus achieved was termed 'analytical knowledge'. A 'closed' system of regression equations, that is, a system of equations in which the number of variables equals the number of equations was called 'synthetic knowledge'. The terminology was clearly borrowed from Henry Moore's *Synthetic Economics* (1929).

Moore's 'Synthetic Economics' was meant to synthesise two bifurcated mathematical approaches in economics, Walras's 'pure' general equilibrium theory and Cournot's statistical approach.[15] However, Walras's equilibrium system was only a static system, while Moore aimed to develop a dynamic economics to 'give, by means of recent statistical methods, a concrete, practical form to the theoretical ideas of moving equilibria, oscillations, and secular change' (Moore 1929: 4). This 'practical form' was to present 'all of the interrelated, economic quantities in a synthesis of simultaneous, real equations' (p. 5).

> There are three special characteristics which I should like the name *Synthetic Economics* to imply: (1) the use of simultaneous equations to express the *consensus* of exchange, production, capitalisation, and distribution; (2) the extension of the use of this mathematical synthesis into economic dynamics where all of the variables in the constituent problems are treated as functions of time; and (3) the still further extension of the synthesis to the point of giving the equations concrete, statistical forms. With these implications *Synthetic Economics* is both deductive and inductive; dynamic, positive, and concrete.
>
> (Moore 1929: 6)

According to Moore, the 'synthetic method' had three advantages. First, it eliminated many controversies in economics as to the causes of phenomena. It showed that each causal relation is only a partial truth; 'that the sum of the partial truths is not the whole truth; that the proper weight and place of each partial truth may be specified; and that the ensemble of the determining conditions may be mathematically expressed' (pp. 6–7).

A second advantage was that it indicated precisely when an economic problem was solved. A problem is not yet solved if there is only a mathematical solution to a system that has as many independent equations as it does unknown quantities. First the equations themselves need to be empirically derived and secondly the problem has to be suitable for a 'real' solution.

But, 'by far the chief advantage' was that 'it gives ground for the hope of introducing into economic life rational forecasting and enlightened control' (p. 8). To solve the problem of the rational forecasting of oscillations, a complete theory of oscillations could be approached by successive approximations. A first approximation would be to take first into account the most important cause of perturbation, and subsequently combining this with the effects of other perturbing causes (p. 9).

According to Tinbergen, two different kinds of synthetic knowledge were possible:

> Either there has to be a certain complex of economic phenomena that, by first approximation, behaves independently of the rest of the economy, and can be lifted *out* and studied separately, or one has to consider economic society as a whole, which can be done in an approximate or a more detailed manner.
>
> (Tinbergen 1933d: 6 trans)

An example of an economic phenomena complex, behaving independently from the rest of an economy, was found in Hanau's investigation of the pork market, Scheme I. Schemes III and IV (see above) could be considered as points of departure for the second possibility of synthetic knowledge.

Quantitative business-cycle theory

In a survey on 'quantitative business-cycle theory', Tinbergen (1935b) systematically and explicitly outlined his criteria for an appropriate business-cycle theory. This fitted into Moore's Synthetic Economics programme: 'The aim of business cycle theory is to explain certain movements of economic variables. Therefore, the basic question to be answered is in what ways movements of variables may be generated' (Tinbergen 1935b: 241). And so, the core of the business-cycle theory was the 'mechanism', that he defined as 'the system of relations existing between the variables; at least one of these relations must be dynamic. This system of relations defines the structure of the economic community to be considered in our theory' (pp. 241–2). However, unlike Moore but in the tradition of Maxwell and Boltzmann, Tinbergen emphasised the distinction between the mathematical form and the economic meaning of the equations:

> The mathematical form determines the nature of the possible movements, the economic sense being of no importance here. Thus, two different economic systems obeying, however, the same types of equations may show exactly the same movements. But, it is evident that for all other questions the economic significance of the equations is of first importance and no theory can be accepted whose economic significance is not clear.
>
> (Tinbergen 1935b: 242)

Apart from the condition that at least one dynamic equation should appear in the mechanism, other mathematical requirements were, as Moore prescribed, that the mechanism should be a 'closed' system of equations, that is, a system that contains as many equations as it does variables, and 'the analytical form of the equations is simplified as much as possible' (p. 242). One way of achieving simplicity was to use Frisch's 'macrodynamic' approach; that is 'the grouping of the elements, which has its statistical counterpart in the calculation of index numbers of all sorts' (p. 243).

After outlining these criteria for a business-cycle theory, Tinbergen discussed 'the most important dynamic relations existing in real economic life which may, or must, be chosen as starting points of an adequate business-cycle theory', which he labelled 'the facts' (p. 243). Tinbergen put forward the mathematical theories of Frisch (1933b), Kalecki (1935, see Chapter 1), Roos (1930) and Vinci (1934) as examples of adequate business-cycle theories. Tinbergen also discussed his own 'lag scheme'. This five-equation scheme was a generalisation of his earlier Scheme IV, the one in which purchasing power was dependent on economic activity.

Mathematical shaping was an essential element of Tinbergen's business-cycle research in the 1930s. Economic theories themselves did not contain any guidelines that could lead to an appropriate formalism. They were either narratives or, if mathematical, only gave descriptions of *static* systems. Mathematical shaping was a trial-and-error process that started with the assumption of a production lag. As Hanau (1928) showed empirically and Aftalion (1927) showed theoretically, lags generate endogenous fluctuations. However, basing dynamics on a production lag alone has several disadvantages. In the first place, as discussed above, to explain a Juglar the assumed production time would have to be far too long. This was why Tinbergen introduced various complications into the schemes. In the second place, the disadvantage of postulating lags is that they must be stated in advance and have a fixed length. 'This has been repeatedly felt as a too rigid representation of reality' (Tinbergen 1933d: 13 trans). Moreover, besides lag relations other dynamic relations are possible, namely those containing differentials and integrals. From physics, Tinbergen knew that second-order differential equations can generate cycles. For example, differentiating (with respect to time) an equation in which a differential and an integral term appear will produce an equation of the harmonic oscillator.

$$a\dot{y}(t) + by(t) + c\int_0^t y(\tau)d\tau = 0 \rightarrow a\ddot{y}(t) + b\dot{y}(t) + cy(t) = 0 \qquad (2.5)$$

An advantage of differential equations is that differentials refer to very small time intervals. Note that $\dot{y} = dy/dt$, where dt can be approximated by a very small difference in time Δt. Thus

$$\dot{y} \approx \frac{y(t) - y(t - \Delta t)}{\Delta t} \qquad (2.6)$$

Considering the shorter time many production processes need nowadays, the appearance of only direct affective causes can be called a realistic feature in view of this. Thus, what really matters is the question just posed: can quantities with an integral character and a differential character, respectively, be found and do these quantities play an important role in the business cycle?

(Tinbergen 1933d: 14–15 trans)

At a meeting of the Econometric Society in Leiden in 1933, Tinbergen raised this question most explicitly: 'Is the theory of harmonic oscillation useful in the study of business cycles?' To deal with this question a special colloquium-lecture by Ehrenfest on harmonic oscillations was planned. Because of Ehrenfest's unexpected death on 24 September, this lecture never took place (Marschak 1934: 187). Tinbergen proposed to start 'from the mathematical nature of harmonic oscillations and seeking among the main economic relations those likely to fit into the harmonic pattern' (p. 188). Accordingly, he marshalled economic relations into two groups: (1) 'differential phenomena', mainly functions of the rate of price change, $\dot{p}(t)$, and (2) 'integral phenomena', mainly functions of $\int pdt$, where p again denotes price. Statistical tests, however, persuaded him not to give too much credit to most of the phenomena of group (2), because the correlations he had hitherto found were too small (p. 188).

In his 1935 survey, Tinbergen discussed this issue again. To make 'closer approximations to reality' (1935b: 277), differentials, $\dot{p}(t)$, and integrals, $\int pdt$, were added to the lag schemes. Thus, in general, the reduced form equation of a business-cycle scheme would have the following shape:[16]

$$\sum_1^n a_i p(t - t_i) + \sum_1^n b_i \dot{p}(t - t_i) + \sum_1^n c_i \int_0^{t-t_i} p(\tau)d\tau = 0$$

The requirement was that the parameters satisfy the 'wave condition' and the 'long wave condition'. The 'wave condition' indicated that the solution to the above reduced form equation should consist of a sine function, $p(t) = C\lambda^t \sin(\omega t)$, so that the time shape of $p(t)$ is cyclic. The 'long wave condition' prescribed that the cycle period should be long compared with the 'time units' and that the cycle should not differ 'too much from an undamped [sic] one' (p. 280). According to Tinbergen, these conditions will be 'a guide in a statistical test of the different schemes as to their accord with reality' (p. 280). As a first approximation to these conditions, Tinbergen put $\lambda = 1$ and $\omega = 0$. Then the period of the cycle, $2\pi/\omega$, goes to infinity. Both conditions taken together implied that

$$\sum_1^n c_i = 0 \qquad\qquad (2.7)$$

In other words, mechanisms 'only then lead to long, not too much damped waves when the integral terms are of small importance' (p. 281).

Tinbergen also considered a second approximation of the long wave conditions by assuming that $\lambda = 1 + \delta$ and $\omega = \varepsilon$, where both δ and ε are very small. Again this resulted in restrictions on the parameters of the possible mechanisms. Tinbergen considered several mechanisms for their ability to explain the business cycle. The wave conditions were used to detect the correct mechanism by comparing the order of magnitude required by the conditions with the estimated parameter values. But to find out whether these possible mechanisms 'can explain real business cycles and which of them resembles reality' (p. 281) statistical verification was again the necessary next step in the analysis.

Tinbergen's modelling programme

Tinbergen's research programme in the first half of the 1930s can be briefly characterised as a combination of two methods, mathematical shaping and statistical verification. Mathematical shaping generated potential business-cycle mechanisms, which had to be verified empirically. Tinbergen was the first to succeed in modelling a real economy on the basis of this new programme. In 1936, he presented his very first macroeconometric model of the Dutch economy to the Dutch Society of Economics and Statistics. The paper was read and published in Dutch, but in the same year Tinbergen was commissioned by the League of Nations to perform statistical tests on business-cycle theories. The results were published in a two-volume work, *Statistical Testing of Business-Cycle Theories* (1939a, 1939b). The first contained an explanation of a method of econometric testing as well as a demonstration based on three case studies, to show what could be achieved. The second volume developed a model of the United States: the second macroeconometric model in the history of economics.

Tinbergen wrote several reports on his work at the League of Nations. They provide us with an explicit account of what early modelling practice entailed. On several occasions, Tinbergen stressed the necessity of simplification.

> Mathematical treatment is a powerful tool; it is, however, only applicable if the number of elements in the system is not too large. Subjects, commodities and markets have, therefore, to be combined in large groups, the whole community has to be schematised to a 'model' before anything fruitful can be done. This process of schematisation is, of course, more or less arbitrary. It could, of course, be done in a way other than has here been attempted. In a sense this is the 'art' of economic research, depending partly on the attitude in which the approach is made.
>
> (Tinbergen 1937: 8)

The model was viewed as a system of equations governing the movements of the various elements in an economic community. This system consisted of 'a network of causal relationships', 'relationships of definition', and 'technical or institutional connections' (p. 8).

The 'method' Tinbergen employed to understand the causation of business-cycle phenomena 'essentially starts with *a priori* considerations about what explanatory variables are to be included. This choice must be based on economic theory or common sense' (Tinbergen 1939b: 10). Tinbergen was quite aware of the fact that economists did not agree upon which were the most important causes of the business-cycle phenomenon. From Ehrenfest he had learned:

> to formulate differences of opinion in a 'nobler' way than merely as conflicts. His favourite formulation was cast in the general form: if *a* > *b*, scholar A is right, but if *a* < *b*, then scholar B is right. The statement applied to a well-defined problem, and both *a* and *b* would generally be sets of values of elements relevant to the problem treated, with possibly a number of components of qualitative nature.
>
> (Tinbergen 1988: 67)

This method was exactly the method he would adopt in his work for the League of Nations:

> It is rather rare that of two opinions only one is correct, the other wrong. In most cases both form part of the truth ... The two opinions, as a rule, do not exclude each other. Then the question arises in what 'degree each is correct'; or, how these two opinions have to be 'combined' to have the best picture of reality.
>
> [We can] combine these different views, viz. by assuming that the movements ... can be explained by some *mathematical function* of all the variables mentioned. We then have not a combination in the physical sense – an addition of two quantities or of two amounts – but a combination of influences. In many cases the mathematical function just mentioned may be approximated by a linear expression.
>
> (Tinbergen 1936b: 1–3)[17]

The equations that were chosen were linear with parameters that remain constant over time. 'The use of linear relations means much less loss of generality than is sometimes believed' (Tinbergen 1939b: 11). The values of the parameters were found by multiple regression analysis. Applying 'statistical tests of significance' checked the accuracy of these results. Apart from these statistical tests, 'economic tests of significance' were used. 'The most important one is that of their algebraic sign, which in most cases the economist knows on *a priori* grounds' (p. 13).

The aim was to better understand the mechanism of business cycles by developing an increasing number of relations in order to represent the network of causal connections that make up the business-cycle mechanism. This should be pursued until a 'complete system' of 'elementary equations' was obtained. Completeness will be achieved when a system has as many relations as there are variables to be explained.

The word 'complete' need [sic] not to be interpreted in the sense that every detail in the complicated economic organism is described. This would be an impossible task which, moreover, no business-cycle theorist has ever considered as necessary. By increasing or decreasing the number of phenomena, a more refined or a rougher picture or 'model' of reality may be obtained; in this respect, the economist is at liberty to exercise his judgement.

(Tinbergen 1939b: 15)

Tinbergen's method can be presented graphically as shown in Figure 2.4. Each model equation had to be assessed in two ways, 'deductively' (indicated by the arrow ($\downarrow$) and 'inductively' ($\uparrow$)). Economic significance was obtained by deducing possible causal factors and conditions on the parameter values from economic theories. Statistical analysis was used to decide which factors were statistically significant and to measure how great their influence was.

The procedure Tinbergen employed to test existing business-cycle theories, consisted of two stages. First, the variables that a given theory provides must be tested by multiple regression analysis, and second, the system of numerical values found for the causal relations must be tested to see whether it really yields a cyclic movement when used in the reduce form equation.

This meant that the final model was not merely the result of theoretical and statistical considerations. Mathematical assessment was still part of the modelling process but, now, less prominently. The resulting mathematical shape of the models was made up of linear difference equations. The differentials and integrals that had played such an important role in the earlier representations of causal connections were gone.

The integrals were omitted because 'some calculations have shown that they have no large influence on the shape of the shorter fluctuations' (Tinbergen 1939b: 130). It appeared that the integrals, now called 'cumulants', in the reduced form equation influenced the possible movements of the system in two ways:

(i) The period and degree of damping [sic] of the cyclical movement are to some extent affected by the presence of such terms.

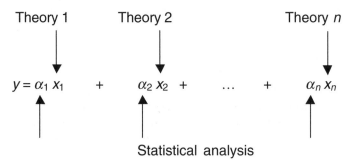

Figure 2.4 Tinbergen's method

(ii) Besides that, the cumulants introduce an additional root into the characteristic equation, which is real and positive, giving rise to a one-sided movement. This movement is explosive (away from the equilibrium situation) if the algebraic sum of all coefficients of cumulation terms in the final equation [reduced form equation] is positive; the movement is damped (gradual approach of the equilibrium situation) if that sum is negative.

(Tinbergen 1939b: 147)

However, the cumulants appearing in the reduced form equation were 'not all, and perhaps not even the most important of, the cumulants to which the economic mechanism gives rise in reality' (Tinbergen 1939b: 149). In many other cases, cumulations could not be distinguished from trends and so remained 'hidden'. A rough estimate of the possible effects of cumulants (including the hidden ones) showed that they would change the dampening factor at the most by ±0.05. Because of the hidden cumulants, the sign of the sum of the coefficients for the cumulants could not be determined, but Tinbergen assumed that the positive real root lay somewhere between 0.75 and 1.25, which leaves the possibility of either a dampened or an explosive one-sided movement. The latter possibility had to be rejected as it was not in accordance with movements observed in reality. The influence of the former on the cyclical movement would only be moderate. 'To sum up, on the ground of their small influence under (i) and our ignorance of their effect under (ii), it seemed both advisable and justified to keep all terms containing cumulants out of the elimination process' so they will not show up in the reduced form equation (p. 149). Although Tinbergen did not mention this, the result was consistent with his earlier result in his 1935 survey paper that the sum of the coefficients of the integrals should be small (equation (2.7)) to satisfy the wave conditions.

The differentials disappeared because Tinbergen changed his views on the meaning and role of lags in the mathematical relations. In his earlier business-cycle schemes, lags meant production lags and referred to time intervals of about one to two years. One of the main reasons for introducing differentials was that they represented more immediate reactions. But in later macroeconometric models, lags did not have this specific economic meaning any more; they came to indicate time units of, for example, one month. If time-lags are time units, $\Delta t = 1$, differentials can be approximated by differences, cf. equation (2.6): $\dot{y} \approx y(t) - y(t-1)$.

Conclusions

Although the term 'model' originally referred to a material object, it has now lost its physical substance in economics. Nevertheless, as Morrison and Morgan (1999) have shown, models still function *as if* they were material representations. Their representative power enables us to learn something about the thing they represent:

we do not learn much from looking at a model – we learn more from building the model and manipulating it. Just as one needs to use or observe the use of a hammer in order to really understand its function, similarly, models have to be used before they will give up their secrets. In this sense, they have the quality of a technology – the power of the model only becomes apparent in the context of its use.

(Morrison and Morgan 1999: 12)

In other words, Morrison and Morgan treat models as instruments.

Morrison and Morgan's account of the understanding that is gained by building and using models fits into a longer tradition that started with what Galileo took to be intelligible and the conception of intelligibility that he developed. Machamer (1998) shows that Archimedean simple machines, such as the balance, the inclined plane, and the screw, combined with the experiences gained using them, constituted Galileo's conception of both theory and experiment.

Intelligibility or having a true explanation for Galileo had to include having a mechanical model or representation of the phenomenon. In this sense, Galileo added something to the traditional criteria of mathematical description (from the mixed sciences) and observation (from astronomy) for constructing scientific objects (as some would say) or for having adequate explanation of the phenomena observed (as I would say). … To get at the true cause, you must replicate or reproduce the effects by constructing an artificial device so that the effects can be seen.

(Machamer 1998: 69)

This mode of scientific understanding was also emphasised by Thomson (see also above): 'I never satisfy myself until I can make a mechanical model of a thing. If I can make a mechanical model I understand it' (Thomson [1884] 1987: 206). In this tradition, understanding a phenomenon became the same as 'designing a model imitating the phenomenon; whence the nature of material things is to be understood by imagining a mechanism whose performance will represent and simulate the properties of the bodies' (Duhem 1954: 72). (For a more recent, philosophically related discussion, see Cartwright's 'simulacrum' account of models: 'the success of a model depends on how much and how precisely it can replicate what goes on' (Cartwright 1983: 153).)

In his paper, 'Bildtheorie and scientific understanding', Henk De Regt (1999) shows how 'Bilder' – images – fulfilled an explanatory task in Boltzmann's philosophy of science, or, in other words, how they functioned as tools for understanding. The kind of images Boltzmann preferred, as being most intelligible, were mechanical pictures. As De Regt (1999: 121–2) argues, 'it is the practical success of mechanicism – possibly linked with our familiarity with mechanical systems from daily experience – that has made it into a criterion for intelligibility in science'.[18]

What, then, is meant by having perfectly correct understanding of a mechanism? Everybody knows that the practical criterion for this consists in being able to handle it correctly. However, I go further and assert that this is the only tenable definition of understanding a mechanism.

(Boltzmann [1902b] 1974: 150)

Intelligibility is not the only advantage of simple mechanical models. Not only do they provide a mechanism to explain a phenomenon under investigation, they supply the mathematics to describe it. Maas (2001, forthcoming b) presents us with an example of how the balance functions in the work of William Stanley Jevons (1835–82), founder of modern economics. Morgan (1999) and Boumans (2001, see also Chapter 6) investigate how the balance provided the appropriate mechanism for developing the Quantity Theory of Money in the work of Irving Fisher (1867–1947). In the 1930s, the exemplar of a simple machine used to understand business cycles was the pendulum. As we have seen above, Tinbergen took harmonic oscillation – the mathematical representation of the pendulum – as a starting point for analysing the business cycle. Moreover, Frisch's classic Rocking Horse model of the business cycle (1933b) was a pendulum (or rocking horse) hampered by friction but frequently hit by a stick (or water, see above) to maintain the cycle.

Intelligible as these physical analogies may be, and useful in that they provide the necessary mathematical shapes, the schemes derived from these analogies still lack any economic meaning: they are not yet images – models – of economic reality. According to Tinbergen, economic meaning is gained in two ways, 'deductively' and 'inductively' (see Figure 2.4). Economic theories indicate which economic factors are relevant and provide conditions concerning parameter values. Statistical analysis is used to decide which factors are statistical significant and to measure how much influence they have.

To see a model as an image implies that there is no unique view but that several perspectives or focuses are possible, depending on the model builder's purpose. Tinbergen adjusted his schemes mathematically until he got the right wavelength (see, for example, his application of the so-called wave conditions above). This is the same kind of adjustment of parameters as Kalecki had carried out in his design of a business-cycle model (discussed in Chapter 1). This 'tuning' is an essential part of modelling besides tests for economic and statistical significance.

Models as conceived by Tinbergen are Hertzian images. They must be *correct*, i.e. represent the relationships of the phenomenon at hand; *distinct*, i.e. represent the essential phenomenological characteristics as far as possible; and *simple*, i.e. need as few as possible empty relations. However, models do not have to be logically permissible. Appropriateness (distinctness and simplicity) is far more important than logical rigour. Dealing with contradictory theoretical statements is not a matter of choosing between them but a matter of degree that should be settled by measurement. Contrary to Gibbs' tendency to rigorous logic, in which self-consistency became more important than correspondence to reality, modelling arose in a tradition in which understanding means being able to deal with the representing mechanism. The difference between a Gibbsian and a Boltzmannian epistemology leads to different methodologies, which will be discussed in more detail in Chapter 6.

The idea that a model is both the snapshot of an economy (picture) and the camera that took it (instrument) derives from Kevin Hoover's discussions of modelling in econometrics. Hoover (1994) sees econometrics as an observational science analogous to astronomy. Therefore, econometric models should not be assessed as to whether they are valid or not, but as to whether they are useful or not. Moreover, the standard by which the usefulness of an observation instrument is judged varies according to what one seeks to observe.

Tinbergen used an 'adaptive strategy' in his business-cycle research, not a 'competitive strategy' which is the 'official' strategy of econometricians. These labels are from Hoover (1995b), who uses them to distinguish between two different types of empirical assessment strategy in econometrics. A competitive strategy is very briefly indicated as 'theory proposes, estimation and testing disposes' (Hoover 1995b: 29). Typical for this strategy is that theories – and not models – compete with one another for the support of data. The adaptive strategy begins with a simple and unrealistic model. 'It sees how much mileage it can get out of that model. Only then does it add any complicating and more realistic feature' (p. 29). Unlike the competitive strategy, the aim is never to test and possibly reject theory, but to construct models whose output resembles the phenomenon in question more and more closely.

Hoover (1995b) discusses both strategies in the context of real-business-cycle models to distinguish between 'calibrators' and 'estimators'. Whether Tinbergen was a 'calibrator' or an 'estimator' can only be settled in Chapter 5 where calibration is discussed. The main difference relevant here is that in the context of real-business-cycle models only a single core theory is involved, whereas Tinbergen had to assess a wide range of theories. These theories were not tested separately, but built in one model, see Figure 2.4, and then checked for their statistical and mathematical significance.

Tinbergen's adaptive strategy (and those of contemporaries Ragnar Frisch 1933b and Michal Kalecki 1935) is the trial and error process of baking a cake without a recipe as described in Chapter 1. In this kind of modelling, mathematical moulding plays a specific role. First, by the choice of a mathematical analogy: Tinbergen used the equation of the harmonic oscillator (see equation (2.5)), Kalecki used Tinbergen's mathematical representation of the ship-building mechanism (see equation (2.4)), and Frisch used the equation describing a pendulum hampered by friction. Then they pursued an adaptive strategy until all ingredients were integrated. In the integration process, 'tuning' was essential. The parameter values were chosen such that the model could precisely mimic specific facts about the cycle. This tuning is essential to ensure that the mathematical representation has empirical significance.

3   Autonomy

... nature is the realization of the simplest conceivable mathematical ideas. I am convinced that we can discover, by means of purely mathematical constructs, those concepts and those lawful connections between them which furnish the key to the understanding of natural phenomena. Experience may suggest the appropriate mathematical concepts, but they most certainly cannot be deduced from it. Experience remains, of course, the sole criterion of physical utility of a mathematical construction. But the creative principle resides in mathematics. In a certain sense, therefore, I hold true that pure thought can grasp reality as the ancients dreamed.

(Albert Einstein, quoted in Holton 1973: 234)[1]

Introduction

Although most accounts on causality discuss the specific roles that statistics and theory should have, it is taken for granted that they at least are useful in finding causal structures.[2] The role for mathematics is not so obvious. However, before the so-called Probabilistic Revolution in econometrics, specification of causal relations was not a matter of economic-theoretical and statistical significance alone. According to Ragnar Frisch's (1933a) original econometric ideal, all three 'viewpoints', economic theory, statistics and mathematics, were necessary, but not by themselves sufficient: 'It is the *unification* of all three that is powerful. And it is this unification that constitutes econometrics' (Frisch 1933a: 2). As we have seen in Chapter 2, mathematical moulding, that is, the use of formal analogies and tuning, was considered as an essential tool in finding significant causal factors. Formal analogies were used to shape the mathematical system such that a similarity between the mathematical system and the system under investigation was obtained. In what respect the model is similar depends on the interests of the model maker and/or user. The degree of similarity is achieved by tuning, and is also interest relative.[3] To detach the idea of tuning from the context of business-cycle research, we now define tuning more generally (than in Chapter 2) as the adjustment of the parameter values till the model's output has the same selected set of characteristics as the phenomenon to be explained by this model.

However, the founding ideal of the Econometric Society, that is to say the union of mathematics, economics and statistics, was lost in later econometric-modelling practices. In the 1940s, mathematical moulding disappeared from the econometric scene, as Mary Morgan describes in her *History of Econometric Ideas* (1990):

> Between the 1920s and the 1940s, the tools of mathematics and statistics were indeed used in a productive and complementary union to forge the essential ideas of the econometric approach. But the changing nature of the econometric enterprise in the 1940s caused a return to the division of labour favoured in the late nineteenth century, with mathematical economists working on theory building and econometricians concerned with statistical work.
>
> (Morgan 1990: 264)

The importance of mathematical moulding disappeared in the changeover from methods to specify causal mechanisms of business cycles to new methods to identify economic structures: that is to say, the invariant relationships underlying the workings of an economy. Mathematical moulding could fulfill its essential role in modelling business cycle mechanisms because of the close connection between mathematical representations of the business-cycle phenomenon and those of the explanatory mechanism. When the econometric programme shifted its focus from mechanisms explaining phenomena to uncovering structural relationships, feedback from the phenomenon back to the mechanism was lost and the role of mathematical moulding ceased to exist.

The works of the Jan Tinbergen, discussed in Chapter 2, show how mathematics was and could be used for specification purposes. As we have seen, the method Tinbergen employed to arrive at a causal explanation of the business-cycle phenomenon started with *a priori* economic-theoretical considerations about which explanatory variables should be included. Some of the explanatory variables did appear as differential or integral terms in the model equation. The equations were chosen to be linear and the values of the parameters were found by multiple regression analysis. Applying statistical tests of significance measured the accuracy of these results. Moreover, the parameter values found for the causal relations were adjusted to make sure that the model yields a cyclic movement with characteristics in accordance with those of the actual business cycle. As a result of this latter assessment – tuning – it became apparent that integral terms were not of any significance and therefore could be neglected. Differentials were approximated by differences. Thus, after starting with mixed differential–difference–integral equations, Tinbergen ended up with representations of the business-cycle mechanism that used only difference equations.

In response to Tinbergen's reports on this method, Frisch ([1938] 1995) showed that the initial close relationship between the mathematical representation of the business cycle and the mathematical representation of its mechanism was lost in the transformation to difference equations. As a result, it was no longer possible to identify all relevant causal factors. 'Passive observation' alone is not sufficient to detect them, statistics alone cannot reveal inactive but potential factors. Without any feedback from phenomena, we have to rely on economic theory to provide us with a complete list of factors. A similar critique was brought forward by John Maynard Keynes. Although unjustly addressed to 'Professor Tinbergen's Method', it certainly applies to the later Cowles Commission approach.

> Am I right in thinking that the method of multiple correlation analysis essentially depends on the economist having furnished, not merely a list of the significant causes, which is correct so far as it goes, but a *complete* list? For example, suppose three factors are taken into account, it is not enough that these should be in fact *veræ causæ*; there must be no other significant factor. If there is a further factor, not taken account of, then the method is not able to discover the relative quantitative importance of the first three. If so, this means that the method is only applicable where the economist is able to provide beforehand a correct and indubitably complete analysis of the significant factors. The method is one neither of discovery nor of criticism. It is a means of giving quantitative precision to what, in qualitative terms, we know already as the result of a complete theoretical analysis.
>
> (Keynes 1939: 560)

In other words, taking a strong *apriorist* position means that econometrics becomes a method not of testing or of discovery, but of measurement.

Haavelmo (1944) discussed the problem of finding a complete list of causal factors under the heading of the 'problem of autonomy'. However, the problem of autonomy was broader than this; it also covered the problem of invariance. This latter issue concerns the identification of the relationships between causal factors that remain unaffected by changes elsewhere in the system. The problem of listing causal factors and the problem of invariance are closely related in which the requirements of as well as economic-theoretical, statistical and mathematical significance all have equal weights.

Ragnar Frisch's memorandum

Although both volumes of Tinbergen's *Statistical Testing of Business-Cycle Theories* were officially published by the League of Nations in 1939, copies of Tinbergen's research were circulated in advance in 1938, and were evaluated at a special Business Cycle Conference in Cambridge (England) in July of that year (see Morgan 1990: 125; and Hendry and Morgan 1995: 57). Frisch did not attend this meeting but wrote 'rather hurriedly' a memorandum, 'Statistical versus theoretical relations in economic macrodynamics'.[4]

> The present memorandum does not discuss details of the various equations which Tinbergen has obtained and whose coefficients he has determined statistically. My main concern has been to discuss what equations of this type really *mean*, and to what extent they can be looked upon as 'A Statistical Test of Business Cycle Theories'.
>
> (Frisch [1938] 1995: 407)

The memorandum discussed two problems. The first problem was the question 'what sorts of equations it is possible to determine from the knowledge of the time shapes that are actually produced' (p. 416). The answer to this question was that only the so-called 'coflux equations' were discoverable. The second and deeper problem was that these coflux relations may not come near to resembling the more 'fundamental' equations that form the 'essence of theory', the so-called 'autonomous equations' (p. 417). Frisch deduced from his analysis that 'it is *only coflux* relations that are determined by Tinbergen, and the lack of agreement between these equations and those of pure theory cannot be taken as a refutation of the latter' (p. 419).

Frisch's analysis of the first problem, here labelled as the 'identification problem',[5] stimulated various members of the Cowles Commission to work on identification in the 1940s (Hendry and Morgan 1995: 57). The second problem, the 'problem of autonomy', was crucial in the development of the concept of structural equations (see Aldrich 1989). Although both problems are closely related, solving the first does not imply a solution to the second. While Frisch, Haavelmo and Koopmans considered the above 'identification problem' to be in principle a mathematical problem, it will be shown that the 'autonomy problem' remains basically an empirical problem.

To understand the nature of both problems, they will be discussed in the same way as their original treatment in Frisch's memorandum. We start with the identification problem. This problem deals with the relation between the 'form' of the equations representing the assumed relations between the economic variables, the so-called 'variates', and the 'time shape' of these variates.

Frisch defined the form of a difference equation,

$$\sum_{i\theta} a_{i\theta} x_i (t - \theta) = 0 \tag{3.1}$$

as the $i\theta$ range of the summation that determines the terms involved in the equation.[6] The time shape of a variate is defined as the sum of the exponentials that make up this variate,

$$x_i(t) = \sum_{k=1}^{n} C_{ik} e^{\gamma_i t} \tag{3.2}$$

In the memorandum, the identification problem was phrased in terms of 'reducibility' and 'irreducibility' and was linked to the time shapes of the variates (3.2).

It is clear that the property of irreducibility must be important when we are studying the nature of those equations that can be determined from the knowledge of the time shapes of the functions that are to satisfy the equations.
(Frisch [1938] 1995: 413)

The (ir)reducibility of an equation was defined with respect to a set of functions. An irreducible equation of the form (3.1) is 'one whose coefficients are *uniquely determined* and allow of no degree of freedom *if the equation is to be satisfied by this set of functions* (apart from the arbitrary factor of proportionality which is always present in the case of a homogeneous equation)' (p. 413).

By inserting the function $x_i(t)$ defined in formula (3.2) into equation (3.1), one can derive algebraically the following rule:[7]

> Rule about reducibility: If the functions with respect to which reducibility is defined are made up of n exponential components ..., the equation is certainly reducible – and hence its coefficients are affected in a more or less arbitrary manner – if it contains more than $n + 1$ terms. And it may be reducible even if it contains $n + 1$ terms or less.
>
> (Frisch [1938] 1995: 414)

In other words, only equations that contain at the most $n + 1$ terms may be irreducible – uniquely identified – with respect to the time shape of a variate. For example, if the time shape of a variate is a (dampened, undampened or anti-dampened) sine function then it is equivalent to a combination of two exponential components and therefore cannot identify an equation with more than three terms.

However, the time shapes of the variates do not satisfy just one equation but form the actual solution of the complete system, including those determined by the initial conditions. Frisch called an equation that is identified by the time shape of this actual solution a 'coflux' equation. The other equations were called 'superflux' equations. The word 'flux' suggested that both kinds of equations were defined with respect to the time shape actually possessed by the phenomena. Thus, only 'coflux equations and no other equations are discoverable from the knowledge of the time shapes of the functions that form the actual solution' (p. 416).

> This is the nature of *passive observations*, where the investigator is restricted to observing what happens *when all equations in a large determinate system are actually fulfilled simultaneously*. The very fact that these equations are fulfilled prevents the observer from being able to discover them, unless they happen to be coflux equations.
>
> (Frisch [1938] 1995: 416)

Should one bother about these other equations that are not discoverable through passive observation? Frisch's answer was yes; the other equations, the superflux equations, are well worth knowing because they have a higher degree of 'autonomy'. These were the equations that 'maintained unaltered while other features of the structure were changed' (p. 417).

> The higher this degree of autonomy, the more *fundamental* is the equation, the deeper is the insight which it gives us into the way in which the system

functions, in short, the nearer it comes to being a *real explanation*. Such relations form the essence of 'theory'.

(Frisch [1938] 1995: 417)

Unfortunately, autonomy is 'not like the irreducibility a mathematical property of a closed system ... but is built on some sort of knowledge outside this system' (p. 416). Passive observation only leads to coflux equations, and generally speaking, these relations are far from able to give information about the autonomous structural relations. Therefore, it is necessary to use active observation, namely experimentation, as Frisch recommended.

In his memorandum of 1938, the concept of autonomy was not further explicated. Ten years later, in an account of the work being done and studies planned for the next few years at the University Institute of Economics in Oslo, Frisch gave a more explicit description of what he meant by the idea of autonomy:

> Take any equation and ask the question: is the technical and institutional setting which surrounds it and the behaviour of the individuals involved such that this particular equation will *hold good* even though other equations involving the same variables are destroyed through technical, institutional or behaviouristic changes or through the fixation of some specific variables in the system, for instance through a specific economic measure. This, it seems, is the only way in which it is possible to define a 'causal' relation as distinguished from an incidental covariation between economic magnitudes.

(Frisch 1948: 368–9)

Mathematical moulding

Frisch used assumptions about the time shapes of the variates to establish the conditions for identification. Or more specifically, irreducibility was a relation between the terms of the equation in question and the number of exponential components of the function satisfying that equation. It is remarkable that through the whole 1938 memorandum Frisch seems to assume that the time shape of the actual solution of the complete system, including those determined by the initial conditions, is that of a sine function, whether dampened, undampened or anti-dampened. In any case, the actual solution is assumed to consist of at most a small number of exponentials. Moreover, because a sine function is made up of two exponentials, Frisch expected that equations of more than three terms could not be identified. He thus believed that 'in a big system of structural equations it would be quite exceptional if all the equations should be irreducible with respect to that particular solution which turns out to be the final one' (Frisch [1938] 1995: 417). Although he was right to worry about arriving at autonomous equations, his pessimism concerning the identification of irreducible equations was related to an inadequate understanding of difference equations. He treated them as differential equations and this led to confusion about the shape of the solution of a difference equation (see also Chapter 1).

Differential equations (like equation (3.3)) are solved by assuming the solution to be an exponential function (see function (3.4)).[8]

$$x^{(n)} + a_1 x^{(n-1)} + \ldots + a_n x = 0 \tag{3.3}$$

$$x(t) = C e^{\gamma t} \tag{3.4}$$

By inserting this exponential function into the differential equation, the so-called characteristic equation can be derived:

$$\gamma^n + a_1 \gamma^{n-1} + \ldots + a_n = 0 \tag{3.5}$$

The order of the differential equation (n) determines the number of roots of this characteristic equation. The roots of the characteristic equation ($\gamma_1, \ldots, \gamma_n$) can be real or complex. Complex roots lead to periodic solutions (trigonometric functions) and real roots to exponential solutions. The general solution of the differential equation is a finite weighted sum of these solutions:

$$x_i(t) = \sum_{k=1}^{n} C_{ik} e^{\gamma_i t}$$

The weights, C_i, are determined by n initial conditions, e.g. $x(0)$, $x^{(1)}(0)$, ..., $x^{(n-1)}(0)$.

Frisch used the same method to solve difference equations. As a result the general solution is again a weighted sum of trigonometric functions. But now the number of terms summed is not determined by the order of the difference equation. The sum consists of an infinite number of terms and the weights are determined by the initial movement, that is the movement during an initial period of the length of the smallest time lag, θ, and from Fourier analysis we know that this can be any arbitrary movement.

The actual solution of the complete system is a weighted sum of terms satisfying each equation separately. In other words, if one starts with a general infinite sum of weighted exponentials, each equation can be seen as a limiting condition on the set of weights. Frisch implicitly assumed that both the system equations and the initial conditions would reduce the infinite sum of trigonometric functions until a finite sum remained (he even seems to assume that only one sine function would be left). However, although each condition on the weight system establishes a relation between the weights, such a condition is not necessarily a reduction of the number of exponential terms in the summation. So, there are neither theoretical nor empirical grounds to assume that only finite sums of exponential form the actual solution of the whole system.

In general, the actual solution of the complete system including initial conditions is an infinite sum of exponentials. Identification problems arise whenever an equation contains more terms than the number of exponential components that form the time shape of the actual solution (see the above 'rule about reducibility'). So, in case of an infinite sum of exponentials, identification is not a problem for any equation that consists of a finite number of terms, which is usually the case. As a result, the time shapes of the variates, if taken as an infinite sum of exponentials, can identify the complete list of causal factors.

As we have seen in Chapter 2, Tinbergen used the characteristics of the business cycle to acquire information about the causal structure: tests of mathematical significance were used to infer the shape of the equations of the mechanism plus the relevant causal factors. So, an essential part of the model-building process is mathematical shaping: a mathematical formalism is sought that is able to generate the relevant characteristics of the phenomena that should be explained or described. Next, the parameters are quantified in such a way that the model precisely picks out these characteristics. This latter stage has been called tuning. In Chapter 1 we have seen that because mathematical shaping and testing for mathematical significance are two sides of the same coin in the model-building process, justification is built in. One of the examples discussed there showed that Kalecki (1935) tuned his parameters such that his model generated a maintained cycle with a period of 10 years. Boumans (1999) discusses a second example of a model that was built in the same period as Tinbergen's modelling work: Frisch's (1933b) business-cycle models. Frisch tuned the parameters such that his model generated three dampened cycles of which two had a period in accordance with the observed cycle periods.

This practice of mathematical moulding was criticised by Haavelmo in his paper, 'The inadequacy of testing dynamic theory by comparing theoretical solutions and observed cycles' (1940). On the basis of an example, Haavelmo demonstrated that ' "correction" of *the form of* a priori *theory* by pure inspection of the *apparent shape* of time series is a very dangerous proceeding and may lead to spurious "explanations"' (Haavelmo 1940: 321). The example he gave showed that when an apparent trend, that is 'not strongly justified on *a priori* reasons', is built into the model, things are often assumed to be structural whereas they are merely the effect of cumulation of random events and thus, in fact, spurious.

Haavelmo's warning about the danger of building the time shapes of variables into a model was one of the arguments for cutting off the empirical feedback from the phenomenon in question to modelling its causal mechanism. Haavelmo's 1940 paper was the basis for his later 1944 paper on autonomy. In it he showed that when apparent shapes of times series, like temporary trends, are confused with structure the real explanation for the apparent changes in structure is in fact 'the disappearance of spurious elements introduced in our theory by the trend fitting' (p. 321). It should be noted, however, that Haavelmo only discussed the danger of building in temporary appearances which are mistaken as steady characteristics of the phenomena, or in other words, as stylised facts about the phenomena. It would be thirty years before the strategy of using facts about a phenomena to assess parameter values remerged under the new name: 'calibration', see Chapter 5. This strategy could only flourish once the high-days of the Cowles Commission approach were over.

Trygve Haavelmo's probability approach

Haavelmo's (1944) 'The probability approach in econometrics' echoed Frisch's memorandum in many respects, in particular its terminology, but it is important to be aware of the change in its scope. There was not only a shift from linear to non-linear equations, and the concomitant change in mathematical technique from linear algebra to implicit function theory, but the point of departure also differed (see Aldrich 1994: 205–6). Haavelmo envisaged a situation in which the form of the equations are given by the relevant economic theory and the unknowns are the values of the economic structural parameters, while to Frisch all that is given is the possibility that there are one or more linear relations between the variables. Nevertheless, Haavelmo also distinguished between the identification problem and the autonomy problem. The problem of identification, here called 'problems of estimation' or 'problem of arbitrary estimates', was that 'one or more of the parameters to be estimated might, in fact, be *arbitrary* with respect to the *system* of equations' (Haavelmo 1944: 84). Haavelmo described this 'statistical side of the problem of autonomous relations' as follows:

> Suppose that a certain set of economic variables actually satisfies a *system* of (static or dynamic) equations, each of which we expect to have a certain degree of autonomy, so that we are interested in measuring the constant parameters involved (e.g. certain elasticities). From this equation system we can, by algebraic operations, derive an infinity of confluent systems. Suppose that, in particular, it is possible to derive an infinity of new systems which have exactly the same *form* as the original system, but with *different values of the coefficients* involved. ... Then, if we do not know anything about the values of the parameters in the original equation system, it is clearly not possible to obtain a unique estimate of them by any number of observations of the variables.
>
> (Haavelmo 1944: 84)

Haavelmo, in line with Frisch, emphasised that economic research is mainly built on '*passive observations* of facts, instead of data obtained by rationally planned experiments' (p. 85). Thus,

> we can obtain only such data as are the results of the economic system *as it in fact is*, and *not* as it *would be* under those unrestricted hypothetical variations with which we operate in economic theory, and in which we are interested for the purpose of economic policy.
>
> (Haavelmo 1944: 85)

The problem of estimation came down to a study of the properties of the joint probability distribution of the random (observable) variables in a stochastic equation system. Within this framework, two 'fundamental' problems could be formulated, namely the 'problem of arbitrary parameters' and the problem of 'best estimates'. The first problem was that if two stochastical equation systems lead to the same joint probability law of the observable random variables, we cannot distinguish between them on the basis of observations (see Haavelmo 1944: 88 and 91). The second problem was how to find the best estimate for the parameters given a specific sample, in other words a straightforward statistical problem. The first problem was considered a problem of 'pure mathematics'. 'This problem, however, is of particular significance in the field of econometrics, and relevant to the very construction of economic models' yet 'this particular mathematical problem does not seem to have attracted the interest of mathematicians' (p. 92). The problem was described using Frisch's term 'reducibility', but with a slightly different meaning. Reducibility was not defined with respect to linear difference equations but to the more general functional equations and was not linked to the exponentials satisfying these equations any more but to the general functions of the parameters. As a result, reducibility was now defined in terms of whether or not the partial derivatives of the functional equations, with respect to the parameters, were linear dependent.

Thus, while the dual problem of estimation could be tackled in a mathematical and statistical way, the problem of autonomy remained, as in Frisch's memorandum, 'a matter of intuition and factual knowledge; it is an art' (p. 29). The problem of autonomy was worded as the problem of 'judging the degree of persistence over time of relations between economic variables', or more generally speaking, 'whether or not we might hope to find elements of invariance in economic life, upon which to establish permanent "laws"' (p. 13). The problem of autonomy results from the fact that real economic phenomena cannot be 'artificially isolated from "other influences"' (p. 14). We have to deal with passive observations, and these are

> influenced by a great many factors not accounted for in theory; in other words, the difficulties of fulfilling the condition 'Other things being equal'. But this is a problem common to all practical observations and measurements; it is in point of principle, not a particular defect of economic time series.
>
> (Haavelmo 1944: 18)

To explore the problem of autonomy, we consider the following more concrete problem. Let y denote an economic variable, the observed values of which may be considered as results of planned economic decisions taken by individuals, firms, etc. And let us start from the assumption that the variable y is influenced by a number of causal factors, $x_1, x_2, \ldots$.

> Our hope in economic theory and research is that it may be possible to establish constant and relatively *simple* relations between dependent variables, y (of the type described above), and a relatively *small* number of independent variables, x. In other words, we hope that, for each variable, y, to be 'explained', there is a relatively small number of explaining factors the variations of which are practically decisive in determining the variations of y.
>
> (Haavelmo 1944: 22–3)

Haavelmo distinguished between two different notions of 'influence', namely 'potential influence' and 'factual influence'. Let y be a theoretical variable defined as a function of n independent 'causal' variables $x_1, x_2, \ldots, x_n$:

$$y = F(x_1, \ldots, x_n) \tag{3.6}$$

Then, the 'potential influence' of the factor x_i upon y is defined as $\Delta_i y$ given by

$$\Delta_i y = F(x_1, \ldots, x_i + \Delta x_i, \ldots, x_n) - F(x_1, \ldots, x_i, \ldots x_n) \tag{3.7}$$

To compare the size of the influence of each of the variables x_i, one has, for any point $(x_1, x_2, \ldots, x_n)$, to choose a set of displacements $\Delta x_1, \Delta x_2, \ldots, \Delta x_n$, which are considered to be of equal size according to some standard, e.g. equal percentages of $x_1, x_2, \ldots x_n$ respectively.

The notion 'factual influence' refers to a set of N observed values of y corresponding to a set of $N \times n$ observed values of the variables $x_1, \ldots, x_n$, and is determined according to some 'outside principle':

Determine the minimum with respect to c_i of Q_i

$$Q_i = \sum_{j=1}^{N} \left[F\left(x_{1j}, \ldots, x_{ij}, \ldots, x_{nj}\right) - F\left(x_{1j}, \ldots, c_i, \ldots, x_{nj}\right) \right]^2 \tag{3.8}$$

The factual influence upon y of the variable x_i is then defined as: $C\sqrt{Q_i^{\min}}$.

To clarify this complicated definition of 'factual influence', let us assume that F is a linear function of the independent causal factors: $F(x_1, \ldots, x_n) = a_1 x_1 + \ldots + a_n x_n$. Then $c_i = \bar{x}_i$ and thus

$$Q_i^{\min} = a_i^2 \sum_{j=1}^{N} \left(x_{ij} - \bar{x}_i\right)^2 = N a_i^2 \sigma_{x_i}^2 \tag{3.9}$$

Taking into account that, $\sigma_y^2 = a_1^2 \sigma_{x_1}^2 + \ldots a_n^2 \sigma_{x_n}^2$ one can read the factual influence of the variable x_i upon y as that part of the standard deviation of y that is caused by the variation of factor x_i.

According to Haavelmo, the distinction between potential and factual influence was fundamental.

> For, if we are trying to explain a certain observable variable, y, by a system of causal factors, there is, in general, no limit to the number of such factors that might have a *potential* influence upon y. But Nature may limit the number of factors that have a nonnegligible *factual* influence to a relatively small number.
> (Haavelmo 1944: 24)

Thus, the relationship $y = F(x_1, \ldots, x_n)$ (see equation (3.6)) explains the actual observed values of y, provided that the factual influence of all the unspecified factors together were very small as compared with the factual influence of the specified factors $x_1, \dots, x_n$.

> This might be the case even if (1) the unspecified factors varied considerably, provided their potential influence was very small, or if (2) the potential influences of the unspecified factors were considerable, but at the same time these factors did not change much, or did so only very seldom as compared with the specified factors.
>
> (Haavelmo 1944: 25)

However, 'our greatest difficulty in economic research' does not lie in establishing simple relations, but rather in the fact that the empirically found relations, derived from observation over certain time intervals, are 'still simpler than we expect them to be from theory, so that we are thereby led to *throw away* elements of a theory that would be sufficient to explain apparent "breaks in structure" later' (p. 26). The problem is that we may throw away those elements that have had a very small factual influence because these factors did not change much (case 2), and not because the potential influence was very small (case 1). This refers to the so-called 'problem of autonomy of economic relations'. Some of these relations have very little autonomy because their existence depends upon the simultaneous fulfillment of a great many other relations. Highly autonomous relations are those that 'describe the functioning of some parts of the mechanism *irrespective* of what happens in some *other* parts' (p. 28). This is the 'principal task of economic theory': to establish those relations that might be expected to possess as high a degree of autonomy as possible.

Haavelmo called any relation that was derived by combining two or more relations a confluent relation. In general, a confluent relation has a lower degree of autonomy than the relations from which it is derived. This gives rise to the problem that an infinite number of systems of confluent equations will derive from a system built up of equations that have a certain degree of autonomy.

> How can we actually distinguish between the 'original' system and a derived system of confluent relations? That is *not* a problem of mathematical independence or the like; more generally, it is not a problem of pure logic, but a problem of actually *knowing something* about real phenomena, and of making realistic assumptions about them.
>
> (Haavelmo 1944: 29)

Autonomous relations are those relations that could be expected to have a high degree of invariance with respect to various changes in the economic structure. However, this kind of invariance should not be equated with the observable degree of constancy or persistence of a relation. The degree of autonomy referred to 'a class of hypothetical variations in structure, for which the relation *would be* invariant, while its actual persistence depends upon what variations *actually occur*' (p. 29).

In scientific research – in the field of economics as well as in other fields – our research for 'explanations' consists of digging down to more fundamental relations than those that appear before us when we merely 'stand and look'. Each of these fundamental relations we conceive of as invariant with respect to a much wider class of variations than those particular ones that are displayed before us in the natural course of events. Now, if the real phenomena we observe day by day are really ruled by the simultaneous action of a whole system of fundamental laws, we see only very little of the whole class of hypothetical variations for which each of the fundamental relations might be assumed to hold.

(Haavelmo 1944: 38)

The problem of autonomy of economic relations

Haavelmo's approach of finding invariant relationships without being able to set up *ceteris paribus* conditions can be explicated by the following model: Let y be an economic variable whose behaviour is determined by a function, F, of independent causal factors $x_1, x_2, \ldots$

$$y = F(x_1, x_2, \ldots) \tag{3.10}$$

The way in which the factors x_i might influence y can be represented by the following equation:

$$\Delta y = \Delta F(x_1, x_2, \ldots) = \frac{\partial F}{\partial x_1} \Delta x_1 + \frac{\partial F}{\partial x_2} \Delta x_2 + \ldots \tag{3.11}$$

The deltas, Δ, indicate a change in magnitude. The terms $\frac{\partial F}{\partial x_i}$ indicate how much F will proportionally change due to a change in magnitude of factor x_i.

Suppose we are trying to discover a law that could explain the phenomenon y. In principle, there are an infinite number of factors, $x_1, x_2, \ldots$, that could influence the behaviour of y, but we hope that it may be possible to establish a constant and relatively simple relation between y and a relatively small number of explanatory factors, x. In a laboratory, we would artificially isolate a selected set of factors from the other influences, in other words we would take care that *ceteris paribus* (CP) conditions are imposed: $\Delta x_{n+1} = \Delta x_{n+2} = \ldots = 0$, so that a simpler relationship can be investigated:

$$\Delta y_{CP} = \frac{\partial F}{\partial x_1} + \Delta x_1 + \ldots + \frac{\partial F}{\partial x_n} \Delta x_n \tag{3.12}$$

Moreover, in a controlled experiment the remaining factors, x_i, can be varied in a systematic way to gain knowledge about the $\frac{\partial F}{\partial x_i}$ and, so, establish the relationship between y and a limited number of factors $x_1, \ldots, x_n$.

However, in economics, we are not able to carry out 'experiments that *we should like to make* to see if certain real economic phenomena – when *artificially isolated* from "other influences" – would verify certain hypotheses' (Haavelmo 1944: 14). We can only passively observe 'the stream of experiments that Nature is steadily turning out from her own enormous laboratory' (p. 14). Having only passive observations available, Haavelmo's distinction between potential and factual influence is fundamental to judge the degree of persistence over time. Taking into account that by definition:

$$\frac{\partial F}{\partial x_i} \approx \frac{F(x_1, \ldots, x_i + \Delta x_i, \ldots, x_n) - F(x_1, \ldots, x_i, \ldots, x_n)}{\Delta x_i}$$

and for a fixed set of displacements, say $\Delta x_i = \Delta_i$, Haavelmo defined the potential influence of a factor x_i as

$$\Delta_i y = F(x_1, \ldots, x_i + \Delta x_i, \ldots, x_n) - F(x_1, \ldots, x_i, \ldots, x_n) \approx \frac{\partial F}{\partial x_i} \Delta_i. \qquad (3.13)$$

As we can infer from equation (3.13), the potential influence is a property of the shape of the function F, or as Haavelmo put it: 'for a given system of displacements $\Delta x_1, \Delta x_2, \ldots, \Delta x_n$, the potential influences are, clearly, formal properties of the function F' (pp. 23–4).

Then, the factual influence can be represented by $\frac{\partial F}{\partial x_i} \Delta x_i$. This can be seen by defining $\Delta x_{ij} = x_{ij} - c_i$ and rewriting $Q_i^{\min}$ as:

$$Q_i^{\min} = \sum_{j=1}^{N} \left[F(x_{1j}, \ldots, c_i + \Delta x_{ij}, \ldots, x_{nj}) - F(x_{1j}, \ldots, c_i, \ldots, x_{nj}) \right]^2$$

$$\approx \sum_{j=1}^{N} \left[\frac{\partial F}{\partial x_i} \Delta x_{ij} \right]^2 = \left(\frac{\partial F}{\partial x_i} \right)^2 \sum_{j=1}^{N} (x_{ij} - c_i)^2$$

$\frac{1}{N} \sqrt{\sum_{j=1}^{N} (x_{ij} - c_i)^2}$ can be seen as a kind of average deviation of x_i from c_i and can thus be represented by Δx_i. In particular, if F is a linear function of the x's, then Δx_i is the standard deviation of x_i (see above). The factual influence is defined as the square root of $Q_i^{\min}$ and thus can be represented as $\left(C = 1/\sqrt{N} \right)$:[9]

$$C\sqrt{Q_i^{\min}} = \frac{\partial F}{\partial x_i} \Delta x_i \qquad (3.14)$$

We usually passively observe (*PO*) a limited number of factors that have a non-negligible factual influence:

$$\Delta y_{PO} \approx \frac{\partial F}{\partial x_i} \Delta x_1 + \ldots + \frac{\partial F}{\partial x_n} \Delta x_n \tag{3.15}$$

Thus, the relationship $y = F(x_1, \ldots, x_n)$ explains the actual observed values of y, provided that the factual influence of all the unspecified factors together are very small as compared with the factual influence of the specified factors $x_1, \ldots, x_n$.

The problem, however, is that it is not possible to identify the reason for the factual influence of a factor, say x_{n+1}, being negligible, $\frac{\partial F}{\partial x_{n+1}} \Delta x_{n+1} \approx 0$. We cannot distinguish whether its potential influence is very small, $\frac{\partial F}{\partial x_{n+1}} \approx 0$, or whether the factual variation of this factor over the period under consideration was too small, $\Delta x_{n+1} \approx 0$. We would like only to 'throw away' the factors whose influence was not observed because their potential influence was negligible to start with. At the same time, we want to retain factors whose influence was not observed because they varied so little that their potential influence was veiled.

The variation of x_{n+1} is determined by other relationships within the system. In some cases a virtually dormant factor may become active because of changes in the economic structure elsewhere. However, deciding whether a factor should be accounted for in the relationship under investigation should not depend on such changes. The relationship should be autonomous with respect to structural changes elsewhere.

How autonomous an equation is depends on our knowledge of the potential influence of each factor, $\frac{\partial F}{\partial x_i}$, which will inform us about the formal properties of the function F (see Haavelmo 1944: 24). Both Frisch and Haavelmo were pessimistic about whether it was possible to acquire knowledge about the autonomy of an equation through passive observation alone (therefore they both advocated experiments in economics). However, the problem is not insurmountable if we use our knowledge about the time shapes of the phenomenon we want to explain. Facts about the time shape of y can be fed back to the form F of the relation being investigated. However, this only works if facts about the time shape of the phenomenon are invariant and stable, and not just temporary characteristics. As we discussed earlier, Haavelmo considered this strategy to be 'very dangerous' and therefore abandoned it. Frisch, also, mistakenly, believed that the time shapes were not sufficient to gain knowledge about the complete list of causal factors.

Unlike Haavelmo, Frisch and Tinbergen used (stylised) facts about the time shape of the business-cycle phenomenon. For Tinbergen, whether integral terms (hidden or not in the observations) should be included in the business-cycle mechanism depended on assumptions about the periodicity and amplitude of the business cycle. Frisch's Propagation and Impulse model (1933b) also used time shapes to gain knowledge about the business cycle's generating mechanism. However, his 1938 memorandum shows that the possibility to identify the full list of causal factors depends on the connection between assumptions about the mathematical representation of the business cycle and assumptions about the mathematical representation of the explaining mechanism.

Tjalling Koopmans' identification of structural equations

Haavelmo's design rules for econometrics were considered to be an alternative to the experimental methods of science (Morgan 1990: 262). However, although researchers at the Cowles Commission[10] adopted Haavelmo's 'blueprint' for econometrics (Morgan 1990: 251), they scrapped the term 'autonomy' because it was believed that structural relations were autonomous (see Aldrich 1989). The reason for believing this was that Haavelmo had pointed out the possibility that the empirically found relationships may be simpler than theory would suggest. This could lead researchers to discard potential influences that could explain shifts in these relationships (see above). This problem could be avoided by building models as comprehensive as possible, based on *a priori* theoretical specifications. As Christ (1994: 53) observes, the Cowles Commission theoretical econometric work 'did not have much to say about the process of specifying models, rather taking it for granted that economic theory would do that, or had already done it'.

The Cowles Commission view (see e.g. Christ 1994) was that to understand a particular aspect of economic behaviour, it is necessary to have a system of descriptive equations. These equations should contain relevant observable variables, be of a known form (preferably linear), and have estimatable coefficients. The Cowles Commission programme aimed to provide an appropriate method to choose the variables relevant to a particular problem so as to obtain a suitable system of equations and estimate the value of the parameters. However, 'little attention was given to how to choose the variables and the form of the equations; it was thought that economic theory would provide this information in each case' (Christ 1994: 33). This position was explicitly expressed by Tjalling Koopmans (1910–85), director of Cowles Commission research, in a paper jointly written with Herman Rubin and Roy B. Leipnik, 'Measuring the equation system of dynamic economics'. The paper was published in 1950, but had already been presented at a Cowles Commission conference in 1945 on statistical inference in economics. It is striking to read in the first sentences the evidence that the role of the requirement of mathematical significance no longer appeared:

> The analysis and explanation of economic fluctuations has been greatly advanced by the study of systems of equations connecting economic variables. The construction of such a system is a task in which economic theory and statistical method combine. Broadly speaking, considerations both of economic theory and of statistical availability determine the choice of the variables.
>
> (Koopmans, Rubin and Leipnik 1950: 54)

The paper focused on linear systems of difference equations of the following general form:

$$\sum_{i=1}^{G}\sum_{\tau=0}^{T}\beta_{git.}y_i(t-\tau)+\sum_{k=1}^{K}\sum_{\tau=0}^{T}y_{git}z_k(t-\tau)=u_g(t)$$

$$g=1,2,...,G; \quad t=1,2,...,T$$

(3.16)

There are G equations containing both G 'endogenous' variables $y_i(t)$ and K 'exogenous' variables $z_k(t)$. The latter were defined as variables that influence the endogenous variables but are not themselves influenced by the endogenous variables.

In the measurement of a system of equations, two separate problems can be distinguished: the problem of the identification of each equation and the problem of the estimation of the parameters of each equation. The problem of identification originated from the fact that systems as shown in equation (3.16), which can be seen as a specification of the joint probability distribution of the observable variables, can be written in many different ways. 'Under no circumstances whatever will passive statistical observation permit [the econometrician] to distinguish between different mathematically equivalent ways of writing down that distribution' (p. 64). However, only one specific way of writing was of importance, and that was the 'structural representation':

> The study of a system of equations like [(3.16)] derives its sense from the postulate ... that there exists one and only one representation in which each equation corresponds to a specified law of behavior (attributed to a specified group of economic agents), to a specified technical law of production, or to a specified identity. Let us call these particular equations the *structural equations*, because they are the elements of which the dynamic economic structure of society is composed. ... Any discussion of the effects of changes in economic structure, whether brought about by gradual trends or by purposive policies, is best put in terms of changes in the structural equations. For those are the elements that can, at least in theory, be changed one by one, independently. For this reason, it is important to have the system [(3.16)] in a form in which the greatest possible number of its equations can be identified and recognised as structural equations.
>
> (Koopmans, Rubin and Leipnik 1950: 63)

So, the problem was to identify among all linear combinations of the equations the 'structural equations' that alone reflect specified laws of economic behaviour, of the technique of production, or of economic accounting.

However, because the econometrician has no 'experimental control' over economic variables,

> the only way in which he can hope to identify and measure individual structural equations implied in that system is with the help of a priori specifications of the form of each structural equation. The most important instrument of

> identification is a specification as to *which variables may enter into which structural equations with which possible time lags.*
>
> (Koopmans, Rubin and Leipnik 1950: 64)

Although the three authors acknowledge both Frisch and Haavelmo's preliminary work on the problem of identification, they do not address the problem of autonomy.

> The first systematic discussion of the problem of identification was given by Frisch in an unpublished memorandum [1938]. Frisch's terminology is rather different from that employed here, and the concepts are slightly different in that the disturbances and their distribution are not explicitly introduced in his formulae. Nevertheless, the underlying ideas are to a large extent the same, and the present authors desire to acknowledge their indebtedness, and to emphasize the support found in Frisch's memorandum for the discussion of the problem of identification in this article. ... The same point is emphasized by Haavelmo, who has continued and extended Frisch's work in a very general discussion [Haavelmo, 1944 pp. 91–8] of one central problem in identification: the formulation of conditions under which *all* structural relations of the system can be identified.
>
> (Koopmans, Rubin and Leipnik 1950: 69–70)

Modern textbook accounts on identification are based on Koopmans' work (Koopmans, Rubin and Leipnik 1950; Koopmans and Hood 1953). Identification is taught in terms of the conditions under which a certain structure can be identified among all the permissible structures embodied in a mathematically complete theoretical model. Since the model usually takes a linear form, such conditions are usually referred to as 'rank' and 'order' conditions. As can be seen from the above quotation by Koopmans *et al.*, Frisch's memorandum is acknowledged to be the first systematic discussion of the problem of identification. However, Frisch had another name for it: 'irreducibility'. The difference between the meaning of identifiability in modern terms and Frisch's irreducibility can be shown by the following two conditions.

Let us assume a linear equation:

$$\beta_1 y_1(t) + \dots + \beta_G y_G(t) + \gamma_1 x_1(t) + \dots + \gamma_K x_K(t) = 0$$

where the $y_i(t)$ denote current endogenous variables at time t and the $x_i(t)$ indicate exogenous variables (current or lagged) and lagged endogenous variables, the so-called predetermined variables.

Identification *à la* Koopmans can be achieved by putting *a priori* restrictions on the coefficients. When the restrictions are solely exclusion restrictions, the necessary condition for identifiability can be formulated as

$$m \leq K + 1 \qquad\qquad (3.17)$$

where *m* denotes the number of variables included (left over after exclusion) in the equation.

In his memorandum, Frisch only considered models with endogenous variables (lagged or current). His rule of reducibility stated that if the equation is irreducible (identified) then

$$m \leq n + 1 \tag{3.18}$$

where *n* denotes the number of exponential components of the functions with respect to which reducibility is defined. This condition is only a sufficient condition (not a necessary condition), because he showed that the equation is reducible for $m = n + 1$ when there is a certain relation between the lags.

A comparison between these two 'order' conditions, (3.17) and (3.18), shows that Frisch defined identification with respect to the solution of the equation, whereas Koopmans' definition refers to the number of predetermined variables in the model, *K*.

In Koopmans, Rubin and Leipnik (1950), the problem of autonomy was avoided by implicitly assuming that structural equations are autonomous and considering that the identification problem was only 'concerned with the unambiguous definition of the parameters that are to be estimated – a logical problem that precedes estimation' (p. 70). Only Haavelmo kept the term 'autonomy' alive. If one looks at the index of the 1950 monograph of the Cowles Commission, which also contained the chapter of Koopmans, Rubin and Leipnik discussed above, one finds only one reference to 'autonomous relation', and that was in Haavelmo's chapter 'Remarks on Frisch's confluence analysis and its use in econometrics'. In it he described an autonomous relation as a relation that 'would hold regardless of whether or not other economic relations were fulfilled' (Haavelmo 1950: 263). This is again the case in the follow-up of the 1950 monograph, namely the 1953 monograph *Studies in Econometric Method*, edited by William. C. Hood and Tjalling Koopmans.[11] There is only one reference to 'autonomous equations' in the index, in Girshick and Haavelmo's chapter on 'Statistical analysis of the demand for food: examples of simultaneous estimation of structural equations'. But now 'structural' and 'autonomous' are taken as synonyms.

> Why is it that we are interested in one particular member of this infinite set of true systems? It is because, in setting up the original model, we believe that there is one particular system of equations that is a system of *autonomous*, or *structural* equations, that is, equations such that it is possible that the parameters in any one of the equations could *in fact* change, e.g. by the introduction of some new economic policy, *without* any change taking place in any of the parameters of the other equations.
>
> (Girshick and Haavelmo 1953: 106)

The reason why researchers at the Cowles Commission believed that the structural equations were autonomous is that the empirically found relationships may be simpler than theory would suggest. This could lead researchers to overlook potential influences, 'it might be that the data, as given by economic time series, are restricted by a *whole system* of relations, such that the series do not display enough variations to verify each relation separately' (Haavelmo 1944: 18). Moreover, there may be factors that were not only overlooked because they were not revealed empirically but were also not yet accounted for in theory. However, as passive observers 'we cannot clear the data of such "other influences", we have to try to introduce these influences in the theory, in order to bring about more agreement between theory and facts' (p. 18). Thus, it was assumed that the problem of autonomy could be avoided by building models to be as comprehensive as possible.

Causal ordering

The problem of autonomy in fact consisted of two related but principally different problems. One was the problem of finding causal factors even if they are dormant. The method of discovering them was originally (Tinbergen and Frisch) based on feedback from facts about the phenomenon in question. In the Cowles Commission (Haavelmo and Koopmans) account, this problem was resolved by aiming to build models as comprehensive as possible based on *a priori* theoretical considerations. The second related problem of autonomy was the problem of invariance with respect to changes in the system of relations. However, if (it is assumed that) the full set of causal factors is given, then invariance is not an empirical problem any more. In that case, ordering the listed causal factors in a specific way can pinpoint invariance.

This problem of causal ordering of a given set of causal factors had already been discussed in Haavelmo's 'Probability approach' paper.

> [M]odern economists have stressed very much the necessity of operating with relations of the mutual-dependence type, rather than relations of the cause–effect type. However, both types of relations have, I think, their place in economic theory; and, moreover, they are not necessarily opposed to each other, because a system of relations of the mutual-dependence type for the economy *as a whole* may be built up from *open* systems of causal relations within the various *sectors* of the economy. The causal factors (or the 'independent variables') for one section of the economy may, themselves, be dependent variables in another section, while here the dependent variables from the first section enter as independent variables.
>
> (Haavelmo 1944: 22)

This ordering of causal factors was, as Haavelmo admitted, of a 'relative character'. It depended on what one wanted to explain and was not yet linked to invariance.

Haavelmo's idea of ordering was adopted by Koopmans (1950) in his study on which variables should be taken as given, 'exogenous', and which variables should be explained, 'endogenous'. He therefore distinguished between two 'main principles': the 'departmental principle' and the 'causal principle'. The departmental principle treated those variables that are wholly or partly outside the scope of economics as exogenous, for example climate, earthquakes, population, technological change, and political events. The causal principle regarded as exogenous those variables that influence, but are not influenced by, the remaining (endogenous) variables.[12]

It was Herbert Simon's paper 'Causal ordering and identifiability' (1953) that linked causal ordering with invariance. The context of Simon's essay was a debate between the Cowles Commission, as the proponent of simultaneous equation models, and Herman Wold as the proponent of recursive chain models.[13] One of the issues in the debate was causality and its representation and interpretation in economic models. Although the Cowles Commission group mainly ignored the issue, it was taken seriously and discussed in greater depth by Simon (1953). While Simon and Wold disagreed on certain notions about causal systems – asymmetries and relationships versus time sequences and variables – they came closer to each other with respect to the need for causal systems and their purpose for intervention analysis and policy decisions (Morgan 1991: 248–9).

One of Wold's concerns was that Simon's causal ordering was based on definitions imposed on the structure without regard to underlying economic behavioural relationships: 'the concepts to be defined all refer to a model – a system of equations – and not to the "real" world the model purports to describe' (Simon 1953: 51).

The definition of causal ordering was limited to complete ('self-contained' in Simon's terminology) 'linear structures'. A complete linear structure is an independent and consistent set of linear non-homogeneous equations that has exactly as many equations as it does variables. The first step was to show that a complete linear structure can be decomposed into a number of distinct 'minimal' complete subsets and a 'remainder'. Minimal complete subsets were defined as complete subsets of a linear structure that do not themselves contain complete (proper) subsets. When there are one or more minimal complete proper subsets of the structure and the remainder is not empty, the structure is said to be 'causally ordered'. The next step was to repeat the partitioning as follows. The equations of the minimal subsets are solved and the values of its variables are substituted in the equations of the remainder. The result is again a complete structure, called the 'derived structure of first order'. If the 'first order' structure is also causally ordered, the process can be repeated leading to a 'second order' structure and so on. Finally, a point will be reached when the remainder of the nth decomposition is empty. The result of this process is a complete ordering of disjunct subsets of the equations from the original structure. A consequence of this ordering is that each variable appears as an endogenous variable in one and only one complete subset, and that it appears in a structure of higher order as an exogenous variable. Thus, there exists a one-to-one correspondence between the minimal subsets of equations and the subsets of variables that occur as endogenous variables in these equations. By employing this distinction between exogenous and endogenous variables, Simon defined a causal ordering of the sets of variables endogenous to the corresponding complete subsets of equations:

> Let β designate the set of variables endogenous to a complete subset B; and let γ designate the set endogenous to a complete subset C. Then the variables of γ are *directly causally dependent* on the variables of β ($\beta \rightarrow \gamma$) if at least one member of β appears as an exogenous variable in C.
>
> (Simon 1953: 57)

To Simon, this causal ordering also had an operational meaning; it specified which variables would be affected by intervention at a particular point of the structure.

> We found that we could provide the ordering with an operational basis if we could associate with each equation of a structure a specific power of intervention, or 'direct control'. That is, any such intervention would alter the structure but leave the model (and hence the causal ordering) invariant. Hence, causal ordering is a property of models that is invariant with respect to interventions within the model, and structural equations are equations that correspond to specified possibilities of intervention.
>
> (Simon 1953: 66)

The operational meaning of causal ordering was pictured as follows:

> We suppose a group of persons whom we shall call 'experimenters'. If we like, we may consider 'nature' to be a member of the group. The experimenters, severally or separately, are able to choose the nonzero elements of the coefficient matrix of the linear structure, but they may not replace zero elements by nonzero elements or vice versa (i.e. they are restricted to a specified linear model). We may say that they *control directly* the values of the nonzero coefficients.
>
> (Simon 1953: 65)

Turning any zero element into a non-zero one would change the causal structure. So, causal ordering only had operational meaning within certain limits: 'we must have a priori knowledge of the limits imposed on the "experimenters" – in this case knowledge that certain coefficients of the matrix are zeros' (p. 65). Simon did not give any indication how to attain this a priori knowledge. In fact, this is Haavelmo's problem of autonomy – the problem of finding which coefficients are zero and which are not – which in principle remains an empirical problem. Although 'nature' was seen to be a member of the group of 'experimenters', it was not clear which experiment it was performing (see Chapter 4).

The problem of causality, or in other words the problem of invariance, was reduced to a mathematical problem of clever transformations of the matrices in this framework. As such it was logically connected with the concept of identifiability. Identifiability was obtained by specifying *a priori* that certain coefficients in the model must be zero and any such specification in a complete structure defines the causal ordering.

Conclusions

Originally, in business-cycle analysis, whether a potential causal factor was added to the business-cycle mechanism depended on whether it was theoretically as well as statistically and mathematically significant. Mathematical significance of a causal factor depended on considerations of whether the model containing that factor generated the appropriate facts about the phenomenon. Because feedback from the phenomena was cut off, the Cowles Commission approach was not to discover or test but only to identify and measure. Because Simon showed that a linear system of equations was identified if and only if it was causally ordered, causality also disappeared from the scene.

> Identification seemed to be the more pressing problem to econometricians focused on the problems of estimation. Equivalence meant, in some respects, causality could be ignored without loss. And identification itself had noncausal roots in the problem of the measurement of demand. Causal language simply faded away.
>
> (Hoover 2001: 147)

Hoover (1994) shows that the Cowles Commission approach, which he labels as 'strong apriorism', is just one of the two strategies to secure invariance. In his view, it is better to see econometrics as an observational science such as astronomy. Because observations made by econometric instruments are observations of confluent relations, one should adopt a strategy of 'weak apriorism'. Theory guides observations but observation can suggest which elements of a theory are unsatisfactory: 'Measurement requires prior theory; equally, theory requires prior measurement' (p. 73). Nevertheless, as Hoover emphasises,

> econometric observations would be practically useless if they were completely unstable. We must, therefore, count on finding some stability and on supplementing econometric observations with other information, say institutional facts, if we are to distinguish between real changes in structure and our inability to focus our observations.
>
> (Hoover 1994: 75–6)

It was this class of stable facts about business cycles that originally were used to solve the problem of autonomy.

4 Design of experiments

But even in mechanics long chains of deductive reasoning are directly applicable only to the occurrences of the laboratory. By themselves they are seldom a sufficient guide for dealing with the heterogeneous materials and the complex and uncertain combination of the forces of the real world.

(Marshall 1920: 771)

Introduction

Margaret Morrison and Mary Morgan (1999) have argued that models function as 'instruments of investigation'. We can learn about the world from them and about theories because they involve some form of representation. They either represent an aspect of the world or an aspect of theories about the world, or both. As indicated in Chapter 1, we confine ourselves to models that provide mathematical representations of aspects of the empirical world. The relevant question about instruments is not 'How true are they?' but 'How accurate are these instruments?' In general, to assess an instrument's accuracy we test it: that is, we investigate the correspondence between the representation itself and the aspect of the world that is to be represented. The accuracy of this correspondence depends on the complexity of the system under investigation and our ability to construct representations of it. This is, in principle, a technical problem, labelled by Kevin Hoover (1988: 218–20) as the 'Cournot problem' after the man who formulated it explicitly, Antoine Augustin Cournot (1801–77):

The economic system is a whole of which all the parts are connected and react on each other. … It seems, therefore, as if, for a complete and rigorous solution of the problems relative to some parts of the economic system, it were indispensable to take the entire system into consideration. But this would surpass the powers of mathematical analysis and of our practical methods of calculations, even if the values of all the constants could be assigned to them numerically.

(Cournot [1838] 1971: 127)

This means that testing, too, is dependent on the complexity of the system at hand and the techniques available to deal with it. These techniques of modelling and testing not only include mathematical methods but also computational devices. As will become apparent in this chapter, the history of macroeconomic modelling is intrinsically linked to the rise and development of artificial intelligence.[1]

The Walrasian programme provided an answer to the Cournot problem by setting up a manageable interdependent system to represent a whole economy. A modern version of this programme is the Cowles Commission approach. This was a combination of the Walrasian method, which attempts to construct a mathematical skeleton of system, and econometrics, to put empirical flesh on the bones of the system. The Cowles Commission for Research in Economics, founded in 1932, was

> dedicated to research in economic theory and measurement. It seeks to make additions to fundamental knowledge about society, through theory construction, through measurement for testing of theory, through development of methods of measurement, and through application of results in specific areas.
>
> (Cowles Commission 1952: 2)

The Cowles Commission approach, as a research programme in the Lakatosian sense, contains in its hard core the following elements (see also Chapter 3):

a   that the economy may be characterised as a set of autonomous and simultaneous behavioral (causal) relations with structural features captured by the parameters of these relations; and

b   that these relations are essentially stochastic.

> (De Marchi and Gilbert 1989: 5)

The positive heuristic corresponding to this hard core is simply stated as: 'build, identify, estimate and assess the parameter estimates of structural models conforming to the theory of optimising agent behaviour, stochastically formulated' (De Marchi and Gilbert 1989: 6).

Naive model tests

The Cowles Commission's solution to the problem of autonomy, discussed in Chapter 3, was to build more and more comprehensive models. The idea was to build in as many potential influences as possible. In the 1940s, Lawrence Klein was commissioned to build Cowles Commission type models of the United States economy in the tradition of Tinbergen's macroeconometric modelling. The programme's aim was to build increasingly comprehensive models to improve their predictability so that they could be used as reliable instruments for economic policy. The implications of a policy change could then be forecasted. One of the early results was a monograph *Economic Fluctuations in the United States* (Klein 1950).[2] It presented three models of the United States economy, called models I, II and III, made up of from three to fifteen equations containing parameters estimated using the least-squares and maximum-likelihood methods.

For model III, the largest model, the 'limited-information maximum likelihood method' was used. This method, developed by two members of the Cowles Commission, Theodore W. Anderson and Herman Rubin (1949, see also Anderson 1950), was a new, more economical way of obtaining estimates. It yielded estimates of only one or a few of the equations at a time and used considerably less information to get them. As a result, 'the estimates are obtained by mathematically simpler, and in most cases less laborious, computational methods' (Koopmans, Rubin and Leipnik 1950: 111, see also Anderson 1950: 321). The simplification of computational problems is obtained at the cost of increasing sampling variances of the estimates, which means a reduced efficiency of the method of estimation. Klein's fifteen-equation model was 'the largest model hitherto fitted by the new technique; and it presents a statistical test of the hypothesis that the deviations are random as assumed, as well as tests of several economic hypotheses' (Christ 1952: 41).

Andrew W. Marshall (1950a, 1950b) and Carl F. Christ (1951) conducted tests on Klein's fifteen-equation model III. 'These two studies were among the first to act on the precept that econometric models, like any other theories, must be tested by their performance in making predictions' (Christ 1952: 49). An important part of Marshall and Christ's tests was a comparison of the predictive power of Klein's model against that of simple extrapolation models, the so-called 'naive models'. The concept of 'naive models' was introduced into econometrics by Marshall at a joint session of the Econometric Society and the American Statistical Association in New York, on 29 December 1949 ('Report of the New York meeting', 1950: 264–7; Littauer 1950: 151–5). Milton Friedman was working on a similar idea, although he gave the concept a different name (Christ 1951: 57n). During that session Marshall presented the results of his M.A. thesis, 'A Test of Klein's Model III for Changes of Structure' which has never been published, except for two short abstracts (Marshall 1950a, 1950b; see Qin 1993, 138n). He tested Klein's model III in two ways (see Christ 1951: 55–9; Qin 1993: 137–8). Both ways used the calculated residual for Klein's structural equations for the post-sample period of 1946–7.

Marshall's first test examined each residual for 1946 and for 1947, to see whether they were larger than would be expected, under the hypothesis that Klein's model described 1946 and 1947 as well as it did the sample period (1921–41). This was done separately for each structural equation by means of a tolerance interval for the calculated residuals. Because of this procedure, Christ called this test the 'structural equation tolerance interval test', or SETI test for short.

The second test examined each calculated residual for 1946 and 1947 to see whether it was larger than the error one would expect to make when using naive models. Two naive models were used for testing. The first, 'naive model I', says that next year's value of any variable will equal this year's value plus a random normal disturbance ε_t^I with zero mean and constant variance. The second, 'naive model II', says it will equal this year's value plus the change from last year to this year plus a random normal disturbance ε_t^{II} with zero mean and constant variance.

Naive model I: $y_{t+1} = y_t + \varepsilon_t^{I}$ (4.1)

Naive model II: $y_{t+1} = y_t + (y_t - y_{t-1}) + \varepsilon_t^{II}$ (4.2)

The results of these tests were that three equations were rejected on the basis of these naive model tests and two equations on the basis of the SETI test.

Christ (1951) revised Klein's model, estimated it with the data for 1921–47, and tested the results against 1948 data. He distinguished between two groups of tests: 'tests of internal consistency' and 'tests of success in extrapolation and prediction'. The first group comprised tests dependent only on data available for use in the estimation process; the second group comprised tests that used post-sample data and 'therefore are of higher authority' (Christ 1951: 67). This second group consisted of the SETI tests, the naive model tests, and an additional comparative test of the goodness of fit of different estimation methods on the grounds of their predictive abilities.

The results of the naive model tests were remarkable. Each of the two naive models predicted seven out of thirteen endogenous variables better than did the reduced-form equations, as estimated by the ordinary least-squares method. Naive model I was better at predicting in fifteen cases out of twenty-one, and naive model II predicted better in thirteen cases out of twenty-one in comparison to the reduced form, as estimated by the restricted least-squares method. So, 'the econometric model used here has failed, at least in our sample consisting of the one year 1948, to be a better predicting device than the incomparably cheaper naive models' (Christ 1951: 80). In defence of this econometric modelling approach, Christ put forward the argument that econometric models are preferable to naive models because they are better at predicting the effects of alternative policy measures (p. 80).

Milton Friedman's instrumentalism

An important critique of the Cowles Commission approach came from Milton Friedman. He doubted the validity of the Cowles Commission method of econometric modelling on the basis of the poor results obtained by Marshall and Christ's post-model forecasting tests. Friedman's 'Comment' (1951) on Christ's paper was very critical towards the Cowles Commission programme but approved of Marshall and Christ's post-model tests, in particular the naive model tests. 'Economics badly needs work of this kind. It is one of our chief defects that we place all too much emphasis on the derivation of hypotheses and all too little on testing their validity' (Friedman 1951: 107). The validity of the equations should not be determined by high correlation coefficients,

> the fact that the equations fit the data from which they are derived is a test primarily of the skill and patience of the analyst; it is not a test of the validity of the equations for any broader body of data. Such a test is provided solely by the consistency of the equations with data not used in the derivation, such as data for periods subsequent to the period analyzed.
>
> (Friedman 1951: 108)

Friedman had been critical about this kind of econometric modelling for some time. In a review of Tinbergen's work for the League of Nations (Friedman 1940), Friedman noted that 'Tinbergen's results cannot be judged by ordinary tests of statistical significance' because the variables

> have been selected after an extensive process of trial and error *because* they yield high coefficients of correlation. Tinbergen is seldom satisfied with a correlation coefficient less than .98. But these attractive correlation coefficients create no presumption that the relationships they describe will hold in the future.
>
> (Friedman 1940: 659)[3]

To emphasise this point, Friedman approvingly quoted Wesley C. Mitchell who aimed a similar criticism towards Karl Karsten's (see Chapter 2) and Irving Fisher's attempts to find curves that fit the data with the highest attainable correlation coefficient:

> The proposition may be ventured that a competent statistician, with sufficient clerical assistance and time at his command, can take almost any pair of time series for a given period and work them into forms which will yield coefficients of correlation exceeding ±.9. ... So work of the sort which Mr. Karsten and Professor Fisher have shown how to do must be judged, not by the coefficients of correlation obtained within the periods for which they have manipulated the data, but by the coefficients which they get in earlier or later periods to which their formula may be applied.
>
> (Mitchell 1927: 266–7)

Friedman did not consider naive models as competing theories of short-time change, but as standards of comparison, the 'natural' alternative hypotheses – or 'null' hypotheses – against which to test the hypothesis that the econometric model makes good predictions (Friedman 1951: 109). On the basis of Christ's exercise, then, one should reject the latter hypothesis. Friedman opposes Christ's argument that these models are preferable to naive models because of their ability to predict consequences of alternative policy measures, by claiming that naive models can make such predictions, too. One can simply assert that a proposed change in policy will have no effect. The assertion that the econometric model can predict the consequences of policy changes, according to Friedman, is a 'pure act of faith'. And because of 'the fact that the model fails to predict one kind of change is reason to have less rather than more faith in its ability to predict a related kind of change' (p. 111).

Friedman interpreted the disappointing test results as evidence that econometric modelling of an economy as a whole was premature, and cannot be achieved until dynamic models of parts of the economy are adequately developed:

> As I am sure those who have tried to do so will agree, we now know so little about the dynamic mechanisms at work that there is enormous arbitrariness

in any system set down. Limitations of resources – mental, computational, and statistical – enforce a model that, although complicated enough for our capacities, is yet enormously simple relative to the present state of understanding of the world we seek to explain. Until we can develop a simpler picture of the world, by an understanding of interrelations within sections of the economy, the construction of a model for the economy as whole is bound to be almost a complete groping in the dark. The probability that such a process will yield a meaningful result seems to me almost negligible.

(Friedman 1951: 112–13)

Friedman's lack of faith in the macroeconometric programme sent him in another research direction – namely, that of partitioning, the so-called 'Marshallian approach'[4] (Hoover 1988: 218–25):

Man's powers are limited: almost every one of nature's riddles is complex. He breaks it up, studies one bit at a time, and at last combines his partial solutions with a supreme effort of his whole small strength into some sort of an attempt at a solution of the whole riddle.

(Marshall [1898] 1925: 314; quoted in Friedman 1949: 469)

This Marshallian approach of partitioning echoed in his comment on macro-modelling:

The direction of work that seems to me to offer most hope for laying a foundation for a workable theory of change is the analysis of parts of the economy in the hope that we can find bits of order here and there and gradually combine these bits into a systematic picture of the whole.

(Friedman 1951: 114)

This opinion was increasingly held in the applied circle. Many applied modellers shifted their interest in macro-modelling away from a whole economy to parts of economic activities in which economic theories were relatively well developed (Qin 1993: 138–9).

Marshall's approach of partitioning was based on his use of the *ceteris paribus* clause. The sentence immediately following his quote above shows how: 'In breaking it up, he uses some adaptation of a primitive but effective prison, or pound, for segregating those disturbing causes, whose wanderings happen to be inconvenient, for the time: the pound is called *Cæteris Paribus*' (Marshall [1898] 1925: 314; see also 1920: 366). In his discussion of Marshall's methodology, J. Daniel Hammond notes:

Ceteris paribus is a way of dealing with the complex nature of reality, where every event is the result of a number of causes. *Ceteris paribus* serves as a 'pound' into which factors are placed, to be dealt with one at a time. Properly used, *Ceteris paribus* does not presume simple unicausal relationships. On the contrary it is useful precisely because causal relationships are complex and man's powers of reasoning are limited.

(Hammond 1991: 99)

Marshall considered this method to be appropriate in the early stages of economic analysis. The advantage of the use of the *ceteris paribus* pound was that issues could be handled 'more exactly'. However, it had the disadvantage, noted by Marshall, that the more an issue was narrowed 'the less closely does it correspond to real life' (Marshall [1898] 1925: 314). In the next stages, however, correspondence to reality could be regained at the expense of exactness. 'With each step of advance more things can be let out of the pound; exact discussions can be made less abstract, realistic discussion can be made less inexact than was possible at an earlier stage' (p. 315).

For Friedman, the ability to predict was the quality of a model that should be evaluated, not its realisticness.[5] This methodological standpoint was spelled out in his well-known article 'The methodology of positive economics' (1953)[6] and is generally considered as an economic science version of 'instrumentalism':

For some policy-oriented economists, the intended job is the generation of true or successful predictions. In this case a theory's predictive success is always a sufficient argument in its favor. This view of the *role* of theories is called 'instrumentalism'. It says that theories are convenient and useful ways of (logically) generating what have turned out to be true (or successful) predictions or conclusions.

(Boland 1979: 508)

Friedman's anti-realistic position was most expressly worded in his famous dictum: 'Truly important and significant hypotheses will be found to have "assumptions" that are wildly inaccurate descriptive representations of reality, and, in general, the more significant the theory, the more unrealistic the assumptions (in this sense)' (Friedman 1953: 14).

However, a 'lapse into instrumentalism' is unnecessary, as Alan Musgrave (1981) has shown in his discussion of the different kind of assumptions that could be distinguished in Friedman's paper. According to Musgrave, Friedman's instrumentalist position stems from his failure to distinguish three different types of assumption: negligibility, domain and heuristic assumptions. A negligibility assumption is the assumption that a factor that could be expected to affect the phenomenon under investigation actually has no effect upon it, or at least no detectable effect (Musgrave 1981: 378). A domain assumption is the assumption that an expected factor is absent and so is used to specify the domain of applicability of the theory concerned (p. 381). A heuristic assumption is made if a factor is considered to be absent or negligible in order to simplify the 'logical' development of the theory (p. 383).

In fact, there is also a fourth type of assumption in Friedman's paper, although this is only mentioned in a footnote and not labelled separately by Musgrave. They belong to the kind of 'as-if p' assumptions where p is an analogous mechanism, and not an idealisation in the sense of one of the other three assumptions. In other words, p is a simulacrum: 'something having merely the form or appearance of a certain thing, without possessing its substance or proper qualities' (*OED* 1933). This definition is used by Cartwright (1983) to denote what models are, stressing the 'anti-realist' aspect of models (see Chapter 2). She could have used the term 'simulation', but probably didn't because it refers to the assumption of false appearances for the sake of deception. But in the social sciences today the term is employed without this connotation of deception: 'the assumption of the appearance of something without having its reality' (Dawson 1962: 1–2).

To clarify Friedman's anti-realisticness position, let us consider an example he used, namely a Galilean fall experiment. The point of departure is the same as in Haavelmo's 'Probability Approach', namely the problem of not being able to carry out controlled experiments, and so being dependent on passive observations alone. The idea behind a controlled experiment is to create a specific environment – a laboratory – in which the relevant variables are manipulated in order to take measurements of particular parameters with the aim to discover the relationship between these variables, if any. However, these laboratory conditions cannot be set up to investigate macroeconomic relationships. We can only be passive observers who have to unearth lawful relationships by inferring from the data supplied by Nature the underlying 'designs' of the experiments Nature performs. This approach will always fall short of a controlled experiment. We can only observe experiments as they occur in the open air and are not able to manipulate any of the relevant objects.

> Unfortunately, we can seldom test particular predictions in the social sciences by experiments explicitly designed to eliminate what are judged to be the most important disturbing influences. Generally, we must rely on evidence cast up by the 'experiments' that happen to occur. The inability to conduct so-called 'controlled experiments' does not, in my view, reflect a basic difference between the social and physical sciences both because it is not peculiar to the social sciences – witness astronomy – and because the distinction between a controlled experiment and uncontrolled experience is at best one of degree. No experiment can be completely controlled, and every experience is partly controlled, in the sense that some disturbing influences are relatively constant in the course of it.
> (Friedman 1953: 10)

Galileo had designed his experiments such that although carried out in the *open air* with *specific* objects, the law he found applies to *all* bodies in *vacuum*. The empirical regularity he found by his fall experiments is a very simple one:

$$s \propto t^2$$

Distance (s) is proportional to time (t) squared. From this empirical finding Galileo inferred a law of falling bodies that states that the acceleration of a body dropped in a vacuum is a constant and is independent of the mass, composition and shape of the body, the manner of dropping it, etc.

The question is to what extent can the law of falling bodies be applied outside a vacuum.[7] According to Friedman, to answer this question one has to take into account the kind of object that is to be dropped. Galileo's law works well if applied to compact balls. 'The application of this formula to a compact ball dropped from the roof of a building is equivalent to saying that a ball so dropped behaves *as if* it were falling in a vacuum' (Friedman 1953: 16). Air resistance is negligible for compact balls falling relatively short distances, so they behave approximately as described by Galileo's law. In other words, for compact balls we can apply the negligibility assumption.

The problem, now, is to decide for which objects the air resistance is negligible. Apparently, this is the case for a compact ball falling from the roof of a building, but what if the object is a feather or the object is dropped from an airplane at an altitude of 30,000 feet? One of the traditional criteria on laws is that they must contain no essential reference to particular objects or systems. In contrast to this traditional view, Friedman argues that a specification of the domain of objects and systems for which a generalisation applies should be attached to the generalisation.

To deal with this problem of specification, two options are possible. One is to use a more comprehensive theory – the Cowles Commission approach – 'from which the influence of some of the possible disturbing factors can be calculated and of which the simple theory is a special case' (p. 18). However, the extra accuracy it yields may not justify the extra costs of achieving it, 'so the question under what circumstances the simpler theory works "well enough" remains important' (p. 18). The second option is to select the phenomena for which the theory works. That is to say, to indicate the domain for which the 'formula' works, for example, the law of falling bodies (outside a vacuum) holds for compact balls and not for feathers. This means that one should specify the domain for which a generalisation holds, but this should be done independently of this generalisation. Thus, one should not incorporate this specification into the generalisation itself, as the Cowles Commission programme aimed at. Having a generalisation that has been success-fully used to model and explain certain phenomena, it is a separate empirical question what the full range of phenomena is that can be explained by it and of which the answer can not already been built into this generalisation (see Woodward 2000: 231 in which this issue is extensively discussed). For which previously unexplained phenomena the generalisation must hold, must be discovered empirically.

> The important problem in connection with the hypothesis is to specify the circumstances under which the formula works or, more precisely, the general magnitude of the error in its predictions under various circumstances. Indeed, ... such a specification is not one thing and the hypothesis another. The specification is itself an essential part of the hypothesis, and it is a part that is peculiarly likely to be revised and extended as experience accumulates.
>
> (Friedman 1953: 18)

Summarising Friedman's strategy of finding explanations, a hypothesis or theory should consist of three parts: first, a model containing only those forces that are assumed to be important – in other words, each model implies negligibility assumptions; second, a set of rules defining the class of phenomena for which the model can be taken to be an adequate representation – these are (independent) domain specifications; and third, specifications of the correspondence between the variables or entities in the model and observable phenomena.

Friedman is not an anti-realist, he only opposes the approach in which models are aimed as 'photographic reproductions', which he unfortunately – because misleadingly – labels as 'the realism of its assumptions'. By a realistic assumption he means an as comprehensive as possible description of reality. The uselessness of such striving for realisticness was illustrated in a hyperbole:

> A completely 'realistic' theory of the wheat market would have to include not only the conditions directly underlying the supply and demand for wheat but also the kind of coins or credit instruments used to make exchanges; the personal characteristics of wheat-traders such as the color of each trader's hair and eyes, his antecedents and education, the number of members of his family, their characteristics, antecedents, and education, etc.; the kind of soil on which the wheat was grown, its physical and chemical characteristics, the weather prevailing during the growing season; the personal characteristics of the farmers growing the wheat and of the consumers who will ultimately use it; and so on indefinitely.
>
> (Friedman 1953: 32)

So, for Friedman the relevant question to ask about the assumptions of a theory is not whether they are descriptively realistic, 'for they never are', but whether they are 'sufficiently good approximations for the purpose in hand' (p. 15).

To clarify Friedman's position within the framework developed in Chapter 3, a comprehensive explanation of the motion of a falling body can be represented by the following equation (cf. equation (3.11)):

$$\Delta y = \Delta F\left(x_1, x_2, \ldots\right) = \frac{\partial F}{\partial x_1} \Delta x_1 + \frac{\partial F}{\partial x_2} \Delta x_2 + \ldots \qquad (4.3)$$

Suppose that y is the motion of a body, x_1 is gravity, x_2 air pressure, and x_3, x_4, … are other specifications of the circumstances (e.g. temperature, magnetic forces). The law of falling bodies says that in a vacuum ($x_2 = 0$, but the notion of 'vacuum' in this law in fact also supposes that interference by other disturbing causes is absent: $x_3 = x_4 = \ldots = 0$) all bodies fall with the same acceleration regardless of mass, shape or composition: $\frac{\partial F}{\partial x_1}$ is equal for all bodies. However, in the open air, the shape and the substance of the falling body determine which of the interfering factors can be considered as having negligible influence (i.e. $\frac{\partial F}{\partial x_i} \approx 0$). For example, air resistance is negligible for compact balls falling relatively short distances, so they behave as if they are falling in vacuum. However, for feathers the air pressure does interfere. Similarly, magnetic forces act on steel balls and not on wooden balls, etc. To conclude, one has to specify the class of phenomena for which a specific model is an adequate representation.

Musgrave (1981) conjectures a chronological ranking in the use of the assumptions:

> what began as a negligibility assumption may be changed under the impact of criticism first into a domain assumption, then into a mere heuristic assumption; and that these important changes will go unnoticed if the different types are not clearly distinguished from one another.
>
> (Musgrave 1981: 386)

In contrast to this view, my reading of Friedman's methodology is that the model based on negligibility assumptions should be maintained and that it is the domain of phenomena for which the model holds that should be explored empirically. Friedman advocated a Marshallian partitioning, not on the basis of *ceteris paribus* assumptions as generally is assumed, but according to a combination of negligibility assumptions and domain specifications.

Herbert Simon's hierarchical-system approach to complexity

While Friedman avoided the problem of complexity by Marshallian partitioning and only focusing on some parts, Herbert Simon dealt explicitly with complexity. Although he used the same method of partitioning – as will be shown below – the interaction between the subsystems was an essential part of his analysis.

The contributions of Simon are extremely vast and diverse, ranging from philosophy and methodology of science, applied mathematics, through various aspects of economics, computer science, management science, political science, cognitive psychology to the study of human problem-solving behaviour. In his review of Simon's contributions to economics, Albert Ando (1979) formulates a theme that runs consistently throughout Simon's writings:

> to construct a comprehensive framework for modeling and analyzing the behavior of man and his organizations faced with a complex environment, recognizing the limitation of his ability to comprehend, describe, analyze and to act, while allowing for his ability to learn and to adopt.
>
> (Ando 1979: 83)

One of the research areas was therefore to find a description of that complex environment so that it is both comprehensible and manageable for decision makers.

Very early in his career, Simon found that the description of a very complex system can be simplified by considering them as hierarchic, a strategy that can be found in several of Simon's articles dealing with complexity. The first time of mentioning the idea of hierarchical systems as representations of complex systems, like the human mind, was in a comment on John von Neumann's talk, 'General theory of automata', at the Harvard Meeting of the Econometric Society in 1950. In his talk, von Neumann warned against taking the brain–computer analogy too literally. Simon (1951) who was a discussant at this session on the theory of automata, observed that, 'the significant analogy was not between the hardware of computer and brain, respectively, but between the hierarchic organizations of computing and thinking systems' (Simon 1977: 180).

The paper presented by von Neumann was his paradigm paper, 'The general and logical theory of automata' ([1951] 1963), in which the top-down approach of artificial intelligence to deal with complexity was introduced for the first time. In this paper, he explained what he called the Axiomatic Procedure:

> The natural systems are of enormous complexity, and it is clearly necessary to subdivide the problem that they represent into several parts. One method of subdivision, which is particularly significant in the present context, is this: The organisms can be viewed as made up of parts which to a certain extent are independent, elementary units. We may, therefore, to this extent, view as the first part of the problem the structure and functioning of such elementary units individually. The second part of the problem consists of understanding how these elements are organised into a whole, and how the functioning of the whole is expressed in terms of these elements.
>
> (von Neumann [1951] 1963: 289)

The first part of the problem belonging to the relating discipline, in this case physiology, could be removed by the 'process of axiomatisation':

> We assume that the elements have certain well-defined, outside, functional characteristics; that is, they are to be treated as 'black boxes'. They are viewed as automatisms, the inner structure of which need not to be disclosed, but which are assumed to react to certain unambiguously defined stimuli, by certain unambiguously defined responses.
>
> (von Neumann [1951] 1963: 289)

Simon's (1962) 'The architecture of complexity' is an elaboration of von Neumann's Axiomatic Procedure. The central thesis of this article is that complex systems frequently take the form of a hierarchic system. A hierarchic system is a system that is composed of interrelated subsystems each, in turn, hierarchic in structure right down to the lowest level of elementary subsystems. Each subsystem can be treated as a 'black box' where the internal structure is irrelevant and only the inputs and outputs are of interest. Therefore, there is inevitably some arbitrariness, related to the researcher's interests, as to when partitioning is necessary and what subsystems are assumed to be elementary.

The first application of Simon's top-down approach, which treats complex systems as hierarchic, can be found in Simon's (1953) 'Causal ordering and identifiability' paper, discussed in Chapter 3. As we have seen, causal ordering, based on a particular partitioning of a system into subsystems, is a special chain of asymmetrical connections between these subsystems.

If one distinguishes between weak and strong interactions and partitions the complex system where interactions are weakest, the analysis of that system can be tremendously simplified. This result was found in a paper, which dealt with the problem of aggregation, entitled 'Aggregation of variables in dynamic systems', co-authored by Alfred Ando, and published in 1961. The aim of this paper was 'to determine conditions that, if satisfied by a (linear) dynamic system, will permit approximate aggregation of variables' (Simon and Ando 1961: 114). This discussion of aggregation was actuated by the disappointing facilities of computer capacities to 'handle matrices of about any desired size, and hence would obviate the need for aggregation' (p. 111).

It appeared that aggregation could be performed in 'nearly decomposable' systems. The notion of 'near decomposability' was clarified by the definition of a decomposable matrix. When a matrix can be arranged in the form

$$P^* = \begin{Vmatrix} P_1^* & & & \\ & \ddots & & \\ & & P_i^* & \\ & & & \ddots & \\ & & & & P_n^* \end{Vmatrix}$$

where the P_i^* are square submatrices and the remaining elements, not displayed, are all zero, then the matrix is said to be completely decomposable. A nearly decomposable matrix is the slightly altered matrix P:

$$P = P^* + \varepsilon C \tag{4.4}$$

where ε is a very small real number, and C is an arbitrary matrix of the same dimension as P^*.[8]

With the aid of both definitions, the dynamic behaviours of the following systems were compared:

$$x(t+1) = x(t)P \text{ and } x^*(t+1) = x^*(t)P^*$$

To present Simon's result, the following notations for the vector $x(t)$ on which P operates, and the vector $x^*(t)$ on which P^* operates, should be adopted:

$$x(t) = \{x_1(t), \ldots, x_i(t), \ldots, x_n(t)\}$$

and

$$x^*(t) = \{x_1^*(t), \ldots, x_i^*(t), \ldots, x_n^*(t)\}$$

where $x_i(t)$ and $x_i^*(t)$ are row vectors of a subset of components of $x(t)$ and $x^*(t)$ respectively. Then

$$x^*(t+1) = \left\{ x_1^*(t)P_1^*, \ldots, x_i^*(t)P_i^*, \ldots, x_n^*(t)P_n^* \right\}$$

The results were:

(1) In the short run, the behavior of $x_i(t)$ will be dominated by roots belonging to P_i^*, so that the time path of $x_i(t)$ will be very close to the time path of $x_i^*(t)$, and almost independent of $x_j(t)$, and P_j^*. 'If we are interested in the behavior of the system at this stage, we can treat the system as though it were completely decomposable' (p. 116).

(2) Unlike P^*, P is not completely decomposable, so that weak links among the subsystems will eventually make their influence felt. But the time required for these influences to appear is long enough so that when they do become visible, within each subsystem the largest root will have dominated all other roots. Thus, at this stage, the variables within each subset, $x_i(t)$, will move proportionally, and the behaviour of the whole system will be dominated by the largest roots of each subsystem.

(3) At the end, however, the behaviour of $x(t)$ will be dominated by the largest root of P, as in any linear dynamic system (p. 117).

Since the variables in each subsystem, after a while, move roughly proportionately according to (2), they may be aggregated into a single variable.

The main theoretical findings of the analysis of the structure of dynamic systems represented by nearly-decomposable matrices were summed up in two propositions, which were also mentioned in slightly more general terms in 'The architecture of complexity':

(a) in a nearly decomposable system, the short-run behavior of each of the component subsystems is approximately independent of the short-run behavior of the other components; (b) in the long run, the behavior of any one of the components depends in only an aggregate way on the behavior of the other components.

(Simon 1962: 474)

By considering a complex system as nearly-decomposable the description of the system can be simplified: only aggregative properties of its parts enter into the description of the interactions of those parts (Simon 1962: 478).

The insights of both Simon's papers on causal ordering and near-decomposability were synthesised in a more recent paper on causality: 'Causal ordering, comparative statics, and near decomposability' by Simon and Iwasaki (1988). The purpose was to extend the account of causality to dynamic and nearly decomposable systems. The question was to what extent the causal analysis of a system is invariant as we pass from a description of the system's dynamics to a description of its equilibrium or steady state, and as we pass from a coarse-grained to a fine-grained description of the system, or vice versa, by disaggregation or aggregation.

(Simon and Iwasaki 1988: 149)

The conclusion was that for hierarchical, nearly decomposable systems causal ordering is not sensitive to the 'grain size' of the analysis. At any level in the hierarchy, the causal ordering that relates to the relative movement of the variables within any single component is (nearly) independent of the causal ordering among components (p. 168).

Because of the indescribable complexity of the world we live in, we necessarily restrict our analyses of events to small or middle-size worlds, abstracted from their large environments and characterized by very small numbers of equations. We see that the notion of causal ordering provides us with a rigorous justification of this essential practice. If the small worlds we choose for study correspond to complete subsets of the mechanisms of the larger world of which they are parts, then simplifying our analysis in this way does not at all invalidate our conclusions.

(Simon and Iwasaki 1988: 160)

Simon's approach of simplifying the analysis of complex systems by treating them – whenever possible – as nearly decomposable systems can be considered as similar to a Marshallian partitioning, not by using a sharp *ceteris paribus* razor but a blunt knife of negligibility assumptions. This kind of partitioning can be very helpful in exploring the kinds of issues that interest social scientists, but which are not suitable for controlled experiments, 'social scientists must use the data generated by a single, complex, uncontrolled experiment that is the history of society in its entirety' (Ando 1963: 1). In Simon's terminology, laboratory experiments are a way to artificially create a decomposable structure: one is able to control the ε of equation (4.4) and to fix it at zero (compare this with his view on controlled experiments in Chapter 3). Unfortunately, this is not applicable to most social phenomena. 'However, nature is not completely unkind to social science' (p. 2). Many of the situations can be represented by nearly decomposable systems.

The question about this approach is: in what sense are the results valid when one such 'nearly' unrelated subsystem is analysed as if it exists in complete isolation? How negligible is the environment of this subsystem? Simon and Ando's analysis shows that for predictions of the behaviour of that subsystem within a given degree of accuracy there is a trade-off between the time interval over which the accuracy of prediction will be maintained and the degree of nearness of that system to a really isolated system. For example, the shorter the time a ball falls, the more air resistance can be neglected.

Characteristics tests

It is not necessary to lose faith in the Cowles Commission programme, as Friedman did, because of the poor forecasting abilities of the early macroeconometric models. In the first place, one might be confident that the forecasting abilities will steadily improve – and, this is, in fact, what happened. In the second place, one may wonder whether measuring success in terms of the ability to extrapolate and predict is the most appropriate standard against which to assess these models. When models are built to gain insight into the mechanism of a certain phenomenon such as, for example, business fluctuations, a more adequate post-model test might be to assess whether the model mimics the relevant characteristics of this phenomenon. For example, Jan Tinbergen's last stage of valuing the United States model (1939b) was to check whether the model as a whole would represent business cycles adequately, discussed in Chapters 2 and 3 under the label of 'mathematical significance'. Indeed, it was this kind of post-model test that provided the Cowles Commission programme with strong support. Irma and Frank Adelman's (1959) computer simulation of the Klein–Goldberger (1955) model of the United States economy – at that time the most advanced macroeconometric model – showed that this model, when shocked by disturbances, could generate cycles with the same characteristics as those of the United States economy. Indeed, the Klein–Goldberger model cycles were remarkably similar to those described as being characteristic of the United States economy by the National Bureau of Economic Research (NBER). From this it was concluded that the Klein–Goldberger model was 'not very far wrong' (Adelman and Adelman 1959: 621).

The Klein–Goldberger model consisted of twenty-five difference equations with a corresponding number of endogenous variables; it was non-linear in character and included lags up to the fifth order. The model had been applied to yearly projections of economic activity in the United States with some success, but its dynamic properties were only analysed using highly simplified assumptions, for example Arthur S. Goldberger's (1958) and John Cornwall's (1958) investigations of linear versions of the model. The innovative element of the Adelmans' research was that, rather than making simplifying assumptions, the complexity of the Klein–Goldberger model was left intact and the equations were programmed for an IBM 650 and simulated for one hundred annual periods. The reason this work was not done earlier was that until then there was no technology available to cope with such a task.[9]

[T]he complexity of the model requires the use of modern high-speed computers for the long-run solution of the system in a reasonable length of time. Since the problem is about the right size for the IBM 650 calculator, and since the appropriate computer facilities exist at the University of California Radiation laboratory, we programmed the equations for that machine.

(Adelman and Adelman 1959: 597)

The IBM Magnetic Drum Calculator Type 650, as it is called in full, was not the first electronic computer, nor was it the largest or the fastest; but it was the first computer to be used extensively in universities. Its popularity was due to the fact that it was relatively cheap, it was easy to use and not easily damaged. The IBM 650 became available to universities around 1955. Because of its availability to faculty and researchers at almost every large university in the United States, it had a major impact on the evolution of computing, computer education, and computer science and engineering research. For example, at the Carnegie Institute of Technology, the IBM 650 played a significant role in the early research on artificial intelligence and cognitive science because it provided Herbert Simon and Allen Newell with the facilities to develop the (first widely used) list-processing language, IPL-V.[10]

In 1959, Irma and Frank Adelman used the IBM 650 to examine the dynamic properties of the Klein–Goldberger model. They were interested in an endogenous explanation of the persistent business fluctuations so characteristic of Western capitalism. Existing theories led to the idea of either dampened or explosive cycles. To the Adelmans, exogenous shocks or externally imposed constraints seemed 'rather artificial', so they looked for a 'more satisfactory mechanism for the internal generation of a persistent cyclical process' (Adelman and Adelman 1959: 596). The purpose of their paper was to investigate whether the Klein–Goldberger model was a good candidate. The first step of their research was to run the program in the absence of additional external constraints and shocks. The exogenous variables were extrapolated by fitting a least-squares straight line to the postwar data. The result was that the variables in the Klein–Goldberger model grow almost linearly with time. Thus, the endogenous part of the model did not contain an explanation of the oscillatory process. Two conclusions could be drawn, either the Klein–Goldberger model is 'fundamentally inadequate' or

> to the extent that the behavior of this system constitutes a valid qualitative approximation to that of a modern capitalist society, the observed solution of the Klein–Goldberger equations implies that one must look elsewhere for the origin of business fluctuations. Under the latter assumptions, cyclical analysis would be limited to an investigation of the reaction of the economic system to various perturbations. And, since the Klein–Goldberger model does present a more or less detailed description of the interactions among the various sectors of the economy, it could be utilized in the examination of the mechanism of response to shocks.
>
> (Adelman and Adelman 1959: 604)

Because it was apparent that the model was stable, even under large exogenous displacements, the next step was to see whether the introduction of relatively minor uncorrelated perturbations into the model would generate cyclical fluctuations analogous to the observed ones. Two types of shocks were introduced. Type I shocks were random shocks superimposed on the extrapolated values of the exogenous quantities, and Type II shocks were random perturbations introduced into each non-definitional model equation. Type I shocks induced cycles with three- to four-year periods in the variables, but the average amplitude of these cycles appeared 'unrealistically small'. Type II shocks also induced cycles with three- to four-year periods, but now the amplitudes were 'reasonably realistic'. Since the effects of Type II shocks were much larger than those of Type I, and because either type of shock may be present in the real economy, further analysis was carried out for a situation in which both shocks were present.

That the amplitudes and the periods of the oscillations observed in this model were 'roughly the same as those which are found in practice' (p. 611) was seen by the Adelmans as 'merely a necessary condition for an adequate simulation of the cyclical fluctuations of a real industrial economy' (p. 611). The question now was whether the shocked model could produce business cycles in the 'technical' sense:

> [I]f a business cycle analyst were asked whether or not the results of a shocked Klein–Goldberger computation could reasonably represent a United States-type economy, how would he respond? To answer these questions we shall apply to the data techniques developed by the National Bureau of Economic Research (NBER) for the analysis of business cycles.
>
> (Adelman and Adelman 1959: 612)

A comparison between the characteristics of the cycles generated by the shocked model and the characteristics summarised in Burns and Mitchell (1946) and Mitchell (1951) was considered to be 'quite a stringent test of the validity of the model' by the Adelmans (p. 612).

The striking result was that when random shocks of a 'realistic order of magnitude' are superimposed on the Klein–Goldberger model equations, the characteristics of the resulting cyclical fluctuations appeared to be are similar to those observed in the United States economy:

> The average duration of a cycle, the mean length of the expansion and contraction phases, and the degree of clustering of individual peaks and troughs around reference dates all agree with the corresponding data for the United States economy. Furthermore, the lead–lag relationships of the endogenous variables included in the model and the indices of conformity of the specific series to the overall business cycle also resemble closely the analogous features of our society.
>
> (Adelman and Adelman 1959: 629)

The Adelmans concluded that 'it is not unreasonable to suggest that the gross characteristics of the interactions among the real variables described in the Klein–Goldberger equations may represent good approximations to the behavioral relationships in a practical economy' (p. 620).

Kim *et al.* (1995) identify four notions for testing in the econometric literature to focus on, and criticise one of them, namely, characteristics testing. Characteristics testing involves matching particular features in an empirical model to specific characteristics in selected data sets. Kim *et al.*'s main criticism is that what is inferred from characteristics tests cannot normally be fed back to confirm the empirical model in cases where the particular characteristics being tested are not unique or essential to the empirical model. Several different empirical models may result in the same characteristics in the data, and it may not always be clear what an essential characteristic is. Characteristics testing cannot capture the essential characteristics in such a way that would facilitate discrimination.

The cases discussed in Kim *et al.*'s essay are the natural rate hypothesis (NRH) tests of the 1970s that had been carried out by Lucas, Sargent and Barro. In their work, the characteristics tests failed to work to provide reverse inference. However, for each case they reduced theory to a simple test relation or single-data characteristics. In my view, this was the main reason that the characteristics test failed to provide reverse inference. The Adelman–Adelman test was 'quite a stringent test' of the validity of the Klein–Goldberger model because the number of matched characteristics was fairly large and the test did go beyond the comparison of cycle lengths and amplitudes.

Robert Lucas's artificial economies

To Robert Lucas, the Adelmans' achievement signalled a new standard for what it means to understand business cycles: 'One exhibits understanding of business cycles by constructing a *model* in the most literal sense: a fully articulated artificial economy which behaves through time so as to imitate closely the time series behavior of actual economics' (Lucas 1977: 11). To see that the Adelman–Adelman test works as a stringent test, Lucas understood that the facts that require explanation should be more detailed in terms of their characteristics than those he used for his NRH tests. In an essay (1977) and in a later account of his business-cycle papers (1981), Lucas admitted that:

> Naturally, my earlier papers recognised to some extent which qualitative facts, because of their central importance, required explanation; but for the most part these were second-hand facts for me, picked up from Phelps or Allan Meltzer or 'common knowledge' around Chicago and Carnegie-Mellon. I was beginning to be concerned that the particular theoretical line I was following might be focused on explaining 'coffee-break' facts only.
>
> (Lucas 1981: 16)

Lucas found these more detailed facts in Friedman and Schwartz's *Monetary History* (1963), Mitchell (1951), and Burns and Mitchell (1946):

> (i) Output movements across broadly defined sectors move together. ... (ii) Production of producer and consumer durables exhibits much greater amplitude than does the production of nondurables. (iii) Production and prices of agricultural goods and natural resources have lower than average conformity. (iv) Business profits show high conformity and much greater amplitude than

other series. (v) Prices generally are procyclical. (vi) Short-term interest rates are procyclical; long-term rates slightly so. (vii) Monetary aggregates and velocity measures are procyclical.

(Lucas 1977: 9)

However, Lucas paraphrased the Adelman–Adelman question above as follows:

The Adelmans posed, in a precise way, the question of whether an observer armed with the methods of Burns and Mitchell (1946) could distinguish between a collection of economic series generated artificially by a computer programmed to follow the Klein–Goldberger equations and the analogous series generated by an actual economy.

(Lucas 1977: 11)

This paraphrasing is important because the characteristics test of the Adelmans is thereby reinterpreted as a Turing test.

Alan Turing (1912–54) was a British mathematician. Among his many accomplishments was basic research in computing science. In 1950, in the article 'Computing machinery and intelligence', which appeared in the philosophical journal *Mind*, Turing asked the question 'Can machines think?' Turing didn't answer this question directly but replaced it by another, described in terms of a game, which he called the 'imitation game':

It is played with three people, a man (A), a woman (B), and an interrogator (C) who may be of either sex. The interrogator stays in a room apart from the other two. The object of the game for the interrogator is to determine which of the other two is the man and which is the woman. … The interrogator is allowed to put questions to A and B … The ideal arrangement is to have a teleprinter communicating between the two rooms. … We now ask the question, 'What will happen when a machine takes the part of A in this game?' Will the interrogator decide wrongly as often when the game is played like this as he does when the game is played between a man and a woman?

(Turing 1950: 433–4)

As one can see, the test is in principle the same as the Adelman–Adelman test: an observer (interrogator) has to decide whether a distinction can be made between a computer output and something from the 'real' world.

The enormous advantage of Turing's approach to artificial intelligence is that it freed scientists from building replicas of the human mind to achieve machine thinking that meets the standard of human intelligence. In the same way, the characteristics test of the Adelmans freed macroeconometricians from having to build 'detailed, quantitatively accurate replicas of the actual economy' (Lucas 1977: 12). In the same way as the criterion of predictability freed Friedman from the Cowles Commission's emphasis on comprehensiveness, characteristic testing legitimised Lucas to work with very simple (and therefore unrealistic) models.

Lucas's approach was not to aim at models as 'accurate descriptive representations of reality', and in this he echoed Friedman's dictum that 'the more significant the theory, the more unrealistic the assumptions':

> [I]nsistence on the 'realism' of an economic model subverts its potential usefulness in thinking about reality. Any model that is well enough articulated to give clear answers to the questions we put to it will necessarily be artificial, abstract, patently 'unreal'.
>
> (Lucas 1980: 696)

The main difference between Friedman and Lucas with respect to ideas about realisticness was that Lucas argued for the use of 'as-if p' assumptions, where p is an analogue system, with the same 'superficial' features as the system under study. This is the type of assumption Musgrave (1981) distinguished beside negligibility, domain and heuristic assumptions but did not label separately (see above). Lucas said,

> I think it is exactly this superficiality that gives economics much of the power that it has: its ability to predict human behavior without knowing very much about the make up and lives of the people whose behavior we are trying to understand.
>
> (Lucas 1987b: 241)

While Friedman, in his empirical work, aimed at modelling by using negligibility assumptions and domain specifications, according to Lucas these model assumptions were not necessary:

> A 'theory' is not a collection of assertions about the behavior of the actual economy but rather an explicit set of instructions for building a parallel or analogue system – a mechanical, imitation economy. A 'good' model, from this point of view, will not be exactly more 'real' than a poor one, but will provide better imitations. Of course, what one means by a 'better imitation' will depend on the particular questions to which one wishes answers.
>
> (Lucas 1980: 697)

As a result, Lucas is not as pessimistic as Friedman about solving the Cournot problem (see Introduction). While Friedman believes that only the Marshallian method of partitioning the problem produces fruitful results, Lucas believes that by constructing 'analogue economies' a Walrasian programme, which fully specifies the optimisation problem which agents face, is a real possibility (Hoover 1988: 224). Therefore, Lucas expects developments in monetary economic and business-cycle theory to arise from 'forces' outside economics, consisting of 'purely technical developments that enlarge our abilities to construct analogue economies': improvements in mathematical methods and improvements in computational capacities (Lucas 1980: 697).

For his views on 'superficiality' Lucas, on several occasions, acknowledges the influence of Herbert Simon's 1969 publication, *The Sciences of the Artificial* (Lucas 1980: 697n; 1987b: 241n; see also Klamer 1984: 47–8). In following up this reference, Hoover (1995b) shows that Simon (1969) provided the materials that could be used to construct a methodological foundation for calibration (the choice of the model parameters to guarantee that the model precisely mimics some characteristics; see Hoover 1995b: 25).

The central object of Simon's account is an artifact, which he defines as

> a meeting point – an 'interface' in today's terms – between an 'inner' environment, the substance and organisation of the artifact itself, and an 'outer' environment, the surroundings in which it operates. If the inner environment is appropriate to the outer environment, or vice versa, the artifact will serve its intended purpose.
>
> (Simon 1969: 7)

The advantage of factoring an artificial system into goals, outer environment, and inner environment is 'that we can often predict behavior from knowledge of the system's goals and its outer environment, with only minimal assumptions about the inner environment' (p. 8). It appears that different inner environments accomplish identical goals in similar outer environments, such as weight-driven clocks and spring-driven clocks. A second advantage is that, in many cases, whether a particular system will achieve a particular goal depends on only a few characteristics of the outer environment, and not on the detail of that environment. So, we 'might look toward a science of the artificial that would depend on the relative simplicity of the interface as its primary source of abstraction and generality' (p. 9). Thus, as Hoover rightly observes: 'Simon's views reinforce Lucas's discussion of models. A model is useful only if it foregoes descriptive realism and selects limited features of reality to reproduce' (Hoover 1995b: 35). However, this does not mean that we can take any inner environment as long as the model succeeds in reproducing the selected features. The inner environment is only relatively independent of the outer environment:

> The independence of the inner and outer environments is not something which is true of arbitrary models; rather it must be built into models. While it may be enough in hostile environments for models to reproduce key features of the outer environment 'as if' reality was described by their inner environments, it is not enough if they can do this only in benign environments. Thus, for Lucas, the 'as if' methodology interpreted as an excuse for complacency with respect to modeling assumptions must be rejected. Simon's notion of the artifacts helps Lucas's both rejecting realism in the sense of full articulation and at the same time, insisting that only through carefully constructing the model from invariants – tastes and technology, in Lucas's usual phrase – can the model secure the benefits of a useful abstraction and generality.
>
> (Hoover 1995b: 36)

In Lucas's view, the ability of models to imitate actual behaviour in the way tested by the Adelmans is a necessary, but not a sufficient, condition to use these kinds of macroeconometric models for policy evaluation. Policy evaluation requires 'invariance of the structure of the model under policy variations' (Lucas 1977: 12). The underlying idea, known as the Lucas Critique, is that estimated parameters that were previously regarded as 'structural' in econometric analysis of economic policy actually depend on the economic policy pursued during the estimation period. Hence, the parameters may change with shifts in the policy regime (Lucas 1976).

Lucas's (1976) paper is perhaps the most influential and most cited paper in macroeconomics (Hoover 1995a) and it contributed to the decline in popularity of the Cowles Commission approach. The Lucas Critique was an implicit call for a new research programme. This alternative to the Cowles Commission programme involved formulating and estimating macroeconometric models with parameters that are invariant under policy variations and can thus be used to evaluate alternative policies. The only parameters Lucas 'hopes' to be invariant under policy changes are the parameters describing 'tastes and technology' (Lucas 1977: 12; 1981: 11–12).

Autonomous automata

In line with his account of artifacts, Simon argues for micro-foundations. The reason is that requiring that a model should mimic specific characteristics is a necessary but not a sufficient condition. Referring to Lucas's list of 'stylised facts' of business cycles (see above), Simon admits that: 'A business cycle theory may be regarded as a plausible first approximation if it can predict (or retrodict) these facts; otherwise it is implausible', but 'many theories, many different sets of structural equations, might fit them' (Simon 1984: 39). Simon goes along with the critique of Kim, De Marchi and Morgan (1995), even if the list of characteristics is expanded. Using additional aggregate empirical data will not help: 'any theory that will reproduce the stylized facts can very likely be fitted to the aggregate data with an R^2 well over 0.9' – an observation consistent with Friedman's critique. As it seems, according to Simon, 'the details of the empirical data that go beyond the stylized facts' are 'well below the noise level, and contain little information that can be used for model identification or prediction' (p. 40). In his view, the strategy for the future development of economics is 'to secure new kinds of data at the micro level, data that will provide direct evidence about the behavior of economic agents and the ways in which they go about making their decisions' (p. 40). To Simon's surprise, Lucas (1980) proved an unlikely supporter of his strategy, 'Support for this thesis comes from surprising directions' (p. 40):

> Our task as I see it ... is to write a FORTRAN program that will accept specific economic policy rules as 'input' and will generate as 'output' statistics describing the operating characteristics of time series we care about, which are predicted to result from these policies. ... The central idea is that *individual* responses can be documented relatively cheaply, occasionally by direct

experimentation, but more commonly by means of the vast number of well-documented instances of individual reactions to well-specified environmental changes made available 'naturally' via censuses, panels, other surveys, and the (inappropriately maligned as 'casual empiricism') method of keeping one's eyes open. Without such means of documenting patterns of behavior, it seems clear that the FORTRAN program proposed above cannot be written.

(Lucas 1980: 709–10)

So, both Lucas and Simon shared the view that micro-foundations are required. Lucas even propagated von Neumann's approach to complexity, that is, a top-down decomposition of the complex system until a certain level is reached, on which the subsystems are treated as black boxes, and of which the input–output relation is well defined. This can clearly be seen by his more recent discussion of models in his 'On the mechanics of economic development' (1988). There he refers to models as 'artificial worlds':

This is what I mean by the 'mechanics' of economic development – the construction of a mechanical, artificial world, populated by the interacting robots that economics typically studies, that is capable of exhibiting behavior the gross features of which resemble those of the actual world that I have just described.

(Lucas 1988: 5)

Artificial worlds are computer-implementable stochastic models, which consist of a set of 'micro-level entities' that interact with each other and an 'environment' in prescribed ways. Artificial worlds are designed to give insight into processes of emergent organisation. In a survey of the use of artificial worlds in economics, David Lane (1993) provides an example of an artificial economy. An artificial economy is an artificial world whose micro-entities represent economic agents and products. Interactions between these micro-entities model fundamental economic activities – production, exchange, and consumption. The purpose of an artificial economy experiment is to discover what kinds of structures of economic regimes can occur and to see how they depend on system parameters and the characteristics of the constituent agents. For example, one of the problems of a general equilibrium model is the problem of coordination: where does this order come from? While general equilibrium modellers start by assuming a Walrasian equilibrium, the designer of an artificial economy is first of all concerned with modelling how economic agents interact. Whether a Walrasian equilibrium will emerge depends on the system parameters and the agent's characteristics. Another example is Nicolaas Vriend's 1995 essay, of which the main objective was 'to present an example of a computational approach to address the following question: How do self-organising markets emerge in the economy, and what are their characteristics?' (Vriend 1995: 205).

However, Lucas only paid lip service to this von Neumann approach without ever applying it to complexity. Lucas is a general equilibrium modeller who bypassed the Cournot problem by adopting the representative-agent model in which one agent or a few types of agents stand in for the behaviour of all (Hoover 1995b: 38). Even his paper, from which the above quotation on artificial worlds is taken, contains three models that are, in fact, representative-agent models. For Lucas, micro-foundations do not mean partitioning as they do for Simon. Lucas employed Turing's approach by representing the economic system by means of an analogue system rendering one representative economic agent. In contrast to Lucas, Simon explicitly dealt with complexity. The procedure that Simon (1962) used to consider systems as 'hierarchic', thus facilitating the investigation of complex systems, is the point of departure of much research dealing with complexity. For example, Lane's artificial worlds are designed to study hierarchic systems in particular (Lane 1993: 90).

The point is to decide on an adequate partitioning and to select the elementary systems that are suitable to be treated as black boxes. When models are only meant to function as forecasting devices, it is possible to consider the whole economy as a black box and to use naive models that contain only a set of rules of thumb. An example is Harvey's term-structure model (1991); this model contains a single equation with only one forecasting variable to forecast economic growth. The forecasting variable is the term structure – the difference between long-term and short-term interest rates – so that 'one needs only a hand-calculator and a copy of a financial newspaper' to obtain forecasts of economic growth (Harvey 1991: 8).

For Lucas, the level of superficiality depends on the kind of questions posed. Lucas's answer to the question, 'Do you think that it is crucial for macroeconomic models to have neoclassical choice-theoretic micro foundations' posed by Snowdon, Vane and Wynarczyk (1994: 221) is 'No'. He, then, is more specific and qualifies his answer by saying that it depends on the purposes you want the model to serve. For short-term forecasting, there is no need for a theoretical foundation.

> But if one wants to know how behaviour is likely to change under some change in policy, it is necessary to model the way people make choices. If you see me driving north on Clark Street, you will have good (though not perfect) predictive success by guessing that I will still be going north on the same street a few minutes later. But if you want to predict how I will respond if Clark Street is closed off, you have to have some idea of where I am going and what my alternative routes are – of the nature of my decision problem.
> (Lucas interviewed by Snowdon, Vane and Wynarczyk 1994: 221)

To use macroeconometric models for policy evaluation, one has to know the properties of the model that are invariant under policy changes, a point on which both Simon and Lucas agreed. However, their views on where invariance occurs differed. Lucas placed invariance in the structural parameters of the unpartitioned box containing one robot agent representing its 'tastes and technology', whereas Simon located invariance at the decomposed elementary micro-level. For each 'small world' the rest of the system is its environment. Simon expected each small box to contain only a simple relationship. Finding your way through

Chicago is similar to the route an ant has to take to cross a beach on the way to its home:

> We watch an ant make his laborious way across a wind- and wave-molded beach. He moves ahead, angles to the right to ease his climb up a steep dunelet, detours around a pebble, stops for a moment to exchange information with a compatriot. Thus he makes his weaving, halting way back to his home.
>
> (Simon 1969: 23)

The ant has a general sense of where home lies, but he cannot foresee all the obstacles that he will encounter on the way. Thus, the ant's path is irregular, complex and hard to describe but this complexity is a reflection of the complexity of the surface of the beach, not of a complexity in the ant.

> An ant/a man viewed as a behaving system, is quite simple. The apparent complexity of its/his behavior over time is largely a reflection of the complexity of the environment in which it/he finds himself.
>
> (Simon 1969: 24, 25, 52)

A black box needs only to contain a simple relationship and, more importantly, 'a simple hypothesis that fits data to a reasonable approximation should be entertained, for it probably reveals an underlying law of nature' (Simon 1968: 448). In other words, simple correlations have a higher probability of being autonomous. This expectation was supported by Harold Jeffreys' (1948) simplicity postulate in Bayesian reasoning. Simon argued the following. If one attaches a high *a priori* probability to the hypothesis that the world is simple:[11] P(simple law) is high; and if one assumes that simple configurations of data are sparsely distributed among all logically possible configurations of data: P(simple configuration of data) is low; then a high posterior probability must be place on the hypothesis that a simple configuration of data in fact reflects approximations to conditions under which a simple law of nature holds:

$$P(\text{simple law} \mid \text{simple conf}) = \frac{P(\text{simple conf} \mid \text{simple law}) \cdot P(\text{simple law})}{P(\text{simple conf})}$$

where P(simple conf | simple law) = 1.

Therefore, when a scientist 'finds that the "facts" summarized by a simple, powerful generalization do not fit the data exactly, his first reaction is *not* to throw away the generalization, or even to complicate it by incorporating additional terms' (Simon 1968: 442). Instead, his explorations would move in two directions: '(1) toward investigations of his measurement procedures as possible sources of the discrepancies; and (2) toward the identification of other variables associated with the deviations' (p. 442). However, in contrast to Haavelmo's method of incorporating these other variables into the model, Simon describes the modelling process of the black boxes in a similar way to the strategy expounded by Friedman:

the scientist would narrow the empirical generalisation by stating the limiting conditions under which it is supposed to hold.

But this process of inference from the facts does not stop with these two stages of (1) finding simple generalisations that describe the facts to some degree of approximation; and (2) finding limiting conditions under which the deviations of facts from the simple generalisation might be expected to decrease; but continues to (3) explaining why the simple generalisation should fit the facts, e.g. Newton's gravitational explanation for Galileo's law.

According to Simon, one should stick to simple generalisations, even when an object's behaviour is complex, and not make the generalisation more complex accordingly. A simple generalisation is more likely to reveal a lawful relationship. In the example of the falling feather, the environment should hold the explanation for the complex behaviour of the feather. In other words, the complexity of the feather's falling movement is a reflection of the complexity of the environment – turbulence – and not of the law of gravity.

The kind of partitioning Simon aimed at was to decompose the system into a hierarchical system until a level is reached where the elementary units ('axioms' in von Neumann's terminology) are bound only by simple relationships. Their simplicity implies that they probably represent autonomous relationships.

Jeffreys' strategy of starting with simple models was built on by Arnold Zellner (1979, 1994) in his so-called SEMTSA approach. Like Friedman, he was dissatisfied with the poor ability of the large-scale macroeconometric models to explain and predict, in comparison to the naive models.[12] His strategy is briefly stated 'Keep It Sophisticatedly Simple' (KISS) (Zellner 2001): start with models as simple as possible and improve the model each time in the direction indicated by all kinds of diagnostic checks on the properties of the model. Because naive models perform better in prediction than complicated models, he suggested starting with this kind of simple models. According to Jeffreys the choice of the simplest form is not a matter of convention, but 'because it is the most likely to give correct predictions' (Jeffreys 1948: 4). Zellner's approach was based on Jeffreys' suggestion that if there are no effective models available to explain a phenomenon, a sophisticatedly simple initial model is that all variation is random (naive model I) unless shown otherwise (Zellner 1988: 14). Thus, when simple relationships are more likely to give correct predictions in unstable environments, then simple relationships have a higher probability of being more autonomous than more comprehensive relationships.

Autonomy versus precision

Economists use models to evaluate different kinds of policy measures. Therefore, they require their models to predict well. Every evaluation of a policy measure is a kind of prediction. They would like to use models for counterfactual analyses, so models must contain autonomous relationships, that is, the model equations should be invariant for a range of policy interventions. At the same time, using models for policy evaluations means that economists aspire to preciseness of the models' predictions. However, there is a tension between autonomy and preciseness. As long as generalisations like 'if I drop it, it falls' remain imprecise they are almost exceptionless, and thus highly autonomous (Hoover 2002: 160). However, if we would specify the 'it' as a feather or a bank note,[13] as Cartwright (1999: 27) did, it becomes clear that any relation that is used to predict when or where an object hits the ground cannot be autonomous. Environmental conditions such as turbulence are very significant. So-called exceptions (when the dropped object does not fall to the ground, because for example it gets caught in a bush) are caused by the environment of the object and do not contradict the generalisation 'if I drop it, it falls' itself. Precise predictions are based on combinations of relationships like the above imprecise, autonomous generalisation and those that describe the specific circumstances. As a result, these combined relationships are more confluent (and thus less autonomous) but more precise.

Haavelmo's advice was to incorporate as many potential influences as possible into the model to achieve the highest degree of autonomy. The researchers at the Cowles Commission, assuming that their model equations were autonomous, strived for more comprehensiveness to achieve more precise predictions. They recommended building models in which turbulence is taken account of. The result was that the model's equations became less autonomous. Their pursuit for preciseness went at the cost of autonomy.

Friedman propagated an opposite strategy by recommending to start with modelling those phenomena in which the environmental circumstances are less influential. When and where a very heavy ball hits the ground when thrown from the tower of Pisa can be predicted quite precisely. Turbulence, wind or even a bush standing in the way, do not matter. A good (fall) experiment is one carried out with a heavy ball and not with a feather. But are the equivalents of heavy balls to be found in economics? They are scarce. That is, there are probably only a few examples of influential factors that are so dominant that they push other influences aside.

According to Simon, the simplicity of a relationship is an indication of its lawfulness. His advice is to 'decompose' the falling object from its environment to simplify the analysis. The shorter the period that a prediction applies to, the less influence the environment has and thus the more accurate the prediction becomes.

The above discussion is summarised in Table 4.1.

Table 4.1 Autonomy versus precision

Imprecise	'if I drop it, it falls'	autonomous and exceptionless
Cowles Commission	'it' + circumstances	less autonomous, but more precise
Friedman	look for very heavy balls	autonomous and precise, but rare
Simon	the shorter it falls	more autonomous and precise

Conclusions

The laws of nature are, usually, not found in the 'wild' but in laboratories by means of controlled experiments. The view that we need laboratories to detect laws of nature is most clearly expressed by Nancy Cartwright's account of laws. She defines a law of nature as 'a necessary regular association between properties' (Cartwright 1999: 49). A consequence of her capacities account of laws of nature is that necessary regular associations hold only *ceteris paribus*, which means that 'they hold only relative to the successful repeated operation of a nomological machine' (p. 50). A nomological machine is 'a fixed (enough) arrangement of components, or factors, with stable (enough) capacities that in the right sort of stable (enough) environment will, with repeated operation, give rise to the kind of regular behaviour that we represent in our scientific laws' (p. 50). Fixed patterns of association are a consequence of the operation of factors that have stable capacities arranged in the 'right' way in the 'right' kind of stable environment (see also Cartwright 1999: 138).

As a result of this account, a design of an experiment to discover laws is equal to the design ('blueprint' as Cartwright calls it) of a nomological machine. Although I agree with her that for laws we need a kind of a nomological machine, a right arrangement of stable capacities in the right kind of environment, we differ in opinion about the necessity of stability of the environment. In the social sciences we hardly can assume or arrange a stable environment. We can only control and manipulate things and environments to a certain extent. The conventional reading of '*ceteris paribus*' is 'other things being equal', but it can also be read as 'other things being absent'. If read as in the latter case, one could also call it '*ceteris absentibus*' (see Mäki 1998a). In terms of controllability, the *ceteris paribus* clause can be interpreted as 'other things are held constant or absent'. But as has already been said, both forms of conditioning the circumstances are very difficult if not impossible to attain.

Therefore Cartwright is rather pessimistic about finding or using lawful relationships. But in my view we do not need to require stable environments for discovering them. The works of Friedman and Simon show different strategies to gain knowledge about lawful relationships – without being able to do controlled experiments – by modelling the data such that they function as designs of good experiments.

Besides releasing the presumption that we need stable environments to discover lawful relationships, the works of these economists, including Haavelmo, also enforce a reconsideration of what is meant by a lawful relationship in the social sciences. Philosophers have traditionally employed various standard criteria to distinguish laws from other types of generalisations. These criteria take the forms of laws that are said to be exceptionless generalisations and to make no reference to particular objects or spatio-temporal locations and to have a very wide scope. James Woodward (2000) shows that these criteria are not helpful either for understanding what is distinctive about laws of nature or for understanding the features that characterise explanatory generalisations in, for example, the social sciences. 'In general, it is the range of interventions and changes over which a generalisation is invariant and not the traditional criteria that are crucial both to whether or not it is a law and to its explanatory status' (Woodward 2000: 222).

Woodward's idea of invariance is that a generalisation describing a relationship between two or more variables is invariant if it would continue to hold – would remain stable or unchanged – as various other conditions change. The set or range of changes over which a relationship or generalisation is invariant is its domain of invariance. So, invariance is a relative matter: a relationship is invariant with respect to a certain domain.

As we have seen, it is this notion of invariance that is useful for understanding explanatory practice in the social sciences and not the concept of a law of nature fulfilling the above-mentioned traditional criteria. However, it will be shown that the domain of invariance the social scientists are concerned with in finding explanatory generalisations is larger than the domain that Woodward assumes to be crucial for their explanatory status.

Two sorts of changes can be distinguished that are relevant to the assessment of invariance. First, there are changes in the background conditions to a generalisation, that is changes that affect other variables besides those that figure in the generalisation itself. Second, there are changes in those variables that figure explicitly in the generalisation itself. In his discussion of invariance, Woodward emphasises that only a subclass of this latter sort of changes is important, namely changes that result from an intervention, that is changes that result from a causal process having the right causal characteristics as described in his paper. The reason he gives for this is that some background conditions are causally independent of the factors related by the generalisation in question and therefore of no importance. However, other background conditions might be causally connected to some of the factors related by the generalisation, and changes in these conditions might disrupt the relationship. A relationship that holds in certain specific background conditions and for a restricted range of interventions might break down outside of these.

The interesting questions for social scientists are not only whether a relationship is invariant under certain specific kinds of changes and interventions but also under which changes it remains invariant; they want to know the domain of changes for which it holds. Social scientists are faced with constantly changing background conditions and they would like to know whether the relationships on which they base their policy advices still hold tomorrow.

Although Woodward considers the notion of invariance under interventions as the key feature that a generalisation must possess if it is to play an explanatory role, he admits implicitly that discussion of invariance in various sciences is broader than only in terms of intervention. He views an intervention as an idealisation of an experimental manipulation – by human beings or Nature – and probably therefore de-emphasises the role of unstable background conditions. However, when he discusses the idea that invariance comes with degrees, he uses the notion of Haavelmo's autonomy ('just another name for what we have been calling invariance' (p. 215)) to clarify the relativistic characteristic of invariance. In Haavelmo's account of autonomy, invariance is not only defined with respect to interventions but also to changes in background conditions, as we have seen in Chapter 3.

In Woodward's account of explanation in relation to invariance, the difference between laws and invariant generalisations is considered as a matter of degree: laws are generalisations that are invariant under a large(r) and (more) important set of changes. So, any strategy to find laws outside a laboratory has to deal with the question: invariant with respect to what domain? In economics (and econometrics) such an account is captured by the notion of autonomy, as we have seen in the research strategies of inferring invariant relationships from passive observations. With the notion of autonomy, Haavelmo provided the framework for dealing with invariance outside the laboratory. He came to the conclusion that the problem of autonomy could be solved by economic theory. As a result, autonomy disappeared from the Cowles Commission research agenda. Members of the Cowles Commission strived for comprehensiveness to attain preciseness.

Friedman reintroduced invariance on the empirical research agenda by criticising the belief that more autonomy could be achieved by more comprehensiveness. He showed that the problem of autonomy was an empirical problem. Invariant generalisations should be not be assessed by exploring the domain of changes for which they hold, but by investigating for which phenomena they hold. However, these domain specifications should not be incorporated into the model equations, as in the Cowles Commission programme, but should be specified independently.

Simon showed how invariance could be inferred from comprehensive models. Decomposing a system where the interactions between subsystems are negligible in the short run might lead to simple relationships that have a high probability of being invariant.

In general, philosophers link the possibility of finding lawful relationships with the ability to do controlled experiments and therefore tend to be pessimistic about finding these relationships in the social sciences. This chapter has discussed different strategies that question this presupposition of the necessity of laboratories. One replaces this presupposition for the presupposition that theory will solve the problem of autonomy, the other for the presupposition of the existence of phenomena that can be described by simple invariant relationships and the third for the presupposition that laws of nature are simple. The fourth strategy is based on the presumption that computer-simulated laboratories are adequate alternatives to 'real' laboratories made of thick concrete walls and heavy steel doors.

In the 'equilibrium business-cycle programme' dominated by Lucas's instructions, it became standard practice to run an experiment with an artificial economy:

> One of the functions of theoretical economics is to provide fully articulated, artificial economic systems that can serve as laboratories in which policies that would be prohibitively expensive to experiment with in actual economies can be tested out at much lower cost.

> (Lucas 1980: 696)

These kinds of simulations can be considered as substitutes for controlled experiments. Irma Adelman (1968) defines the simulation of economic processes as 'the performance of experiments upon an analogue of the economic system and the drawing of inferences concerning the properties of the economic system from the behavior of its analogue' (p. 268). It is crucial that she considers an analogue as an 'idealization of a generally more complex real system, the essential properties of which are retained in the analogue' (p. 268). In other words, she emphasises the Hertzian requirement of appropriateness (see Chapter 2). To the extent that the analogue used in the simulation represents the relevant properties of the economic system under study, experimentation with the analogue can be used to infer the results of analogous experiments with the real economy.

There are two ways of arriving at appropriate models. One way is von Neumann's Axiomatic Procedure to partition the system under investigation into elementary units. According to Simon, each 'axiom' should represent a simple empirical relationship, the simpler they are the more likely they are to be autonomous. The alternative route is Turing's method to build imitation games with autonomous parameters.

We can only learn from a model if it is an idealisation. However, this idealisation does not necessarily have to be done by way of *ceteris paribus* or *ceteris neglectis* assumptions. Analogue systems, provided that they contain the stable properties of the system under investigation, can also inform us.

5 Measurement

Measurement is the link between mathematics and science. The nature of
measurement should therefore be a central concern of the philosophy of science.

(Ellis 1968: 1)

Introduction

In order to evaluate economic policy, models are built and used to produce numbers
to inform us about economic phenomena. Although phenomena are investigated
by using observed data, they themselves are in general not directly observable. To
'see' them we need instruments, and to obtain numerical facts about the phenomena
in particular we need measuring instruments. This view is a result of James
Woodward's (1989, see also Bogen and Woodward 1988) account on the distinction
between phenomena and data. According to Woodward, phenomena are relatively
stable and general features of the world and therefore suited as objects of
explanation and prediction. Data, that is, the observations playing the role of
evidence for claims about phenomena, on the other hand involve observational
mistakes, are idiosyncratic and reflect the operation of many different causal factors
and are therefore unsuited for any systematic and generalising treatment. Theories
are not about observations – particulars – but about phenomena – universals.

Woodward characterises the contrast between data and phenomena in three ways.
In the first place, the difference between data and phenomena can be indicated in
terms of the notions of error applicable to each. In the case of data the notion of
error involves observational mistakes, while in the case of phenomena one worries
whether one is detecting a real fact rather than an artifact produced by the peculiarities
of one's instruments or detection procedures. A second contrast between data and
phenomena is that phenomena are more 'widespread' and less idiosyncratic, less
closely tied to the details of a particular instrument or detection procedure. A third
way of thinking about the contrast between data and phenomena is that scientific
investigation is typically carried on in a noisy environment, an environment in which
the observations reflect the operation of many different causal factors.

The problem of detecting a phenomenon is the problem of detecting a signal
in this sea of noise, of identifying a relatively stable and invariant pattern of

some simplicity and generality with recurrent features – a pattern which is not just an artifact of the particular detection techniques we employ or the local environment in which we operate.

(Woodward 1989: 396–7)

Underlying the contrast between data and phenomena is the idea that theories do not explain data, which typically will reflect the presence of a great deal of noise. Rather, an investigator first subjects the data to analysis and processing, or alters the experimental design or detection technique, in an effort to separate out the phenomenon of interest from extraneous background factors. 'It is this extracted signal rather than the data itself which is then regarded as a potential object of explanation by theory' (p. 397).

Because facts about phenomena are not directly measured but must be inferred from the observed data, we need to consider the reliability of the data. These considerations cannot be derived from theory but are based on a closer investigation of the experimental design, the equipment used, and need a statistical underpinning. This message was well laid out for econometrics by Haavelmo (1944), see Chapter 3.

The data [the economist] actually obtains are, first of all, nearly always blurred by some plain errors of measurement, that is, by certain extra 'facts' which he did not intend to 'explain' by his theory. [So] one should study very carefully the actual series considered and the conditions under which they were produced, before identifying them with the variables of a particular theoretical model.

(Haavelmo 1944: 7)

The kinds of models discussed in this chapter function as detection instruments – more specifically, as measuring instruments. In measurement theory, measurement is the mapping of a property of the empirical world into a set of numbers. In Chapter 4 we have seen that a 'good' model for policy requires invariance, located in some of the relationships or in some of the parameters. We have also discussed a few strategies to uncover invariance from the data. But we haven't discussed yet how we arrive at informative numbers. There are beautiful examples of cases in which nature is ruled by numbers, but they are rare. Pythagoras discovered the wonderful harmonic progression in the notes of the musical scale, by finding the relation between the length of a string and the pitch of its vibrating note. Thrilled by this discovery, he saw in numbers the elements of all things. Looking at the organic nature, one discovers a sequence of numbers that seems to rule, for example, the arrangement of the florets of a sunflower. This sequence is 1, 1, 2, 3, 5, 8, 13, …, and can be attained by successively adding the last two numbers. If these numbers are placed in ratios of each other, the so-called Fibonacci sequence: $^1/_1$, $^1/_2$, $^2/_3$, $^3/_5$, $^5/_8$, $^8/_{13}$, …, they converge to the ratio known as the Golden Section, which appeals to our aesthetic sense of ratios. But otherwise, the book of Nature is not written in numbers, numbers are the work of man. To attain numbers that will inform us about phenomena, we have to measure, that is, we have to find appropriate mappings of the phenomena. We do this kind of mathematisation by modelling the phenomena in a very specific way.

Theories are incomplete with respect to the facts about phenomena. Though theories explain phenomena, they often (particularly in economics) don't have built-in application rules for mathematising the phenomena (see Chapter 2). Moreover, theories don't have built-in rules for measuring the phenomena. For example, theories tell us that metals melt at a certain temperature, but not at which temperature (Woodward's example); or they tell us that capitalist economies give rise to business cycles, but not the duration of recovery. In practice, by mediating between theories and the data, models may overcome this dual incompleteness of theories. As a result, models that function as measuring instruments are located on the theory–world axis mediating between facts about the phenomena and data, see Figure 5.1. The dotted line in Figure 5.1 represents the indication that theories do not provide (quantitative) facts about phenomena.

This chapter will concentrate on three necessary steps for measurement (whether or not provided by theory): (1) the search for a mathematical representation of the phenomenon, (2) this representation about the phenomenon should cover an as far as possible invariant relationship between facts and data, and (3) calibration of the model.

Mathematical representation

The dominant measurement theory of today is the representational theory of measurement. The core of this theory is that measurement is a process of assigning numbers to attributes or characteristics of the empirical world in such a way that the relevant qualitative empirical relations among these attributes or characteristics are reflected in the numbers themselves as well as in important properties of the

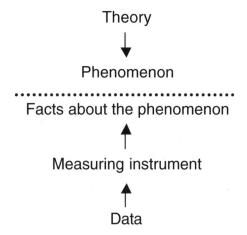

Figure 5.1 Position of models as measuring instruments on theory–world axis

number system. In other words, measurement is conceived of as establishing a homomorphism[1] between a numerical and an empirical structure. In the formal representational theory this is expressed as:

> Take a well-defined, non-empty class of extra-mathematical entities Q ... Let there exist upon that class a set of empirical relations $R = \{R_1, \ldots, R_n\}$. Let us further consider a set of numbers N (in general a subset of the set of real numbers Re) and let there be defined on that set a set of numerical relations $P = \{P_1, \ldots, P_n\}$. Let there exist a mapping M with domain Q and a range in N, $M: Q \to N$ which is a homomorphism of the empirical relationship system $<Q, R>$ and the numerical relational system $<N, P>$.
>
> (Finkelstein 1975: 105)

This is diagrammatically represented in Figure 5.2, where $q_i \in Q$ and $n_i \in N$. Mapping M is a so-called 'scale of measurement'. Measurement theory is supposed to analyse the concept of a scale of measurement. It distinguishes various types of scales and describes their uses, and formulates the conditions required for the existence of scales of various types.[2]

The problem, however, is that the representational theory of measurement has turned too much into a pure mathematical discipline, leaving out the question of how the mathematical structures gain their empirical significance in actual practical measurement. The representational theory lacks concrete measurement procedures and devices. This problem of empirical significance is discussed by Michael Heidelberger (1994a, 1994b), who argues for giving the representational theory a 'correlative interpretation', based on Gustav Theodor Fechner's principle of mental measurement.[3]

In his plea for a correlative interpretation, Heidelberger traces the origins of the representational theory of measurement in Maxwell's method of using formal

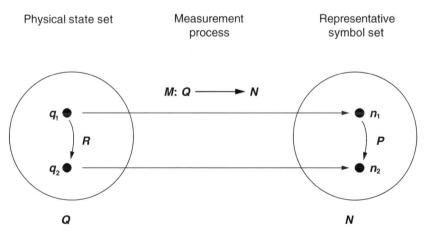

Figure 5.2 Diagrammatic representation of the set-theoretical definition of measurement, a slightly simplified version of Figure 1 in Finkelstein (1975: 105)

analogies, which are the origins of modelling, too, as shown in Chapter 2. As Heidelberger observantly noted, a first glimpse of a representational theory of measurement appeared in Maxwell's article 'On Faraday's lines of force' ([1855] 1965a). In discussing his method of using analogies, the 'representational view' is made *en passant* (see also Chapter 2): 'Thus all the mathematical sciences are founded on relations between physical laws and laws of numbers, so that the aim of exact science is to reduce the problems of nature to the determination of quantities by operations with numbers' (Maxwell [1855] 1965a: 156). In a translation of Maxwell's article by Ludwig Boltzmann (1912), Boltzmann added the following note to the passage quoted above: 'As far as I know, nobody later took up this view that the measurement of magnitudes of space and time by numbers is based on a mere analogy of those magnitudes with the relations obtaining between whole numbers' (Boltzmann 1912: 100; translated by Heidelberger 1994b: 4).

But this is not true. According to Heidelberger, Hermann von Helmholtz (1821–94) took up Maxwell's view and continued to think in this direction. Usually Helmholtz's 1887 article, 'Zählen und Messen, erkenntnis-theoretisch betrachtet' is taken as the starting point of the development of the representational theory. The development since Helmholtz's seminal paper is well described elsewhere[4] and will not be repeated here. But unfortunately, as Heidelberger emphasises, the result of this development is that most followers of the representational theory of today have adopted an operationalist interpretation. This operationalist interpretation is best illustrated by Stevens' dictum:

> [M]easurement [is] the assignment of numerals to objects or events according to rule – any rule. Of course, the fact that numerals can be assigned under different rules leads to different kinds of scales and different kinds of measurements, not all of equal power and usefulness. Nevertheless, provided a consistent rule is followed, some form of measurement is achieved.
>
> (Stevens 1959: 19)

By labelling the current interpretation of measurement as an operationalist one, Heidelberger alluded not only to a strong version of operationalism in which terms in a theory are fixed by giving operational definitions, but also to a weaker one that says that a concept is quantitative if the operational rules are fixed that lead to a numerical value, whatever else the meaning of the concept might be.

The disadvantage of an operationalist interpretation is that it is much too liberal. As Heidelberger rightly argues, we could not make any difference between a theoretical determination of the value of a theoretical quantity and the actual measurement. A correlative interpretation does not have this disadvantage, because it refers to the handling of a measuring instrument. This interpretation of the representational theory of measurement was based on Fechner's correlational theory of measurement. Fechner had argued that

> the measurement of any attribute p generally presupposes a second, directly observable attribute q and a measurement apparatus A that can represent

variable values of q in correlation to values of p. The correlation is such that when the states of A are arranged in the order of p they are also arranged in the order of q. The different values of q are *defined* by an intersubjective, determinate, and repeatable calibration of A. They do not have to be measured on their part. The function that describes the correlation between p and q relative to A (underlying the measurement of p by q in A) is precisely what Fechner called the measurement formula. Normally, we try to construct (or find) a measurement apparatus which realises a 1:1 correlation between the values of p and the values of q so that we can take the values of q as a direct representation of the value of p.

(Heidelberger 1993: 146)[5]

To illustrate this, let us consider an example of temperature measurement. We can measure temperature, p, by constructing a thermometer, A, that contains a mercury column whose length, q, is correlated with temperature. The measurement formula, the function describing the correlation between p and q, $p = f(q)$, is determined by choosing the shape of the function, f, e.g. linear, and by calibration. For example, the temperature of boiling water is fixed at 100, and of ice water at 0.

The correlative interpretation of measurement implies that the scales of measurement are a specific form of indirect scales, namely so-called associative scales. This terminology is from Brian Ellis (1968) who adopted a conventionalist view on measurement. To see that measurement on the one side requires empirical significance – Heidelberger's point – and on the other hand is conventional, we first have a closer look at direct measurement and thereupon we will discuss Ellis's account of indirect measurements.

A *direct* measurement scale for a class of measurands is one based entirely on relations among that class and not involving the use of measurements of any other class. This type of scale is implied by the definition of the representational theory of measurement above, see Figure 5.2. Although, direct measurement assumes direct observability – human perception without the aid of any instrument – of the measurand, we nevertheless need a standard to render an observation into a measurement. A standard is a 'material measure, measuring instrument, reference material or measuring system intended to define, realize, conserve or reproduce a unit or one or more values of a quantity to serve as a reference' (IVM 1993: 45).[6] This means that inserting a standard, s, into the physical state set, see Figure 5.3, should complete Figure 5.2.

However, there are properties, like temperature, for which it is not possible or convenient to construct satisfactory direct scales of measurement. Scales for the measurement of such properties can, however, be constructed, based on the relation of that property, p, and quantities, q^i, with which it is associated and for which measurement scales have been defined. Such scales are termed *indirect*. *Associative* measurement depends on there being some quantity q associated with property p to be measured, such that when things are arranged in the order of p, under specific conditions, they are also arranged in the order of q. In Heidelberger's terminology,

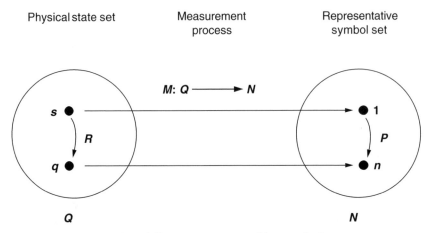

Figure 5.3 Representation of direct measurement with a standard

p and *q* are correlated. This association is indicated by *C* in Figure 5.4. An associative scale for the measurement of *p* is then defined by taking $f(M(q))$ as the measure of *p*, where $M(q)$ is the measure of *q* on some previously defined scale, and *f* is any strictly monotonic increasing function. Associative measurement can be pictured as an extended version of direct measurement, see Figure 5.4.

We have *derived* measurement if there exists an empirical law $F = F(M_1(q^1), \ldots, M_n(q^n))$ and if it is the case that whenever things are ordered in the order of *p*, they are also arranged in the order of *F*. Then we can define $F(M_1(q^1), \ldots, M_n(q^n))$ as a measure of *p*.

The measurement problem then is the choice of the associated property *q* and the choice of *f* (or *F*), which Ellis following Ernst Mach called the 'choice of principle of correlation'.[7] For Ellis, the only kinds of considerations that should have any bearing on the choice of principle of correlation are considerations of mathematical simplicity (Ellis 1968: 95–6). But this is too much conventionalism, even Mach noted that whatever form one chooses, it still should have some empirical significance.

> It is imperative to notice that whenever we apply a definition to nature we must wait to see if it will correspond to it. With the exception of pure mathematics we can create our concepts at will, even in geometry and still more in physics, but we must always investigate whether and how reality correspond to these concepts.
>
> (Mach [1896] 1966: 185)

This brings us back to Heidelberger.

According to Heidelberger (1993: 147), 'Mach not only defended Fechner's measurement theory, he radicalized it and extended it into physics'. To Mach, any establishment of an objective equality in science must ultimately be based on sensation because it needs the reading (or at least the gauging) of a material device

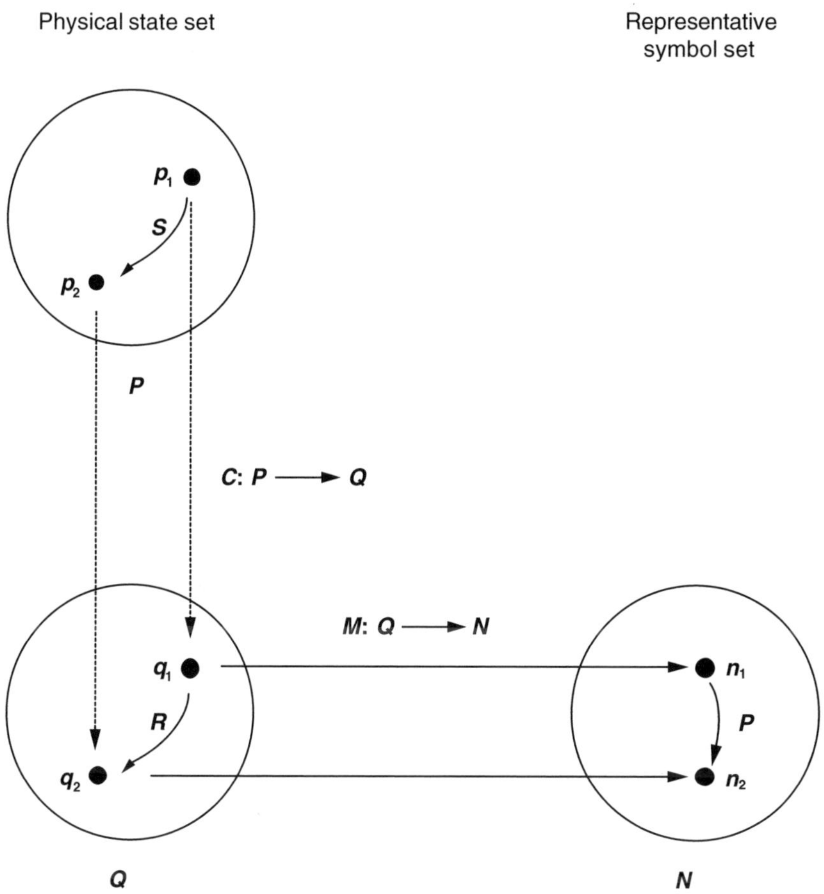

Physical state set

Representative
symbol set

Figure 5.4 Representation of associative measurement

by an observer, see Figure 5.3. The central idea of correlative measurement, which stood in the centre of Mach's philosophy of science, is that 'in measuring any attribute we always have to take into account its empirical lawful relation to (at least) another attribute. The distinction between fundamental [read: direct] and derived [read: indirect] measurement, at least in a relevant epistemological sense, is illusory' (Heidelberger 1994b: 11).

The difference between Ellis's associative measurement and Heidelberger's correlative measurement is that, according to Heidelberger, the mapping of q into numbers, $M(q)$, is not the result of (direct) measurement but is obtained by calibration (see Heidelberger's quote above). To determine the scale of the thermometer no prior measurement of the expansion of the mercury column is required; by convention it is decided in how many equal parts the interval between two fixed points (melting point and boiling point) should be divided. In the same way, a clock continuously measures time, irrespective of its face. The face is the conventional part of time measurement and the moving of the hands the empirical determination of time. This interpretation gives back to measurement the idea that it concerns concrete measurement procedures and devices, taking place in the domain of the physical state sets as a result of an interaction between P and Q, see Figure 5.4.

Although the measuring instrument and the scale of measurement are closely related to each other, there is an essential distinction between both. One is an object of the physical world and the other is an object of the mathematical world. This expresses itself in the different kinds of requirements both have to fulfill,[8] which can be seen by considering more precisely the definitions Ellis provides:

(*a*) Measurement is the assignment of numerals to things according to any determinate, non-degenerate rule.

(*b*) We have a scale of measurement if and only if we have such a rule.

(*c*) Two procedures are procedures for measuring on the same scale, if and only if, wherever they are deemed to be applicable, they would always lead to the same numerical assignments being made to the same things under the same conditions.

(*d*) We have a scale S for the measurement of a given quantity q if, and only if:

   (*i*)   there is a procedure P for measuring on S such that for any object x which occurs in the order of q, x is measurable by P,

   (*ii*) there is no object which is measurable on S which does not occur in the order of q,

   (*iii*) if the objects measurable on S are arranged in the order of the numerical assignments, they are thereby arranged in the order of q.

(Ellis 1968: 41–3)

It may be doubted whether condition (*d.i*) is really a necessary one. Not every quantity is in fact measurable over the whole of its range, because for practical reasons it is not always possible to find an adequate procedure (or to develop a proper instrument) for measuring every object occurring in the order of q. But with respect to scales, one has to make a distinction between the practical problem of finding and developing adequate procedures (and instruments) and the numerical representation of the ordering of quantity q. Ellis included this condition for having a complete scale for the measurement of a given quantity. Although most measuring *instruments* in general only work for a limited range, the scale must apply for the whole range. What the whole range is, is qualitatively indicated by theory, e.g. whether there is an upper bound, or an under bound, or no boundaries at all.

Invariance

Measurement, including the measuring instrument being used, is based on a correlative relation between the measurand, p, and the associated quantity, q. To gain a better understanding of measurement we must have a closer look at the nature of the correlative relation. The various authors refer to it in terms of an empirical lawful relationship, in the sense that 'when things are arranged in the order of p, under certain specified conditions, they are also arranged in the order of q' (Ellis 1968: 90). It should not be considered as a numerical law, because that would require independent measurements of both p and q. 'For each of the variables in a law there must exist a measurement apparatus with a measurement formula before a law can be established and tested' (Heidelberger 1993: 146–7).[9]

To investigate what a 'lawful relation' means in the context of measurement, it is, just as in Chapter 4, very useful to use Cartwright's account that a law of nature – necessary regular association between properties – holds only relative to the successful repeated operation of a nomological machine. It shows why the empirical lawful relation on which the measurement is based and the measuring instrument are two sides of the same coin. The measuring instrument must function as a nomological machine to fulfill its task. This interconnection is affirmed by Heidelberger's use of correlative relation and measuring instrument as nearly synonymous, Ellis's definition of a lawful relation as an arrangement under specific conditions and Finkelstein's observation that the 'law of correlation' is 'not infrequently less well established and less general, in the sense that it may be the feature of specially defined experimental apparatus and conditions' (Finkelstein 1975: 108).

However, as we have discussed in Chapter 4, in economics we can only control the environment to a certain extent. To gain more insight into how to deal with this problem of the (im)possibility of conditioning the circumstances with respect to measurement, the history of the standardisation of the thermometer is helpful. This history has been extensively explored by the historian and philosopher of science, Hasok Chang. He shows that standardisation was closely linked to the dual measurement problem, namely the choice of the proper associated quantity and the choice of the principle of correlation, which is labelled by him as the 'problem of nomic measurement':

(1) We want to measure quantity X.

(2) Quantity X is not directly observable by unaided human perception so we infer it from another quantity Y, which is directly observable.

(3) For this inference we need a law that expresses X as a function of Y, $X = f(Y)$.

(4) The form of this function f cannot be discovered or tested empirically, because that would involve knowing the values of both Y and X, and X is the unknown variable that we are trying to measure.

(Chang 2001: 251)

Although Chang's paper, 'Spirit, air, and quicksilver: the search for a "real" scale of temperature' (2001) discusses only one part of the measurement problem, namely the choice of the associated property, in this case the choice of the right thermometric fluid, it also gives some hints about solving the problem of the choice of the most appropriate form of f.

Historically, there were three significant contenders: atmospheric air, mercury, and ethyl alcohol. At the end of the eighteenth century, it was generally believed that the mercury thermometer indicated the real degree of heat. But in the nineteenth century people started to question the accuracy of mercury thermometers. To choose among the three candidate contenders all kinds of experiments were suggested. The problem, however, was that the proposed experiments to settle the debate were based on theoretical assumptions about the kind of thermal expansion the fluid would show – the form of f. But to test these expansions one has to carry out measurements for which a thermometer was needed. This circularity was avoided by Henri Victor Regnault's[10] use of the principle of 'comparability': 'If a type of thermometer is to be an accurate instrument, all thermometers of that type must agree with each other in their readings' (Chang 2001: 276).

Until Regnault's experiments it was agreed that mercury thermometers were comparable. Regnault discovered that this was not true: the readings of mercury thermometers made with different types of glass, or even the same type of glass which had undergone different thermal treatments, could not be made to agree with each other. The failure of comparability due to the behaviour of glass was not avoidable by specifying a certain type of glass as the standard glass. 'To do so, one would have needed to specify and control the exact chemical composition of the glass, the process of manufacture, and the method of blowing the thermometer bulb' (Chang 2001: 278). But using gas instead of mercury seemed to be the answer, for the thermal expansion of gas was known to be so great that the expansion of the glass envelope was thereby made negligible. Restricting his attention to thermometers containing air, Regnault found that those made with different densities were quite comparable with each other, certainly better than the mercury thermometers. This result was also summarised by Mach, although he pointed to Pierre-Louis Dulong and Alexis-Thérèse Petit as founders of this method of comparability.

> One of the greatest advantages which a gas offers is its large expansion, and the resultantly great sensitivity of the thermometer. Also, because of this great expansion, the disturbing influence of the varying material of the vessels passes into the background. ... gas expands 146 times as much as glass. The expansion has therefore only a small influence upon the apparent expansion of the gas, and its change with different sorts [of glass] is of negligible influence. ... The choice of material for the vessel, that is the individuality of the thermometer, can only disturb this relation insignificantly: thermometers become comparable to a high degree.
>
> (Mach [1896] 1966: 188)

Dulong and Petit had required that a perfect thermometric substance should expand uniformly, without thinking that this condition was amenable to a direct test. But, according to Chang, the point of this history is that for endorsing the air thermometer as most accurate, Regnault did not need to prove that the expansion of air is uniform, 'he was all too aware of the circularity involved in trying to demonstrate such a proposition experimentally' (Chang 2001: 283).

Regnault's strategy of comparability did not amount to truth, it meant self-consistency for a given type of instrument. It was a falsificationist strategy: 'only a clear *failure* of comparability was useful; that allowed Regnault to eliminate an instrument as a candidate for indicating true temperatures' (Chang 2001: 284). Regnault made his strategy a very effective falsificationist strategy by tightening the circle. For the failure of comparability to be an unequivocal verdict against an assumption about the shape of the measurement formula, Regnault eliminated all other assumptions that could be blamed for the failure. 'Regnault's way of proceeding left no room for attacks against auxiliary hypotheses. Tightening the circle, in the sense of involving fewer assumptions, made the refutation more decisive. Sometimes there is virtue in circularity' (p. 284).

If we want to apply the strategy of comparability in economics, we face the problem that we often cannot create a uniform environment to compare the different instruments, for instance in a laboratory as Regnault did. But when we have a closer look at Regnault's method, we see that the essence of comparability is that it allows one to find an accurate measuring instrument especially when one cannot control all circumstances. As Chang pointed out:

> The requirement of comparability was not new with Regnault. It had been widely considered a basic requirement for reliability in thermometry for a long time. The term is more easily understood if we go back to its origin, namely when thermometers were notoriously unstandardised so the readings of different types of thermometers could not be meaningfully *compared* with one another.
>
> (Chang 2001: 276)

The readings of the thermometers were not comparable with each other because the materials from which the instruments were built were not of the same quality – there were no standards. This quality depended on, for example, the kind of glass or the density of the gas that was used for fabricating the instrument, but also on the craftsmanship of the instrument-maker: circumstances that were not controlled in a laboratory, but were at the same time part of the set-up in which the measurement took place. The strategy of comparability is to find a measuring instrument for which the readings are least influenced by or most independent of the quality of the materials, or in more general terms, the circumstances one cannot control.

In measurement, even in a laboratory, there are always circumstances one cannot control. A measuring instrument is accurate when it is designed, fabricated and used in such a way that the influences of all these uncontrollable circumstances are negligible. For example, a gas thermometer is more accurate than a mercury thermometer, because the expansion of glass is negligible compared with the expansion of gas. Thus, the empirical relation between the expansion of the gas column and temperature is (more or less) invariant and influenced only negligibly by other circumstances.

To avoid the problem of (the lack of) controllability is to design and use measuring instruments in such a way that the influences of all the uncontrollable circumstances are negligible; in other words, a measuring device should be constructed and used such that it fulfills the *ceteris neglectis* condition. This latter condition can be clarified by the same equation we used in Chapter 3 to discuss autonomous equations (3.11):

$$\Delta y = \Delta F\left(x_1, x_2, \ldots\right) = \frac{\partial F}{\partial x_1}\Delta x_1 + \frac{\partial F}{\partial x_2}\Delta x_2 + \ldots$$

where x_i denotes a causal factor of y. Suppose we care about the correlative relation between a property p to be measured and the associated quantity q. The instrument should be constructed and used such that it is sensitive to changes in p and at the same time insensitive to changes in the other circumstances (OC):

$$\Delta q = \Delta F\left(p, OC\right) = \frac{\partial F}{\partial p}\Delta p + \frac{\partial F}{\partial OC}\Delta OC \tag{5.1}$$

where OC is a collective noun of all the other factors, $x_2, x_3, \ldots$, that should have a negligible influence on q. This condition implies requirements on $\partial F/\partial p$ and $\partial F/\partial OC$, namely $\partial F/\partial OC$ must be negligible compared with $\partial F/\partial p$, and, of course, $\partial F/\partial p$ is not affected by changes in p : Δp has no influence on $\partial F/\partial p$. To relate this discussion to a branch in economics where measurement is at the centre of interest – econometrics – we can state that measurement entails that the empirical relation represented by the measurement formula should be autonomous as far as possible. If we can construct the instrument based on an autonomous relationship, we do not have to worry about the extent to which the other circumstances are changing. We can allow the other circumstances to change; they do not have to be controlled as is assumed in the conventional *ceteris paribus* ($\Delta OC = 0$) and *ceteris absentibus* ($OC = 0$) conditions.

Equation (5.1) clarifies the problem of comparability: accuracy of the thermometer was dealt with by searching for the most adequate filling. This was done by selecting filling q as such that $\partial F/\partial OC$ is negligible compared with $\partial F/\partial p$. Analogous to the standardisation of the thermometer, the problem of comparability in cases of economic measurement can be considered as the search for the most autonomous relationships. This leads us to the actual purpose of the strategy of comparability: the search for autonomous relationships. The selection of gas in the case of thermometers is similar to Friedman's strategy (discussed in Chapter 4) of finding those phenomena for which the environment is negligible, like the choice of very heavy balls in a Galilean fall experiment to obtain an autonomous relationship.

A measurement formula must be a representation of a lawful relationship. According to Cartwright, for lawful relationships we need stable environments:

nomological machines. So, in her account measuring instruments can only fulfill their measurement task when they are nomological machines. To build them we must be able to control the circumstances, which is possible (always only to a certain extent) in physics but highly problematic in economics. However, invariant relationships (in both economics and physics) are not always the result of *ceteris paribus* environments but could also occur because the influence of the environment is negligible, in other words invariant relationships could also be *ceteris neglectis* regularities, empirical relations that are autonomous as far as possible.

Calibration

Measurement formulae in economics are based on invariant relationships, but these can still be imprecise generalisations (see Table 4.1). As we have seen in Chapter 4, it seems that we can only attain preciseness at the cost of autonomy. However, as discussed above, measurement consists of two parts: association (correlation) between properties (empirical part) and a mapping into numbers obtained by calibration (conventional part). Preciseness is achieved by determining a scale, that is, by choosing values for the equation's parameters. Thus imprecise generalisations can be transformed into precise relationships – without loss of autonomy – through calibration.

Although calibration is in principle just a matter of convention, in practice the parameter values are not chosen arbitrarily. It will be shown that calibration is also a means to achieve accuracy, which in metrology is defined as the 'closeness of the agreement between the result of a measurement and a true value of the measurand' (IVM 1993: 24).[11] Assessing the measuring instrument for accuracy is the second function of calibration.

Of course, we do not have access to the true value of a measurand without the application of any instrument. The true value is the value obtained by a perfect measurement, but measurements are never perfect, errors will always occur and thus the true value is by nature indeterminate. The method of comparability was exactly meant to assess an instrument's accuracy without the necessity of having knowledge about true values. This led to the strategy of the search for autonomous relationships. However, comparability is a necessary but not a sufficient condition for accuracy. Because true values are unknown, in practice the performance of a measuring instrument is described in terms of precision. Precision is a statement about the closeness to a particular value that the individual measurements of a set of identically performed measurements possess. It expresses how well a measurement process repeats each time the same measurement is made. It is presumed that during the time taken the measurand remains fixed and that the scatter of values is due to the process of measurement. However, this term is not defined in the International Vocabulary of Basic and General Terms in Metrology (IVM, see note 6), one only finds a term that signifies precision in a specific sense, namely 'repeatability' (just after the definition of accuracy). The IVM definition of repeatability is the 'closeness of the agreement between the results of successive measurements of the same measurand carried out under the same conditions of measurement' (IVM 1993: 24).[12] These conditions include the same measurement procedure, the same observer, the same measuring instrument, used under the same conditions, the same location, with repetition over a short period of time (p. 24). However, these are laboratory conditions, not met for macroeconomic measurements. So, we have to go a little bit further down this IVM list of performance definitions, and thus arrive at 'reproducibility': 'closeness of the agreement between the results of measurements of the same measurand carried out under changed conditions of measurement' (IVM 1993: 24). In spite of the fact that we cannot assess the closeness of the agreement between a measurement result and a true value – because we do not know the latter value – we nevertheless expect an accurate measuring instrument to reproduce almost the same result each time we measure the measurand in a state of which we assume it would lead to the same (though unknown) value. For example, we assume that both boiling water and melting ice (under a broad range of different conditions of measurement) each exist at the same temperature. We can use both states to calibrate a thermometer.

To have an interpretation of preciseness adequate for the social sciences, it will from now on be understood in terms of reproducibility. Seen as such, the aim for preciseness is the practical alternative to the aim for accuracy: one assumes that closeness of results is an indication for truth, an assumption that underlies many (if not all) minimal or least error methods in the social sciences; true values are expected where the sum of distances between the expected/assumed/estimated but nevertheless unknown true value and the observations – these distances are the so-called errors – is minimal.

So, calibration is the second necessary requirement of assessing the accuracy of measuring, or more generally detection, instruments. It should be noted that both requirements are still not sufficient to acquire certain knowledge about the true values. This is a consequence of their position on the theory–world axis as depicted in Figure 5.1. Instruments located between data and facts about phenomena on the theory–world axis are not assessed as rendered in the standard account of testing, namely by confronting the output of a model with data (observations). The output of a model is facts about the phenomenon. They are the previously unobservables made visible by the detection instrument. As a matter of fact, independent of any instrument we will never be able to gain knowledge about the true values of the measurands. As a result, only through (the same or other) instruments we can assess the accuracy of an instrument. The accuracy of an instrument is assessed by comparing facts about phenomena with each other, and these facts only exist as outputs of instruments.

If other facts about the same phenomena are available, then the model can be tested by confronting its output with these facts. However, these facts are available (only) because they are also produced by instruments. Thus, confronting a model with phenomenological facts rather means comparing this instrument with another instrument that generated these facts. The assessment of instruments for accuracy takes place by comparing them with one that is chosen to act as standard. In metrology, it is this kind of assessment that is meant by calibration and so is defined as the 'set of operations that establish, under specified conditions, the relationship between values of quantities indicated by a measuring instrument or measuring system, or values represented by a material measure or a reference material, and the corresponding values realised by standards' (IVM 1993: 48).

The general philosophy adopted for the creation of standards is that they should be based upon some principle that is known to be as stable as possible – to meet the requirement of reproducibility. Standards are entirely of man's choice, nothing about the natural world defines them, but they are often based upon naturally occurring phenomena when these possess the required degree of stability.

> In order to compare things measured by different persons it is necessary to assume a standard of measure. Some one must indicate a particular specimen of the thing to be measured as the standard of that quantity and every one else must agree to measure by that standard or by copies of it. This method introduces experiment into mathematics, and greatly disturbs the easy elegance of the adherents of proportions who are not accustomed to the apparatus of the market place; but those who make up their minds to study Nature with measuring rod, time-piece and weights will find that these arbitrary and perhaps inaccurate standards are intended to represent something uniform and independent of any individual man, which depends on an ancient decree and is preserved by the power of Nature but which neither a new decree nor new actions of Nature could restore if it were destroyed.
>
> (Maxwell [1857] 1990: 520)

An example of this approach to base standards on a set of proper invariants is the way in which the international metric organisation aims to link the base units of the International System of Units (SI, see Table 5.1) to the real world not through prototypes,[13] but through the fundamental constants of physics, which are supposed to be universal and unchanging, see Table 5.2. Prototypes are clearly instruments. The prototype of a kilogram is not only the lump of platinum–iridium kept at the International Bureau of Weights and Measures (BIPM, Bureau International de Poids et Mesures), but also the equipment to ensure that the conditions as specified by the Committee for Weights and Measures (CIPM, Comité International des Poids et Mesures) in 1889 are met.[14]

However, do not be deceived by the existence of these so-called fundamental quantities, now and then called 'natural constants'. They simply do not exist in 'wild' nature; they are the results of highly sophisticated experimental measurements.

If there are no standards available because, for example, there are no other facts available than the ones produced by the instrument itself, in other words if the instrument is unique, then the assessment is carried out by investigating the inner workings of the instrument.

An important problem of instruments used to make unobservables visible is how to distinguish between the facts about the phenomenon and the artifacts created by the instrument. Allan Franklin (1986) discusses nine epistemological strategies to distinguish between a valid observation and an artifact. One of these strategies, which he labels as calibration, is 'the use of a surrogate signal to standardize an

Table 5.1 Base units of the International System of Units (SI)

Quantity	SI base unit	Symbol
Length	metre	m
Mass	kilogram	kg
Time	second	s
Electric current	ampere	A
Thermodynamic temperature	kelvin	K
Amount of substance	mole	mol
Luminous intensity	candela	cd

Table 5.2 Fundamental physical constants

Fundamental quantity	Symbol
Velocity of electromagnetic radiation in free space	c
Elementary charge	e
Mass of the electron at rest	m_e
Avogadro constant	N_A
Planck constant	h
Universal gravitational constant	G
Boltzmann constant	k

instrument. If an apparatus reproduces known phenomena, then we legitimately strengthen our belief that the apparatus is working properly and that the experimental results produced with that apparatus are reliable' (Franklin 1997: 31). This kind of calibration is to establish the relationship between values of quantities indicated by the instrument in one specific dimension and the corresponding standard values in the same dimension, to acquire reliability of the values indicated by the instrument in other dimensions. But one should be warned, this kind of calibration does not guarantee a correct result; though its successful performance does argue for the validity of the result (p. 76).

Beside calibration, Woodward (1989) also mentions other possibilities for increasing reliability, but these are not applicable in the case of (macro)economic research: control of possible confounding effects and systematic error, replicability, and data reduction. Control and replication are hardly possible in a macroeconomic environment and data reduction is a luxury economists cannot afford. In the case of macroeconomic research, reliability can mainly be achieved by investigation of the equipment used.

Calibration in economics

These accounts on calibration are unmistakably developed in the natural sciences. To see whether these accounts can help us understanding measurement practices in economics, let us start with Kydland and Prescott's (1982) paradigm new-classical equilibrium, real-business-cycle paper, which is generally acknowledged as the first application of calibration in economics.[15] Kydland and Prescott (1982) introduced calibration to macroeconomics as a means of reducing 'dramatically' the number of free parameters of their business-cycle model (p. 1361). However, since the introduction of Kydland and Prescott's application, calibration has been controversial in economics and generated an enormous pile of literature discussing the meaning and role of calibration in economics. One reason for this is the ambiguous meaning Kydland and Prescott gave to calibration. They characterised calibration in two different ways. First, as 'specifications of preferences and technology … close to those used in many applied studies' and secondly as 'the selection of parameter values for which the model steady-states values are near average values for the American economy during the period being explained' (Kydland and Prescott 1982: 1360). The purpose of the parameterisation was not sufficiently clear, resulting in three different interpretations in economics and econometrics: estimation, testing and gauging.

Generally in econometrics, calibration is seen as a method of estimation (Dawkins *et al.* 2001; Pagan 1994): 'simulating a model with ranges of parameters and selecting elements from these ranges which best match properties of the simulated data with those of historical data' (Gregory and Smith 1990: 57; 1993). In other words, calibration is a simulation-based estimation method, 'the operation of fitting model-parameters to observational data obtained from the real system (within a specified experimental frame)' (Elzas 1984: 51). Simulation-based methods may be useful in parameterising models in which there are unobservable variables or simply analytical intractabilities. Calibration considered as such is in fact 'tuning', as discussed in Chapters 2 and 3: the adjustment of parameter values such that the model's output has the same characteristics as the phenomenon to be explained by this model. An often-used calibration criterion is to measure the difference between some empirical moments computed on the observed variable and its simulated counterpart. The estimator derived by calibrating some empirical moments based on observations and simulations is the so-called Method of Simulated Moments (MSM) estimator (Gouriéroux and Monfort 1996).

An alternative but more criticised interpretation is that calibration is a method for testing a model. If there are no free parameters, then the comparison of a model's data-output moments (or perhaps some other output measure) with those of historical time-series can be thought of as a test of the model. This type of testing is a specific case of 'characteristics testing', as discussed in Chapter 4. If the correspondence between some aspect of the model and the historical record is deemed to be reasonably close, then the model is viewed as satisfactory. If the distance between population and historical moments is viewed as too great, then the model is rejected (Gregory and Smith 1991). A drawback of this procedure is that, unlike in the case of estimation, the method itself does not supply a metric that can judge closeness. However, Watson (1993) provides measures of fit for the calibrated models, based on the size of the stochastic error needed to match the second moments of the actual data exactly.

The ambiguity surrounding calibration methods in econometrics has led to a substantial controversy captured by the heading: calibration versus estimation, in which both labels not only refer to specific methods but more broadly to opposing methodologies, each claiming sound scientific practice. Quah (1995: 1594) caricatures both as 'research styles' that are respectively 'disrespectful of econometrics' and 'disrespectful of economic theory'. Hoover (1995b) stylises calibration as an 'adaptive strategy' and estimation as a 'competitive strategy'. Under the latter strategy, 'theory proposes, estimation and testing disposes' (p. 29). However, the aim of the adaptive strategy is never to test let alone to reject a theory, 'but to construct models that reproduce the economy more and more closely within the strict limits of the basic theory' (p. 29).

Whether there is a difference between estimation and calibration, big or small (Hansen and Heckman 1996; Kim and Pagan 1995), in the discussions so far there is no mention of the interpretation Kydland and Prescott themselves have ultimately given to calibration, namely gauging. In a special symposium: 'Computational Experiments in Macroeconomics' in the *Journal of Economic Perspectives* (1996), Kydland and Prescott explicated the 'tool' they used in their (1982) 'Time to Build' paper. Their 'experiment' was an implementation of Lucas's 'equilibrium business-cycle programme': to run a simulation experiment with an artificial economy (see Chapter 4). This programme not only framed their account of models and theories, but also advanced the view that business cycles should be considered as phenomena in the above-described (that is Woodward's) meaning of the word.

Lucas characterised the business cycle by enumerating seven 'qualitative features' of economic time series (see Chapter 4). By defining the business cycle in this way, Lucas indicated that he considered the business cycle as a general phenomenon of capitalist economies:

> There is, as far as I know, no need to qualify these observations by restricting them to particular countries or time periods: they appear to be regularities common to all decentralized market economies. Though there is absolutely no theoretical reason to anticipate it, one is led by the facts to conclude that, with respect to the qualitative behavior of co-movements among series, *business cycles are all alike.* To theoretically inclined economists, this conclusion should be attractive and challenging, for its suggests the possibility of unified explanation of business cycles, grounded in the *general* laws governing market economies, rather than in political or institutional characteristics specific to particular countries or periods.
>
> (Lucas 1977: 10)

Led by this definition, Prescott (1986) preferred to refer to business cycles as 'business cycle phenomena', 'which are nothing more or less than a certain set of statistical properties of a certain set of important aggregate time series' (p. 10). By explicitly treating the business cycle as a general phenomenon not restricted to particular countries or time periods, the business cycle was considered as a universal and its 'qualitative features' as 'stylised facts'.

According to Kydland and Prescott (1996: 70; 1991: 169), any economic computational experiment involves five major steps: 'pose a question; use a well-tested theory; construct a model economy; calibrate the model economy; and run the experiment'. In their view, a theory is well tested when it 'provide reliable answers to a class of questions' (Kydland and Prescott 1996: 72). Discussing business-cycle research, Prescott (1998: 2) explicitly specified a model as 'a measurement instrument used to deduce the implication of theory'. In line with Lucas's programme, he defined a theory as 'an implicit set of instructions for constructing a model economy for the purpose of answering a question' (p. 2), so that the 'quantitative answer to the question is deduced from the model economy' (p. 3). Comparing economic models with measuring instruments, Kydland and Prescott arrive at an interpretation of calibration – referring to the gauging of measuring instruments, like a thermometer – that comes very close to the one given by Franklin above: 'Generally, some economic questions have known answers, and the model should give an approximately correct answer to them if we are to have any confidence in the answer given to the question with unknown answer' (Kydland and Prescott 1996: 74). This specific kind of assessment is similar to Lucas's idea of testing, although he didn't call it calibration. In Chapter 4 it was argued that Lucas's idea of testing is similar to a Turing test. To have confidence that a computer is intelligent it should give familiar answers to familiar questions. To test models as 'useful imitations of reality' we should subject them to shocks 'for which we are fairly certain how actual economies, or parts of economies, would react. The more dimensions on which the model mimics the answer actual economies give to simple questions, the more we trust its answer to harder questions' (Lucas 1980: 696–7).

The 'harder question' Kydland and Prescott wanted their model to answer was 'What is the quantitative nature of fluctuations induced by technology shocks?' (Kydland and Prescott 1996: 71). And the answer to this question was that 'the model economy displays business cycle fluctuations 70 percent as large as did the US economy' (p. 74). In other words, the answer is supposed to be a measurement result carried out with a calibrated instrument.

But what are the economic questions for which we have known answers? Or, what are the standard facts with which the model is calibrated? The answer is most explicitly given by Cooley and Prescott (1995). They describe calibration as a selection of the parameter values for the model economy so that it mimics the actual economy on dimensions associated with long-term growth by setting these values equal to certain 'more or less constant' ratios. These ratios were the so-called 'stylized facts' of economic growth, 'striking empirical regularities both over time and across countries', the 'benchmarks of the theory of economic growth' (Cooley and Prescott 1995: 3). The naming refers to Nicholas Kaldor's ([1958] 1978) 'stylised facts' of growth, but the ones that are used in the business-cycle literature are those as characterised by Solow (1970) and summarised by Cooley and Prescott as follows:

1   Real output grows at a more or less constant rate.
2   The stock of real capital grows at a more or less constant rate greater than the rate of growth of the labor input.

3   The growth rates of real output and the stock of capital tend to be about the same.
4   The rate of profit on capital has a horizontal trend.
5   The rate of growth of output per-capita varies greatly from one country to another.
6   Economies with a high share of profits in income tend to have a high ratio of investment to output.

(Cooley and Prescott 1995: 3)

Only the first four 'facts' were used. The last two emphasise the differences between countries or economies and are thus not general enough.

Although we have seen that equilibrium business-cycle modellers aim to model from invariants (Hoover 1995b, see Chapter 4), the choice of taking these stylised facts as empirical facts of growth is dubious. Solow remarked that 'There is no doubt that they are stylized, though it is possible to question whether they are facts' (Solow 1970: 2). The danger is that stylised facts may turn out to be more conventional than empirical. Graham Hacche (1979) provided an account of the British–US evidence relating to Kaldor's six stylised facts and showed inconsistencies between economic history and Kaldor's stylised facts.

In any event the data for the United Kingdom provide little support for the hypothesis that there is some 'steady trend' or 'normal' growth rate of capital or output or both running through economic history – which is what Kaldor's stylised facts suggest – unless the interpretation of the hypothesis is so liberal as to bear little meaning.

(Hacche 1979: 278)

In the case of the SI base units the values of some of the physical constants used are fixed by convention, although their stability is not a matter of convention but an empirical fact. In contrast to this observation, whether the stylised facts of growth do have empirical counterparts is seriously doubted; it is not clear whether they should be considered as real invariants found in 'nature' or rather as conventions. Hence, whatever values are chosen for them, they will be seen as arbitrary. And so the same sense of arbitrariness will adhere to the calibration procedure and therefore ultimately to the measurement results.

As the second source for facts to calibrate their models, Kydland and Prescott referred to 'relevant micro observations' (Kydland and Prescott 1982: 1359). But they never provided any coherent framework for extracting macro-parameters from microeconomic data. Besides the problem of whether microeconomic data can be used to fill macroeconomic models, it is not clear whether there is a 'filing cabinet full of robust micro estimates ready to use in calibrating dynamic stochastic general equilibrium models' (Hansen and Heckman 1996: 90).

To summarise the different interpretations of calibration in economics and to link it with its dual function of making an instrument precise and as accurate as possible, we simplify the discussion. Let x_t indicate an aspect of the phenomenon in which we are interested. x_t is not directly observable, only through observations y_t (data) which involve noise v_t:

$$y_t^* = x_t + v_t \tag{5.2}$$

An asterisk is used to indicate that data or facts are already known, that is visible or measured.

To make x_t visible or to measure it, a model, M, is specified of which the y_t function as input and the x_t as output:

$$x_t = M\left(y_t^*, y_{t-1}^*, y_{t-2}^*, \ldots; \alpha_1, \ldots, \alpha_n\right)$$

where $\alpha_1, \ldots, \alpha_n$ are the parameters of the model. Let's assume that one part of the mathematical moulding has already been settled, an appropriate mathematical representation has been chosen or specially developed for the phenomenon at hand. So, the problem is narrowed to the choice of the values for the model parameters, $\alpha_1, \ldots, \alpha_n$.

With the aid of this framework one can show that four different kinds of assessments of instruments exists. Which one is most suitable depends on what is already known about the concerning phenomenon.

Tuning. If the phenomenon at hand has already been made visible by another (standard) instrument, that is all its quantitative characteristics, or in other words all quantitative (stylised) facts about the phenomenon, are known, denoted by x_t^*, then an instrument can be tuned. Tuning is a kind of estimation by adjusting the parameter values, $\alpha_1, \ldots, \alpha_n$, until the output x_t has the same characteristics as the observed phenomenon x_t^*. This is a kind of calibration as defined in the International Vocabulary of Basic and General Terms in Metrology (IVM 1993): establishing the relationship between values of quantities indicated by a measuring instrument and the corresponding values realised by standards (see above). Statistical analysis will not reveal background noise because noise is an intrinsic aspect of data. Tuning is a reliable method to filter out background noise, v_t, leaving us with an accurate and specific signal, x_t.

Characteristics testing. If the parameter values are provided by other independent studies, these values, $\alpha_1^*, \ldots, \alpha_n^*$, can be assessed by characteristics tests: the model with these fixed parameter values should generate an output, x_t, with the same characteristics as the already measured facts about the phenomenon, x_t^*.

Gauging. If only a few quantitative facts about the phenomenon are known, $x_t'^*$, and one wishes to use the instrument to generate other (new) facts, x_t, the known facts can be used to assess the instrument. For a specifically defined input, $y_t'^*$, the output should display these facts, $x_t'^*$. This relation between input and output can be used to adjust the model parameters, $\alpha_1, \ldots, \alpha_n$. This is the kind of calibration as defined by Franklin: the use of a surrogate input to standardise an instrument.

Standardisation. If no quantitative facts are yet available, in other words the instrument is a first-generation type or is unique, the characteristics of the output should satisfy more qualitative features of the phenomenon. This will be discussed in more detail in Chapter 6.

Conclusions

A measurement makes a certain attribute of a phenomenon visible by associating this invisible attribute to a correlated observable attribute or set of observable attributes. The problem of designing a measurement instrument consists of three elements: (1) the choice of a correlation that is as autonomous as possible, (2) the choice of a mathematical representation of this autonomous correlation, and (3) the assessment of the instrument.

An essential part of the design process is calibration to acquire precision. But at the same time, calibration is the method of assessing a measuring instrument: with respect to measuring instruments one cannot disconnect the method of discovery from the method of justification. It is shown that when economic modelling is this specific kind of mapping then the standard account of how models are obtained and assessed does not apply. Such models are not simply derived from theories and subsequently tested against empirical data. Instruments are constructed by integrating theoretical and empirical ideas and requirements in such a way that their performance meets a previously chosen standard. The empirical requirement is that such a model should take account of a selected set of phenomenological facts so that the reliability of the model is not assessed by post-model testing but obtained by calibration (see also Chapter 1 or Boumans 1999).

Appendix 1
Output–inflation tradeoffs

Introduction

In this appendix, it will be shown that seeing models as measuring instruments provides a heuristic that can help improve a model that does not produce satisfactory test results. The heuristic consists of three interconnected aspects: comprehensive mathematical representation, invariance and calibration. This means that to assess a model one first tries to find out to what extent it is able to cover all the data. This is because to qualify as a measuring instrument the model must represent the whole data range. The model defines a mathematical system that fulfills the role of a scale, which must apply to the whole range. Second, of all possible comprehensive representations the model should represent the most invariant correlation under various circumstances. Third, calibration can ensure that the invariant relationship is gauged for appropriate invariants.

The problems of representation, invariance and calibration will be analysed in more detail when we take Robert Lucas's 1973 article 'Some international evidence on output–inflation tradeoffs' as a case study. Lucas's article was an attempt to assess the natural rate hypothesis by a characteristics test. The characteristic that was tested for was the fact that the more volatile demand (the higher the variance of demand), the more unfavourable are the terms of the Phillips tradeoff. Lucas tested his own macroeconomic model of rational expectations and found that his model explained output and inflation rate movements 'only moderately well' (Lucas 1973: 334), although it was enough to capture the natural rate hypothesis. Lucas assumed the stability of two elements: (1) the inter-temporal substitution parameter of supply, and (2) the variance of relative prices.

When one takes a closer look at Lucas's model to discover the reason for these disappointing test results, two things become apparent. First, the model was not defined for every value of the output–inflation tradeoff, in other words representation was not comprehensive. Second, the model did not represent an invariant relationship because the parameters were not stable. Because models should represent the whole data range if they are to be considered as adequate measuring instruments, Lucas' account of output–inflation tradeoffs needs to be extended. However, when extending Lucas's model, one should take care that requirements of invariance are met.

Lucas's model

Before we go on to assessing Lucas's rational expectations model, let us first examine Lucas's model and his own evaluation of it. Lucas postulated that suppliers are rational agents whose decisions depend on relative prices only, placed in an economic setting in which they cannot distinguish relative from general price movements. These suppliers are located in a large number of scattered, competitive markets. Demand for goods in each period is distributed unevenly over markets, leading to relative as well as general price movements. Quantity supplied in each market is the product of a normal or secular component that is common to all markets and a cyclical component that varies from market to market. If we let z index markets and using y_{nt} and $y_{ct}(z)$ to denote the logarithm of these components, supply in market z is

$$y_t(z) = y_{nt} + y_{ct}(z)$$

The secular component follows the trend line:

$$y_{nt} = \alpha + \beta t$$

The cyclical component varies with perceived relative prices and with its own lagged value:

$$y_{ct}(z) = \gamma \{P_t(z) - E[P_t | I_t(z)]\} + \lambda y_{c,t-1}(z)$$

where $\gamma > 0$, $|\lambda| < 1$, $P_t(z)$ is the logarithm of the actual price in market z at time t and $E[P_t | I_t(z)]$ is the expected (logarithm of the) general price level, based on information available in z at time t, $I_t(z)$. The information set available to suppliers in z at time t contains the following elements: the distribution of the general price level, which is known to be normal with mean $\overline{P}_t$ and a constant variance σ^2.

The actual price deviates from the general price level by an amount that is distributed independently of P_t. The deviation of the price in z from the general price level is also denoted by z, where z is normal distributed, independent of P_t, with mean zero and variance τ^2. Then the observed price in z, $P_t(z)$ is the sum of independent, normal variates:

$$P_t(z) = P_t + z$$

Then one can derive that the conditional expectation of the general price level based on this information is equal to

$$E[P_t | I_t(z)] = (1 - \theta)P_t(z) + \theta \overline{P}_t$$

where $\theta = \tau^2 / (\sigma^2 + \tau^2)$.

Combining these results yields the supply function for market z:

$$y_t(z) = y_{nt} + \theta\gamma[P_t(z) - \overline{P}_t] + \lambda y_{c,t-1}(z)$$

Averaging over markets gives the aggregate supply function:

$$y_t = y_{nt} + \theta\gamma[P_t - \overline{P}_t] + \lambda y_{c,t-1} \qquad (A1.1)$$

Demand is stochastic. The demand function for goods is postulated to be of the form:

$$y_t + P_t = x_t \qquad (A1.2)$$

where x_t is an exogenous random shift variable – equal to the observable logarithm of nominal GNP. Further, $\Delta x_t = x_t - x_{t-1}$ is a normal variate with mean δ and variance σ_x^2.

By inserting equation (A1.1) into equation (A1.2), the resulting solutions for price and cyclical component are:

$$P_t = (1 - \pi)(\Delta x_t - \delta) + \overline{P}_t \qquad (A1.3)$$

and

$$y_{ct} = \pi (\Delta x_t - \delta) + \lambda y_{c,t-1} \qquad (A1.4)$$

where

$$\pi = \frac{\theta \gamma}{1 + \theta \gamma} \qquad (A1.5)$$

In other words, Lucas's rational expectations model links output–inflation tradeoffs, π, with rational expectations, θ.[1]

Equation (A1.3) implies that

$$\sigma^2 = (1-\pi)^2 \, \sigma_x^2 \qquad (A1.6)$$

Therefore

$$\theta = \frac{\tau^2}{(1-\pi)^2 \sigma_x^2 + \tau^2} \qquad (A1.7)$$

From the 'definition' of π in terms of θ and γ (equation (A1.5)), and the 'definition' of θ in terms of σ_x^2, π and τ^2 (equation (A1.7)) we have

$$\pi = \frac{\tau^2 \gamma}{(1-\pi)^2 \sigma_x^2 + \tau^2 (1+\gamma)} \qquad (A1.8)$$

Lucas tested the natural rate hypothesis by focusing on a particular implication of his model (equations (A1.3) and (A1.4)), namely equation (A1.8) which represents the output–inflation tradeoff, π, and verified whether this tradeoff varies across countries in the way predicted by its representation.[2] Thus the hypothesis actually being tested was:

Under the assumption that τ^2 and γ are *relatively stable* across countries, the estimated π values should decline as the sample variance of Δx_t increases.

(Lucas 1973: 330, my italics, see Figure A1.1)

The test result was 'somewhat disappointing' (Lucas 1973: 331): the statistics (see Table A1.1) provided only two 'points' (see Figure A1.2): one cloud point was the highly volatile and expansive policies of Argentina and Paraguay, the other cloud point was the relatively smooth and moderately expansive policies of the remaining sixteen countries.

Within each cloud the statistics did not confirm the hypothesis conclusively. For example, compare the regression across the first sixteen countries ($R^2 = .0411$, see Figure A1.3) with the regression across all countries ($R^2 = .4449$, see Figure A1.2). But both clouds taken as points confirmed the hypothesis.

As we have seen, this structure accounts for output and inflation rate movements only moderately well, but well enough to capture the main phenomenon predicted by the natural rate theory: the higher the variance of demand, the more unfavourable are the terms of the Phillips tradeoff.

(Lucas 1973: 334)

Mathematical representation

However, if γ is considered to be 'stable across countries' we see that the tradeoff representation is not a complete representation. It is not defined for tradeoffs, π,

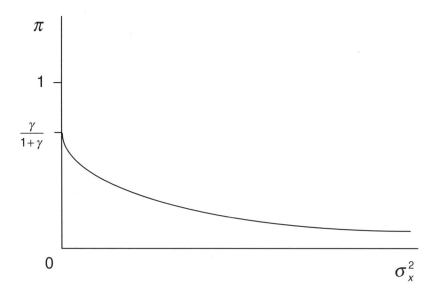

Figure A1.1 Theoretic output–inflation tradeoff. The diagram shows the theoretical relationship between output–inflation tradeoff π and the variance of demand σ_x^2.

Table A1.1 Descriptive statistics

Country	σ_x^2	π
Argentina	0.01555	0.011
Austria	0.00124	0.319
Belgium	0.00072	0.502
Canada	0.00139	0.759
Denmark	0.00084	0.571
West Germany	0.00073	0.820
Guatemala	0.00096	0.674
Honduras	0.00109	0.287
Ireland	0.00111	0.430
Italy	0.00040	0.622
Netherlands	0.00101	0.531
Norway	0.00098	0.530
Paraguay	0.03450	0.022
Puerto Rico	0.00077	0.689
Sweden	0.00041	0.287
United Kingdom	0.00014	0.665
United States	0.00064	0.910
Venezuela	0.00127	0.514

Source: Lucas 1973, adapted from Table 1 and Table 2.

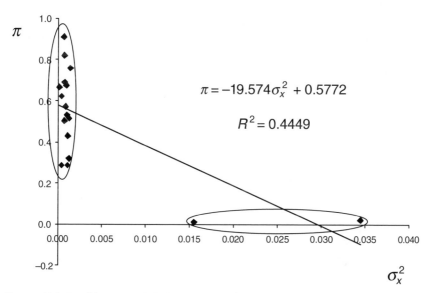

Figure A1.2 Empiric output–inflation tradeoff. The diagram shows the empirical relationship between output–inflation tradeoff π and demand variance σ_x^2. Regression line and correlation coefficient R^2 are added.

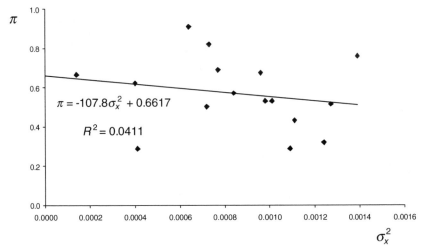

Figure A1.3 Tradeoff of the 16 countries having relatively smooth and moderately expansive policies. The diagram shows the empirical relationship between output–inflation tradeoff π and demand variance σ_x^2 of the 16 countries having a small demand variance. Regression line and correlation coefficient R^2 are added.

between $\gamma/(1+\gamma)$ and one. This can be seen by looking at Figure A1.1 and equation (A1.8). For $\sigma_x^2 = 0$, π has its largest value, namely $\gamma/(1+\gamma)$. But, the empirical measured π can range from zero to one. In an earlier paper that looked at the conditions for testing the Natural Rate Hypothesis, Lucas (1972) used a similar model in which the same problem appeared. Here, again, the range of the empirical tradeoff between zero and one was not predicted by the model; that is to say it did not hold for all parameter values. Nevertheless, he concluded that the empirical range 'is consistent with "reasonable" parameter values' (Lucas 1972: 56).

In order to adjust formula (A1.8) so that it meets the requirement of comprehensiveness, two possible strategies can be distinguished. One is to allow γ to be enormous, in fact, infinitely large so that the model could cover the whole range of π, from zero to one. This is, obviously, not 'reasonable'. The other is that we relax the assumption that γ is stable across countries and allow γ to vary for each country, within a range from zero to infinity. So, although Lucas assumed γ to be 'relatively stable across countries', this assumption cannot be maintained for having a complete representation. Every fixed value for γ would narrow the range too much.

This discussion of the stability of γ is more fundamental to Lucas's work than it appears at first sight. To use macroeconometric models for policy evaluation, one has to know the properties of the model that are invariant under policy changes (the problem of autonomy). According to Lucas, the model invariance is located on the level of the parameters describing 'tastes and technology'. In his 'Econometric policy evaluation: a critique' (1976) where he formulated this well-known critique, Lucas discussed Phillips curves using the same model as discussed here. In that article, Lucas interpreted γ (there labelled as β) as reflecting 'intertemporal substitution possibilities in supply: technological factors such as storability of production, and tastes for substituting labor supplied today for supply tomorrow' (Lucas 1976: 37).

By considering γ as a free parameter, the fact that the points are not on one line (Figure A1.1) but scattered in clouds (Figure A1.2) is now explained by differences in supply elasticity.

Invariance

The second requirement of a measurement formula is that it represents invariant relationships. Lucas assumed that invariance was guaranteed by the stability of γ and τ^2. We have already seen that to have a complete representation, γ cannot be stable, but Daniel Vining and Thomas Elwertowski (1976) also questioned Lucas's assumption that σ^2 (general price variance) and τ^2 (relative price variance) are unrelated, hence, implicitly the assumption that τ^2 could be assumed constant across countries where σ^2 varies. Their paper showed that 'there is strong statistical evidence that the two parameters τ^2 and σ^2 move together' (Vining and Elwertowski 1976: 701). In a modified version of the Lucas model, Alex Cukierman and Paul Wachtel (1979) took account of these findings while preserving Lucas's central hypothesis concerning the relationship of the inflation variance and the terms of the output–inflation tradeoff. In this respect, the most important modification was the introduction into the demand function of a random shock, $w(z)$ whose realisation is specific to market z but whose distribution is common to all markets: $w \sim N\left(0, \sigma_w^2\right)$. As a result, in the amended version of the model, τ^2 equals $\sigma_w^2 / (1 + \theta\gamma)^2$. In the modified version,

$$\pi = \frac{\sigma_w^2 \gamma}{\sigma_x^2 + \sigma_w^2 (1 + \gamma)} \tag{A1.9}$$

which is equivalent to Lucas's expression for π in terms of $\tau^2\left(= (1-\pi)^2 \sigma_w^2\right)$ and $\sigma^2\left(= (1-\pi)^2 \sigma_x^2\right)$ (cf. equation (A1.8), see Lucas 1973: 330):

$$\pi = \frac{\tau^2 \gamma}{\sigma^2 + \tau^2 (1 + \gamma)} \tag{A1.10}$$

Richard Froyen and Roger Waud (1980) tested this modified model against new international statistics. In fact they tested three implications from the amended Lucas model 'if we accept the assumption that γ and σ_w^2 are relatively stable across the populations we consider' (Froyen and Waud 1980: 410):[3]

1   π and σ_x^2 should be negatively correlated (this follows from (A1.8) or (A1.9));
2   σ_x^2 and σ^2 should be positively correlated (follows from (A1.6));
3   π and σ^2 should be negatively correlated (from (A1.6) and (A1.8), or (A1.10)).

Lucas had only tested implication (1).

Froyen and Waud found only evidence for a negative correlation between aggregate price variance, σ^2, and the terms of the output–inflation tradeoff, π (implication 3): 'A higher aggregate price variance will result, *ceteris paribus*, in a lower real output response' (p. 418). The test results did not provide support for the other two correlations (1 and 2). Froyen and Waud therefore suggested including an aggregate supply disturbance in the model to make the model more in accordance with the data. Taking the test results of Vining and Elwertowski (1976) and Froyen and Waud (1980) into account we replace the original model (A1.8) with the amended version of Lucas's model:

$$\pi = \frac{\sigma_w^2 \gamma}{\dfrac{\sigma^2}{(1-\pi)^2} + \sigma_w^2(1+\gamma)} \tag{A1.11}$$

However, γ cannot be considered as a constant – as opposed to what Lucas (1973), Vining and Elwertowski (1976), Cukierman and Wachtel (1979) and Froyen and Waud (1980) assumed – but must be seen as a variable. Therefore, equation (A1.11) is not an equation representing a negative correlation between π and σ^2.[4] Equation (A1.11) depicts a relation between *three* variables, π, σ^2 and γ (σ_w^2 is considered to be stable) and cannot be tested because we do not have independent observations on γ. As such it could be better considered as a definition of γ.

$$\gamma = \frac{\pi}{1-\pi} + \frac{\pi}{(1-\pi)^3} \frac{\sigma^2}{\sigma_w^2} \tag{A1.12}$$

Calibration

We could use this definition to make observations on γ, which means that we could use this definition to measure γ. Then this would be a specific case of indirect measurement, namely derived measurement. As we have seen from the discussion on measurement in this chapter, we do need an autonomous relationship between π and σ^2 to standardise to the above measurement formula. This autonomous relation provides a scale for γ by supplying the parameter value for σ_w^2. In other words, we can gauge the measurement formula with the value for σ_w^2.

From this perspective, we can now use the empirical results above, not to test the measurement formula but as an indication about the parameter values of the autonomous relationship. From Froyen and Waud's work (1980) we know that the autonomous relationship is a negative correlation between π and σ^2. To demonstrate how one could arrive at a calibrated measurement formula, we proceed as if the regression equation (with the highest correlation coefficient) between π and σ^2 is the intended autonomous equation. In other words we aim at preciseness to acquire accuracy. Remember that we have followed a falsification strategy. In other words, we can only eliminate possible candidates, never point out the true ones. Moreover, Haavelmo warned us not to equate autonomous equations with the observable degree of consistency or persistence of an equation (see Chapter 3).

Froyen and Waud (1980) based their study on annual data from the years 1956 to 1976 for ten industrialised countries: Belgium, Canada, France, West Germany, Italy, Japan, Netherlands, Switzerland, the United Kingdom, and the United States. Quarterly data for Canada, Japan, the UK and the US were also examined, but will not be discussed here. These annual data show a regime shift over this period in that they display a significant increase in price variability. For this reason, Froyen and Waud examined the two regimes separately, in three different ways. First, they split the whole period into two equal sub-periods 1957–66 and 1967–76. Second, they split the whole period in each country into the two sub-periods that showed the maximum difference (in ratio form) between the sizes of each country's estimated price variance σ_p^2 calculated for each sub-period. Third, they split the whole period in each country into two sub-periods showing the maximum difference between the sizes of the estimated nominal income variance σ_x^2 calculated for each sub-period. As already mentioned above, the negative correlation between π and σ^2 was 'quite strongly' supported by the cross-country comparisons. For the time period as a whole and for the first sub-period, for each of the three data splits, the correlation coefficient between the estimates of π and σ^2 is significant at the 5% level, for the second sub-period this correlation coefficient is significant at the 1% level. The highest correlation coefficient at the 1% level is for the second sub-period of the first kind of split, namely the period 1967–76: –0.862. I will use the data of this sub-period, see Table A1.2, to estimate the value of σ_w^2.

These data are plotted in Figure A1.4, which also shows the regression line. The Taylor expansion for π about $\sigma^2 = 0$, derived from equation (A1.11), is

$$\pi = \frac{\bar{\gamma}}{1+\bar{\gamma}} - \bar{\gamma}\frac{\sigma^2}{\sigma_w^2} \qquad (A1.13)$$

Table A1.2 Estimates of σ^2 and π for 1967–76

Country	σ^2	π
1. United Kingdom	0.00184	–0.249
2. Canada	0.00062	0.216
3. United States	0.00019	1.097
4. Italy	0.00149	0.045
5. Japan	0.00094	0.399
6. Belgium	0.00047	0.598
7. Switzerland	0.00026	0.937
8. France	0.00038	0.238
9. Netherlands	0.00021	0.860
10. West Germany	0.00023	0.760

Source: Froyen and Waud 1980, adapted from Table 1 and Table 2.

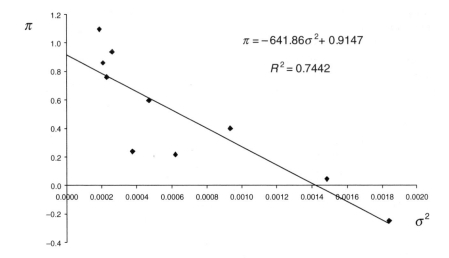

Figure A1.4 Output–inflation tradeoff from Froyen and Waud (1980). The diagram shows the empirical relationship between output–inflation tradeoff π and aggregate price variance σ^2. Regression line and correlation coefficient R^2 are added.

The γ in equation (A1.13) is an average across countries, therefore indicated by $\bar{\gamma}$. If we compare this with the regression line,

$$\pi = 0.9147 - 641.86\sigma^2 \tag{A1.14}$$

we can derive that $\sigma_w^2 = 0.01671$.

If equation (A1.14) is the intended autonomous equation, we now could measure γ for each country with measurement formula (A1.12) calibrated for the inferred value for σ_w^2.

Appendix 2

Filters

Introduction

Filters are a nice example of detection instruments in the sense that they are typical instruments designed to make unobserved components of data visible. For example, in their computational experiment, Kydland and Prescott (1996) used a filter to make visible facts about the business-cycle phenomenon. Moreover, Sydenham (1979, 1982) considers filters as essential part of any measuring system.

> A measuring system comprises a *sensing* stage, in which the original parameter to be measured, called the *measurand*, is transduced into an appropriate equivalent signal. The sensor's role is to extract specific information, to act as an information filter, passing information on the state of a particular chosen parameter existing within a possibly infinite set of definable parameters that totally describe the system.
>
> (Sydenham 1982: 41)

A measuring system conveys information about the system being studied to the observer. It has the dual task of conveying correct messages and of selecting meaningful information from the total information existing about the system under observation.

> A key role, therefore, of the measuring instrument is that of selecting, that is, filtering, from the latent information available the specific information required. Information having defined meaning becomes knowledge. The meaning ascribed to some particular measurement data is entirely a matter of codification by the user.
>
> (Sydenham 1979: 18)

Measuring-instrument output signals in themselves are not necessarily useful knowledge; the coding applied may be incorrect, the signal may contain extraneous information that did not enter the measuring stage from the system under study: the noise of the system that is always present to some extent. Thus, 'measuring instruments are information machines that convey and code, with meaning, knowledge sought' (Sydenham 1979: 20–1). The coding that gives meaning to numbers generated by a measurement is calibration.

A discussion of filters will clarify some problems that go along with the assessment of measuring instruments. As will soon become clear from the discussion below, filters are also assessed by calibration. However, it will appear that the different calibration strategies discussed in this chapter do not work for mathematical filters in the same way as they do for physical instruments. The non-materiality of mathematical filters used in economics prevents calibration being an undisputable strategy for gaining reliability.

The term 'filter' is reminiscent of spectral filters in optics used to modify the spectral transmittance of an optical system. According to the *Dictionary of Statistical Terms* (Kendall and Buckland 1960: 109), a filter is any method of isolating harmonic constituents in a time-series, analogous to filtering a ray of light or sound by removing unsystematic effects and bringing out the constituent harmonics. But one should note an essential difference between a physical filter and a mathematical one; a physical filter removes impurities by withholding them, rather than transforming them like a mathematical filter (Kendall and Stuart 1966: 424).

A well-known filter in time-series analysis is the Kalman filter, first developed by Kalman (1960).[1] Kalman filtering is a method of extracting the behaviour of a signal x_t given observations y_t which are subject to error v_t, so that $y_t = x_t + v_t$, cf. equation (5.2). The term 'filtering' refers to the removal of as much as possible of the error term v_t to give an estimation of the true signal x_t. A prerequisite to the application of the Kalman filter is that the behaviour of the system under study be described through a quantity known as the system 'state', which may be defined in terms of a first order differential or difference equation known as the system equation.

Given the state-space representation of a discrete linear dynamic system the problem is then to estimate the state x_t from the noisy observations $y_1, y_2, \dots, y_t$; in this context, three distinct problems may be distinguished:

a) *filtering*: the measurements $y_1, y_2, \dots, y_t$ are used to form an estimate $\hat{x}_t$ of the state at time t;

b) *smoothing*: the measurements $y_1, y_2, \dots, y_t$ are used to form an estimate $\hat{x}_t$ of x_s at some past time point for $1 \leq s < t$;

c) *prediction*: the measurements $y_1, y_2, \dots, y_t$ are used to form an estimate $\hat{x}_t$ of x_s at some future time point for $s > t$.

(Kalman 1960: 36)

In general, filtering in economics is motivated by one of several objectives:

1 extraction of a component such as a growth, cyclical, or seasonal component,

2 transformation to induce stationarity, or

3 mitigation of measurement error that is assumed to be particularly important at specific frequencies.

(King and Rebelo 1993: 213)

The Hodrick–Prescott filter

Kydland and Prescott (1996) did not use the Kalman filter but the 'Hodrick–Prescott filter' (HP filter). Its application was motivated by objective (1), that is, taking a moving average of the observations to extract one of the components. To simplify the discussion, we focus on time series containing only growth and business cycle components:

$$y_t = y_t^g + y_t^c$$

where y_t^g is the hidden growth component and y_t^c is the hidden business-cycle component. In the subsequent discussion, filtering is understood as a way of detrending by representing the growth component as a moving average of the observed y_t that permits us to extract both components. That is, we assume that

$$y_t^g = \sum_{k=-\infty}^{\infty} g_k y_{t-k} = G(B)y_t$$

where B is the backshift operator with $B^n x_t = x_{t-n}$ for $n \geq 0$. Then, y_t^c is also a moving average of y_t:

$$y_t^c = \left[1 - G(B)\right] y_t \equiv C(B) y_t$$

In the language of filtering theory, both $G(B)$ and $C(B)$ are linear filters.

The specific linear filter suggested by Hodrick and Prescott (1997)[2] determines the trend component series $\{ y_t^g, t = 1, \ldots, T \}$ by minimising

$$\sum_{t=1}^{T} \left(y_t - y_t^g\right)^2 + \lambda \sum_{t=2}^{T-1} \left[\left(y_{t+1}^g - y_t^g\right) - \left(y_t^g - y_{t-1}^g\right)\right]^2 \tag{A2.1}$$

where λ is a fixed parameter. 'The maintained hypothesis, based upon growth theory considerations, is that the growth component of aggregate economic time series varies smoothly over time' (Hodrick and Prescott 1997: 2). The measure of the smoothness of the growth path is the sum of the squares of its second difference. The parameter λ can be interpreted as a penalty on variability in the growth component series. The larger the value of λ, the smoother is the solution series. If λ goes to infinity, the growth component approaches a linear deterministic time trend. If $\lambda = 0$, the growth component series coincides with the observed series and the cyclical component is zero. Hodrick and Prescott propose a value of $\lambda = 1600$ for quarterly time-series data as reasonable, and their recommendation has been widely followed in the literature applying the HP filter.

Gauging

Hodrick and Prescott (1997: 4) considered the following probability model 'for bringing to bear prior knowledge in the selection of the smoothing parameter λ'.

If the cyclical component y_t^c and the second differences of the growth components $\Delta^2 y_t^g$ were identically and independently distributed, normal variables with means zero and variances σ_1^2 and σ_2^2,

$$y_t^c = \varepsilon_t \quad \varepsilon_t \sim N(0, \sigma_1^2)$$

$$\Delta^2 y_t^g = \eta_t \quad \eta_t \sim N(0, \sigma_2^2)$$

the conditional expectation of the y_t^g given the observations would be the solution to the problem (A2.1) when $\lambda = \sigma_1^2 / \sigma_2^2$.

The value of λ is fixed as follows:

> Our prior view is that a 5 percent cyclical component is moderately large, as is a one-eighth of 1 percent change in the growth rate in a quarter. This led us to select $\sqrt{\lambda} = 5/(1/8) = 40$ or $\lambda = 1,600$ as a value for the smoothing parameter.
>
> (Hodrick and Prescott 1997: 4)

At first sight this is remarkable because these data normally can only be inferred when both growth and cyclical component are made visible by a filter. However, the choice of this value must be considered as a kind of calibration, namely gauging: various other values of λ were tried. Standard deviations and auto-correlations of cyclical real GNP for the values of λ equal to 400, 1600 and 6400 were compared and found to change little. The differences between the cyclical component ($\lambda = 1600$) and those obtained with perfect smoothing ($\lambda = \infty$) were depicted in a figure along with the cyclical component. The smoothness of the variation in this difference relative to the variation in the cyclical component was considered indicating 'that the smoothing parameter chosen is reasonable' (p. 5), or as Kydland and Prescott put it: 'With this value, the implied trend path for the logarithm of real GNP is close to the one that students of business cycle and growth would draw through a time plot of this series' (Kydland and Prescott 1990: 9).

The HP filter was gauged by choosing the smoothing parameter such that in one dimension – growth component – the filter reproduces a 'reasonable' picture. The idea of this kind of calibration is that the calibrated instrument produces reliable facts about the business cycle. However, the subsequent literature discussing the HP filter shows that the gauged instrument did not naturally result in confidence in its internal functioning.

The internal functioning of filters

The functioning of linear filters is mainly discussed in terms of the frequencies extracted by taking the Fourier transform of a linear filter, also called the frequency response function of the filter. The frequency response function makes it easier to interpret the effects of filtering. For example, the Fourier transform of the growth filter is

$$G(\omega) = \sum_{k=-\infty}^{\infty} g_k e^{-ik\omega}$$

where i denotes the imaginary number $\sqrt{-1}$ and where ω is the frequency measured in radians.

At a given frequency ω, the frequency response $G(\omega)$ is simply a complex number, so it may be written in polar form as $G(\omega) = |G(\omega)|\exp(-i\Psi(\omega))$. The 'gain' of the linear filter, $|G(\omega)|$, yields a measure – at the specified frequency ω – of the increase in the amplitude of the filtered series over the original series. The phase, $\Psi(\omega)$, yields a measure of the time displacement attributable to the linear filter. Symmetric filters, filters that possess the symmetry property that $g_k = g_{-k}$, have the property that they do not induce a phase shift, because their Fourier transform is real so the frequency response is equal to the (positive or negative) gain function.

King and Rebelo (1993) show that the HP filter takes the form

$$C_{HP}(B) = \frac{\lambda(1-B)^2(1-B^{-1})^2}{1+\lambda(1-B)^2(1-B^{-1})^2}$$

Thus, the HP filter is a symmetric filter and depends only on the value of the parameter λ.

The Fourier transform of the cyclical component filter takes the form:

$$C_{HP}(\omega) = \frac{4\lambda[1-\cos\omega]^2}{1+4\lambda[1-\cos\omega]^2} \tag{A2.2}$$

The cyclical component filter places zero weight on the zero frequency and close to unit weight on high frequencies, see Figure A2.1. Increasing λ shifts the gain function upward, moving a given frequency's gain closer to unity. The larger λ, the more the HP filter looks like an ideal high-pass filter. A high-pass filter removes the low frequencies or long-cycle components and allows the high frequencies or short-cycle components to pass through. An ideal high-pass cyclical filter is a filter for which the frequency's gains are defined as: $C_{high}(\omega) = 0$ for $\omega < \omega^*$ and $C_{high}(\omega) = 1$ for $\omega > \omega^*$.

The effect of filtering can be analysed with a formula linking the spectrum of a stationary process, x_t, with the spectrum of the filtered process, $y_t = F(B)x_t$:

$$g_y(\omega) = |F(\omega)|^2 g_x(\omega) \tag{A2.3}$$

where g denotes the spectrum and $|F|$ the gain of the filter F. A stochastic process is said to be stationary if its first moment is independent of t and if the covariance $\sigma_{t,s}$ depends only on $t - s$.

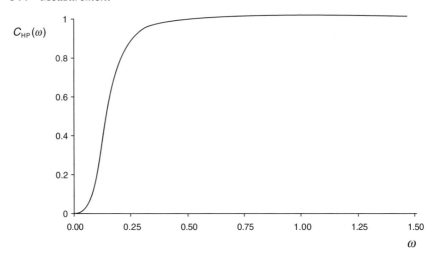

$C_{HP}(\omega)$

Figure A2.1 Hodrick–Prescott filter. The diagram shows the frequency response $C_{HP}(\omega)$ of the Hodrick–Prescott filter, where ω denotes frequency.

Before we continue discussing the HP filter, let us first examine the spectra of two simple processes. First consider a white-noise process, $y_t = \varepsilon_t$. As its name indicates its spectrum is flat, that is, all frequencies are equally important and equal σ_ε^2 :

$$g_{\text{white}}(\omega) = \sigma_\varepsilon^2 \qquad\qquad (A2.4)$$

Second, we consider a random walk, which is a first-order autoregressive process $y_t = y_{t-1} + \varepsilon_t$, ε_t white noise. Then

$$y_t = \frac{1}{1-B}\varepsilon_t$$

Therefore, the spectrum of a random walk is

$$g_{\text{walk}}(\omega) = \frac{1}{2-2\cos\omega}\sigma_\varepsilon^2 \qquad\qquad (A2.5)$$

See Figure A2.2 for the graphs of both spectra; spectrum values are in fractions of σ_ε^2 .

The effect of the HP filter applied to these simple processes can now easily be shown. Substituting equations (A2.2) and (A2.4) into equation (A2.3) yields the spectrum of filtered white noise:

$$g_{\text{filterwalk}}(\omega) = \left|C_{HP}(\omega)\right|^2 g_{\text{walk}}(\omega) = \left[\frac{4\lambda[1-\cos\omega]^2}{1+4\lambda[1-\cos\omega]^2}\right]^2 \frac{1}{2-2\cos\omega}\sigma_\varepsilon^2$$

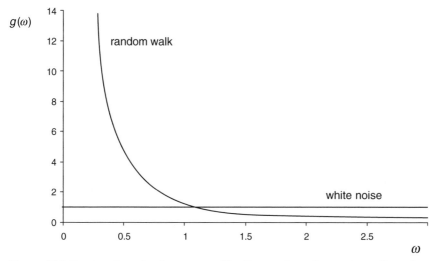

Figure A2.2 Spectra of two simple processes. The diagram shows the spectrum of a random walk and the spectrum of white noise, where ω denotes frequency.

and substituting equations (A2.2) and (A2.5) into (A2.3) yields the spectrum of a filtered random walk:[3]

$$g_{\text{filterwhite}}(\omega) = \left|C_{\text{HP}}(\omega)\right|^2 g_{\text{white}}(\omega) = \left[\frac{4\lambda[1-\cos\omega]^2}{1+4\lambda[1-\cos\omega]^2}\right]^2 \sigma_\varepsilon^2 \qquad (A2.6)$$

See Figure A2.3.

Artifacts

The Hodrick–Prescott filter has been widely adopted in the business-cycle literature to make the business cycle visible. Beside this growing interest in the use of this filter, several studies have appeared in which the HP filter has been critically examined. One of the worries is whether the filter does not in fact lead to spurious cyclical behaviour and distorts the measure of persistence, variability and co-movement – that is, distorts Lucas's stylised facts of the business-cycle phenomenon. Cogley and Nason (1995) assert that 'the filter can generate business cycle periodicity and comovement even if none are present in the original data' (p. 254). Thus, 'it is not clear whether the results should be interpreted as facts or artifacts' (p. 255). Harvey and Jaeger (1993: 231) claim to have shown that 'the uncritical use of mechanical detrending can lead investigators to report spurious cyclical behaviour'. In a note, Jaeger (1994) asserts that applying the HP filter to time series with stochastic trends 'may extract cyclical movements which are entirely spurious' (p. 493).

These papers share a common argument in their claim that the HP filter may extract spurious cycles. This argument in its simplest form runs as follows. If one

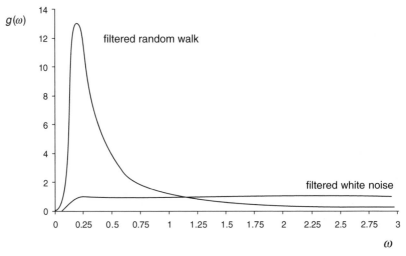

Figure A2.3 Two filtered processes. The diagram shows the spectrum of a random walk
filtered by a Hodrick–Prescott filter and the spectrum of white noise filtered
by a Hodrick–Prescott filter, where ω denotes frequency.

of the components of the time series being investigated is the above-described
random walk, the filtered process contains a peak at a frequency which for $\lambda = 1600$
corresponds to a period of about $(2\pi/0.21 =)$ 30 (see Figure A2.3). Because we
deal with quarterly data, this period of about 7.5 years equals the business-cycle
period.

> Thus applying the standard HP filter to a random walk produces detrended
> observations which have the characteristics of a business cycle for quarterly
> observations. Such cyclical behaviour is spurious and is a classic example of
> the Yule–Slutzky effect.
>
> (Harvey and Jaeger 1993: 234; see also Jaèger 1994: 497)

> [T]he power spectrum for an HP filtered random walk … has a peak at 7.6
> years per cycle. Hence there is business cycle periodicity in the elements of
> $c(t)$ even though the elements of $y(t)$ are random walks.
>
> (Cogley and Nason 1995: 259)

Many textbooks of statistics (e.g. Kendall and Stuart 1966; Malinvaud 1966)
warn against the use of filters or moving averages because they might produce
artificial oscillations due solely to the statistical treatment of the data. This is the
so-called (Yule–)Slutzky effect, after the two statisticians who studied it in detail.
In particular, Slutzky (1937) considered the effects of starting with a white noise
ε_t, taking a two-period moving sum n times, and then taking first differences m
times. If m/n is held constant and $n \to \infty$, then a single frequency is strongly
emphasised by this process and a cycle results.

The question now is whether the application of the HP filter leads also to a Slutzky effect. The HP filter on its own does not enlarge the amplitude of any frequency, so does not emphasise a specific frequency. It only de-emphasises frequencies below 0.21. The problem is that the analysis is not conclusive, spectral analysis can be applied to stationary time series, because stationary time series can be decomposed into orthogonal periodic components. However, in general non-stationary time series do not have a periodic decomposition. It is only shown that the HP filter operates like a high-pass filter when applied to stationary time series. Hence it is not clear yet what the effect of the HP filter is when applied to non-stationary time series.

However, macroeconomic time series often have an upward trend which makes them non-stationary and one of the objectives of filtering is 'transformation to induce stationarity' (see objective of filtering (2) above). To analyse the HP filter effect for these non-stationary cases, Cogley and Nason (1995), Jaeger (1994) and Harvey and Jaeger (1993) split the HP filter into two parts. One part is chosen to make the time series stationary so that subsequently the resulting part can be analysed to see its effect on the stationary data.

To discuss the results the simplest case will be picked out: Cogley and Nason analyse the HP filter effect on difference-stationary time series, that is a time series y_t of which the differenced time series, Δy_t, is assumed to be stationary. In this way the HP filter operates like a 'two-step linear filter': 'Difference $y(t)$ to make it stationary, and smooth $\Delta y(t)$ with an asymmetric moving average filter' (Cogley and Nason 1995: 258):

$$y_t^c = S(B)\Delta y_t$$

where $S(B) = C_{HP}(B)/(1-B)$. The squared gain of $S(B)$ is equal to the spectrum of the filtered random walk (when σ_ε^2 is taken as unit; see equation (A2.6)), so that Figure A2.3 also pictures the squared gain of $S(B)$. If one considers $S(B)$ as a filter, one can easily see that it leads to a Slutzky effect, namely it enormously emphasises a period of 7.5 years. But one cannot infer from this that the HP filter, $C_{HP}(B)$, also has this effect. Properties of the split parts of the filter do not necessarily sum to the properties of the complete filter, they may cancel each other out. The Slutzky effect of the $S(B)$ filter may be nullified by the factor $(1-B)$.

Whether filters lead to spurious cycles or not, the above account of filters shows that calibration does not work for mathematical filters as it does for physical filters. The fact that the HP filter functions as a high-pass filter for stationary data, did not strengthen the belief that the filter works properly for non-stationary data.

Conclusions

Macroeconomic models located on the theory–world axis between phenomena and data are assessed by calibration. The mathematical nature of the filter hindered the success of the calibration. Although the HP filter works well for known phenomena, namely being gauged for the growth component and functioning accurately for stationary processes, it did not produce confidence in its working for non-stationary processes. While in the case of calibration as an investigation of material instruments the move from observing that the tool works properly for known domains to having confidence in its working for unknown domains is legitimised, this is apparently not the case for a mathematical investigation.

6 Rigour

If contradictory attributes be assigned to a concept, I say, that mathematically the concept does not exist.

(Hilbert 1902: 448)

Sometimes control with a single lens is impossible since some incompatible features are required and a compromise becomes necessary calling for further judgement on the part of the designer as to which error should be reduced and to what degree.

(Bracey 1960: 18)

Introduction

The assessment of a model depends not only on whether it fulfills certain theoretical and empirical requirements but also on how these requirements are fulfilled. That is to say, models are also assessed on the basis of how they have been constructed, whether it is done in a rigorous way or not. What is taken to be rigorous depends on the underlying assumption of what a model actually is: whether it is seen as an instrument or as a formal concept. Although one usually thinks of an instrument as being a physical device such as, for example, a thermometer or a ruler, in economics models are non-material. However, despite their non-materiality they function as empirical objects, see Chapter 1. This 'instrumental' view contrasts with the more received formalistic account of mathematical objects, which take an 'axiomatic' view in that they consider models to be formal axiomatic abstractions.[1] Both the 'instrumental' and the 'axiomatic' views will be explored on the basis of specific developments in the history of index number theory. The two quotations above, by Hilbert and Bracey, reflect the difference between the Axiomatic Index Theory and Irving Fisher's work on index numbers and represent the two respective 'axiomatic' and 'instrumental' approaches. While in one approach the existence of inconsistencies is a capital sin, in the other approach it is accepted that the best instrument sometimes has to be a compromise between incompatible requirements.

Since the beginning of the nineteenth century, a large number of price index number formulae have been developed, usually named after their inventors. These include the Paasche and Laspeyre indexes. Parallel to the invention of new index formulae, criteria were being developed to distinguish between them. These parallel developments culminated in Fisher's two classic works on index numbers, *The Purchasing Power of Money* (1911) and *The Making of Index Numbers* (1922). In these, Fisher evaluated index formulae in a systematic way, with respect to a number of 'tests'. Although they are considered as the 'Old and New Testament' (Vogt and Barta 1997: viii) of Axiomatic Index Theory, the axiomatic approach originated from challenges to Fisher's system of tests on grounds of their consistency and the seeming arbitrariness of the choice of tests. This debate started with Ragnar Frisch in 1930, but Axiomatic Index Theory did not acquire its current name and shape – based on functional equation analysis – until 1973 from Wolfgang Eichhorn. In Axiomatic Index Theory, tests are considered as the requirements for the functional form of the index number from which the index formula is to be derived. If these requirements are not consistent, a formula cannot be constructed. So, although Fisher's work is considered to be the ancestor of the Axiomatic Index Theory, his system of tests was criticised because of internal inconsistencies. However, evaluating Fisher's work from an axiomatic perspective leads to misunderstanding his empirical approach to the assessment of index numbers. To gain a better understanding of his work on index numbers, we will examine his background in mathematics, his philosophical thinking and the measuring instruments he invented.

Because rigour and axiomatics are often seen as two sides of the same coin, one might expect an instrumental approach such as Fisher's to be less rigorous. This preconception is unjustified. Giorgio Israel (1981) and Roy Weintraub (1998) have shown that, in the history of mathematics, rigour has not always been identified with axiomatics.[2] Weintraub (1998: 235) showed, for example, that for Volterra the 'opposite of "rigorous" was not "informal" but rather "unconstrained"'. The interpretation of rigour changed under the influence of the Axiomatisation Movement. As a result of this movement,

> a rigorous argument was reconceptualised as a logically consistent argument instead of as an argument that connected the problematic phenomenon to a physical phenomenon by use of empirical data. Propositions were henceforth 'true' within the system considered because they were consistent with the assumptions instead of being 'true' because they could be grounded in 'real phenomena'.
>
> (Weintraub 1998: 237)

Israel discussed the distinction between rigour and axiomatics in relation to the 'crisis of present-day mathematics', namely that the axiomatic trend has emptied mathematical research of any external determination and content to such an extent that the relation to applications has been lost. Although the role of mathematics in applied sciences is growing rapidly – economics is a good example of this – mathematics is still deeply separated from the applied sciences. 'What appears to be missing, is a codification of the rules which should define and guide the use of mathematics as an instrument for the description, interpretation and control of phenomena' (Israel 1981: 219).

Practical issues require a different set of rules than axiomatic problems. This means that the rigour applied in solving practical problems will inevitably be different to the rigour in an axiomatic system. Although a mathematical object cannot exist in an axiomatic system if it has contradictory attributes, it can be build as a model for use as an instrument for calculations, measurement or other purposes. As will be shown later in this chapter, for measurement one should aim for a more general view of mathematical rigour, namely one that demands that a mathematical object can only exist if it is constructed according specific sound rules. This does not, necessarily, include consistency, but what then are these sound rules? This problem can be illustrated by the following analogous case in the history of mathematics: the quadrature of the circle. The quadrature of the circle refers to the problem of constructing a square of equal area to the given circle. If there were no constraints in solving the problem, it would be a simple task. The side of a square equal in area to a circle of radius r has length $r\sqrt{\pi}$. Take a graduated ruler and draw four lines of length $r\sqrt{3.1415927}$ or of any other precision. The problem becomes more complicated, even unsolvable, if there are constraints imposed on the means of construction. A construction consists of a sequence of operations performed on a given configuration, which results in a new element of the figure with certain required properties. In classical Greek geometry, the only two legitimate operations were drawing with a ruler or a compass. These were implied by Euclid's first three postulates (see below). So, a (geometrical) object only existed if it was constructed with ruler and compass. For more than two thousand years people have tried to solve the quadrature of the circle, until in 1882 it was shown to be impossible. Before this conclusion was reached people tried to solve the problem by extending the means of construction by means of so-called sliding rulers ('neuses'), or mechanical – not geometrical – curves or calculating procedures for approximations. The problem of existence in mathematics was not about finding practical constructions, because they already existed, but whether mathematical objects were constructed in a rigorous way, in other words whether the construction procedure was in accordance with sound rules.[3]

As we shall see, the rule implied by Fisher's instrumental approach can best be summed up as: finding the best balance between theoretical and empirical requirements even if these requirements are incompatible. Then, rigour is attained by ensuring the instrument's performance is as close as possible to a certain standard. In Fisher's case, this standard was a specific geometrical form against which the geometrical representations of the candidate instrument were compared, so that the evaluation could be based on the judgment of the eye. Because of its visually appealing geometrical features, the triangle was Fisher's favourite standard of comparison.

The aim of this chapter is to take a closer look at the various characteristics of Fisher's instrumental approach to index numbers in order to identify what kinds of rigour acknowledge the idea of models as instruments. Fisher's empiricist, rather than *a priorist*, inclinations can be traced back to the period in which he was educated as a mathematician, namely the period in which non-Euclidean geometry began to have a major influence on the foundations of mathematics. Fisher's method was to see a scientific problem as if it were the same as the design problem of an instrument. We will have a closer look at a specific invention that will help us to understand his typical approach to solving the index-number problem. In his work, Fisher did not base rigour on consistency. Nevertheless, this was the main target for criticism in Fisher's work on index numbers. The contrast between the two approaches – instrumental versus axiomatic – will be clarified. Fisher's assessment of world maps provides us with an example of his instrumental approach.

Non-Euclidean geometry

Non-Euclidean geometry had a major influence on the foundations of mathematics at the end of the nineteenth century, the period in which Fisher was educated as a mathematician. This new geometry obliged mathematicians to radically revise their understanding of the nature of mathematics and its relation to the physical world.[4] Until about 1800, all mathematicians were convinced that Euclidean geometry was the correct idealisation of the properties of physical space and of figures in that space. But this conviction changed dramatically in the nineteenth century. Towards the end of that century, mathematicians and physicists understood that the properties of space were not given *a priori* but they had to be measured.

There is considerable evidence that Fisher was well informed about this development. In 1890 and 1891, in addition to the courses he was taking in the graduate school, he started teaching geometry at Yale (which he continued to do for several years) (Allen 1993: 36). He even wrote a textbook on geometry, *Elements of Geometry*, with Andrew W. Phillips of the Mathematics Department (Phillips and Fisher 1896). Fisher also took courses under Josiah Willard Gibbs, one of his mentors at Yale (Allen 1993: 37), including one on multiple algebra (and thus also vector analysis). Fisher was also well aware of the philosophical implications of these developments in mathematics. Philosophy intrigued Fisher, and he had taken George Ladd's course on Kant (Allen 1993: 38). Fisher brought geometry and philosophy together in an essay he wrote as a student during the period 1889–90. This handwritten, and never published, essay entitled, 'Mathematical contribution to philosophy: attacking Kant's theory of geometrical axioms' consisted of two parts.[5] The first was a brief history of the origin and development of non-Euclidean geometry and the second part was a discussion about the implications of non-Euclidean geometry to Kant's epistemology. Fisher's essay made no original contribution to philosophy or geometry; it was an elaboration of Hermann von Helmholtz's 'The origin and meaning of geometrical axioms' (1876, 1878). To assess Fisher's understanding of the history and philosophical implications of non-Euclidean geometry, these issues will be described below in parallel to his account.

At the centre of the history of non-Euclidean geometry stood Euclid's fifth postulate, the status of which has occupied mathematicians since the Ancient Greeks. After a list of twenty-three definitions, Euclid's Elements continued with the following five 'postulates':

1   To draw a straight line from any point to any point.
2   To produce a finite straight line continuously in a straight line.
3   To describe a circle with any centre and distance.
4   That all right angles are equal to one another.
5   That, if a straight line falling on two straight lines make the interior angles on the same side less than two right angles, the two straight lines, if produced indefinitely, meet on that side on which are the angles less than the two right angles.

(Heath 1956: 154–5)

If we see these postulates as being abstract descriptions of experience, we notice a difference between the first four and the fifth postulate. The first four are derived from the experience of drawing with a ruler, a compass and a protractor. The fifth postulate is different in that we cannot verify empirically whether those two lines meet, since we can draw only segments, not lines. We can extend the segments further and further (according to postulate 2) to see if they meet, but we cannot go on extending them for ever. Apparently, even Euclid himself recognised the questionable nature of this postulate, for he postponed using it for as long as he could until the proof of his twenty-ninth proposition.

Non-Euclidean geometry arose from attempts to prove Euclid's fifth postulate, the so-called parallel postulate or axiom. In fact, non-Euclidean geometry is a geometry in which the parallel postulate does not hold. Nikolai Ivanovich Lobachevsky (1792–1856) was one of the first who proposed to deny the parallel axiom and to see whether the resulting geometry would lead to a contradiction. It did not, and the geometry he elaborated is now known as Hyperbolic or Lobachevsky geometry. Carl Friedrich Gauss (1777–1855) arrived at the same conclusions and saw its most revolutionary implication, namely that non-Euclidean geometry could be used to describe the properties of physical space as accurately as Euclidean geometry does. Thus the latter is not the necessary geometry of physical space; its physical truth cannot be guaranteed on any *a priori* grounds. Gauss never published his views on the problem of the parallel axiom but he did publish his discussion of curved surfaces. Gauss introduced the concept of 'measure of curvature', now known as the Gaussian curvature of a surface. For a surface of constant curvature, Gauss derived a simple formula relating curvature (K), area and angular measure. He took a geodesic triangle $\triangle ABC$ with vertices A, B, and C and sides geodesic segments. A geodesic segment between two points on a surface is the shortest path lying on the surface between those points. He determined that, if $\angle A$ denotes the measure of angle A, then

$$K \times \text{area } \triangle ABC = \angle A + \angle B + \angle C - 180°$$

The Euclidean space has constant zero curvature whereas the spherical space has constant positive curvature and the pseudo-spherical space has constant negative curvature. As a result, in these three spaces, the sum of the angles of a triangle will be: 180°, greater than 180° and less than 180°, respectively (see Figure 6.1).

| Cylinder | Sphere | Pseudo-sphere |

Figure 6.1 Triangles in three different spaces. The diagram shows a triangle on a cylinder
(Euclidean space: zero curvature), a triangle on a sphere (positive curvature),
and a triangle on a pseudo-sphere (negative curvature).

Source: Phillips and Fisher (1896, p. 527).

Apart from the growing interest to work out different kinds of geometries on
the basis of different parallel axioms, mathematicians began to think of the possible
existence of more than three space dimensions. This notion of multidimensional
space arose from multiple-algebra (vector analysis). Josiah Willard Gibbs made
important contributions to this field. Fisher, in his Josiah Willard Gibbs Lecture
(1930), recalled Gibbs's response to German criticism of the way he violated the
fundamental rules of algebra (such as the commutative rule that $a \times b$ is equal to
$b \times a$), a consequence of his multiple algebra. Gibbs's comment was

> that all depends on what your object is in making those sacrosanct rules for
> operating upon symbols. If the object is to interpret physical phenomena and
> if we find we can do better by having a rule that $a \times b$ is equal not to $b \times a$ but
> to minus $b \times a$, as in the multiplication of two vectors, then, he said, the
> criticisms of the Germans are beside the point.
>
> (Fisher 1930: 231)

Both non-Euclidean geometry and n-dimensional geometry were taken up by
(Georg Friedrich) Bernhard Riemann, in his celebrated paper 'On the hypotheses
which lie at the bases of geometry' (1882), and Helmholtz, in his popularisation
entitled, 'The origin and meaning of geometrical axioms' (1876, 1878).

In the second part of his essay on Kant, Fisher discussed the consequences of
these developments in mathematics for Kant's *apriorism*. Kant maintained that
our minds supply certain modes of organisation, so-called 'intuitions', of space
and time, and that experience is absorbed and organised by our minds in accordance
with these intuitions. As a consequence, certain principles about space exist prior
to experience. According to Kant, these principles, which he called *a priori* synthetic
truths, were those of Euclidean geometry. 'We cannot say perhaps that Kant's

doctrine of space as an *a priori* form of mental intuition is false but we can say without hesitation that the foundations on which he built his theory are false' (Fisher 1890: 6). Because the parallel axiom might be untrue, maybe

> we do live in spherical or pseudo-spherical space. The illustration of the triangle which Kant makes so much use of is the most unfortunate one he could have chosen. For the proposition about the triangle rests directly on the parallel postulate. If this postulate be untrue then is it that the sum of the angles of a triangle are not exactly 180°.
>
> (Fisher 1890: 6–7)

Fisher's conclusion was an echo of Helmholtz's (1878: 214):

> [Geometry] is not possible as a pure science. Its foundation truths are the accumulated consolidated experience of our race but no less experience. We must strip geometry of its pretended dignity of being pure and give it the greater dignity of being the most perfect of the physical sciences.
>
> (Fisher 1890: 9)

Helmholtz's conclusion was in line with his general empiricist philosophy. He rejected the Kantian claim to look upon 'the geometrical axioms as propositions given *a priori* by transcendental intuitions which no experience could either confirm or refute' (Helmholtz 1876: 320). All we know about space, he said, is what we have learned from experience. If we lived in a spherical or pseudo-spherical space, our experience of the world would dictate the adoption of the non-Euclidean geometries of Riemann or Lobachevsky; nothing in our intuition would require us to adopt a 'flat-space' Euclidean system. Thus the only useful test of the validity of the axioms lies in observation and measurement.

Developments like the creation of non-Euclidean geometry and n-dimensional geometry and discoveries such as non-commutative quaternions or vectors, which challenged the accepted principles of numbers, made mathematicians doubt the foundations of mathematics. As long as mathematics dealt with, or was considered to deal with, concepts that had physical meaning, rigour had an empirical basis. By the end of the nineteenth century, the developments mentioned above led to acceptance of the view that all mathematical axioms are arbitrary. David Hilbert's answer to this crisis in the foundations of mathematics was to reintroduce rigour by demanding consistency. As long as mathematics was regarded as telling the 'truth' about nature, the occurrence of contradictory theorems could not arise. When non-Euclidean geometries were created, however, their apparent variance with reality did raise questions about their consistency. This problem was solved by making the consistency of the non-Euclidean geometries depend upon that of Euclidean geometry. Hilbert did succeed in establishing the consistency of Euclidean geometry on the assumption that arithmetic is consistent. But the consistency of the latter had not been established, and Hilbert posed this problem as the second in the list he presented at the Second International Congress in

1900: 'The compatibility of the arithmetical axioms' (Hilbert 1902: 447). It is in the discussion of this problem that he related the existence of a concept to consistency as opposed to giving it an empirical basis, as his quote at the beginning of this chapter shows.

The inventor

Besides being a mathematician and economist, Fisher was a 'gadgeteer, an inventor of gadgets and widgets' (Allen 1993: 135), or as Tobin (1987: 371) worded it: 'Fisher was, on top of everything else, an inventor'. In his work as an economist his approach had the same characteristics as that of a 'great engineer' (Allais 1968: 483). Throughout his life Fisher sought an invention that would provide the foundation for a manufacturing enterprise that would make him rich. He began with a desk-opening-and-closing device that he invented while he was still at school. Next was a piano apparatus that he patented as a Yale freshman (Allen 1993: 135–6). Sometimes he wrote a special article to accompany an invention explaining and recommending its use. He did this for inventions such as a tent for the treatment of tuberculosis (Fisher 1903), a mechanical diet indicator (Fisher 1906), and an icosahedral world map (Fisher 1943). His last invention was a portable stool (Fisher 1997: 301). But the only invention to pay off was the Index Visible Filing System (Fisher 1997: 282).

Fisher did not only invent and develop devices to make money. He was also convinced that for understanding a certain mechanism or phenomenon, visualisation is essential, 'for correct visual pictures usually yield the clearest concepts' (Fisher 1939: 311). Sometimes these pictures showed mechanical devices, because he believed that a 'student of economics thinks in terms of mechanics far more than geometry, and a mechanical illustration corresponds more fully to his antecedent notions than a graphical one' (Fisher [1892] 1925: 24). Fisher ([1892] 1925) used pictures of a hydrostatic mechanism to explain a three-good, three-consumer economy in this PhD thesis.[6] He also used a mechanical balance to illustrate the equation of exchange and a hydraulic system 'to observe and trace' important variations and their effects in the *Purchasing Power of Money* (Fisher [1911] 1963: 108).[7] On other occasions he used geometrical illustrations to visualise properties of a system. For example, he gave a description of a three-dimensional construction of the properties of production factors in his 1939 paper 'A three-dimensional representation of the factors of production and their remuneration, marginally and residually' to help the students 'to see, literally to see with his eyes' (p. 311). He discussed a better method of graphical representation in his paper 'The "ratio" chart, for plotting statistics' (1917). There he recommended the ratio chart, in which only ratios are displayed and compared, because it

> simply utilizes the natural powers of the eye. Consequently, when one is once accustomed to it, it never misleads, but always pictures a multitude of ratio relations at a glance, with absolute fidelity and without the annoyance of reservations or corrections.
>
> (Fisher 1917: 600)

Gibbs may well have been influential in Fisher's efforts to use visualisation. Gibbs's first two publications, 'Graphical methods in the thermodynamics of fluids' and 'A method of geometrical representation of the thermodynamic properties of substances by means of surfaces' ([1873] 1961) dealt explicitly with this issue. In a biographical sketch, Henri Bumstead noted that

> Professor Gibbs was much inclined to the use of geometrical illustrations, which he employed as symbols and aids to the imagination, rather than the mechanical models which have served so many investigators; such models are seldom in complete correspondence with the phenomena they represent, and Professor Gibbs's tendency toward rigorous logic was such that the discrepancies apparently destroyed for him the usefulness of the model. Accordingly he usually had recourse to the geometrical representation of his equations, and this method he used with great ease and power.
>
> (Bumstead [1906] 1961: xii–xiii)

However, Gibbs was not a model builder, see Chapter 2. As Morgan (1999: 351) emphasises 'it was Fisher who broke with the tradition of his teacher and developed constructions which we now recognise as "models" in his texts'. While Gibbs saw geometrical illustrations mainly as aids to the imagination, Fisher stressed the role of visualisations because they helped to understand a system or phenomenon. It connected the unknown to something familiar: to something we have experience of. Fisher made no principled distinction between geometry and mechanics, because geometry, too, was in his view 'consolidated experience'.

Fisher approached a problem by thinking of it in terms of building an instrument. Such an approach can only work if one also has the skills of a designer. Proof of Fisher's ability as designer can be seen in his elegant 'mechanical diet indicator', illustrated in Figure 6.2 (Fisher 1906). This device was designed to 'save labor and at the same time to *visualize* the magnitude and proportions of the diet' (Fisher 1906: 418). It used a clever combination of mechanical and geometrical principles, a combination that also turned out to be very useful in the context of indexes.

The method Fisher proposed for indicating food values worked as follows. The first step was to measure food in terms of calories instead of by weight and to take the portion that contains 100 calories as the fundamental unit. So, the value of each food is indicated by the amount of calories of protein, fat and carbohydrate in the portion. The next step was to represent the food values geometrically in such a way that the portions of protein, fat and carbohydrate formed the coordinates of a point on an isosceles right-angled triangle. The third step was to use this geometrical representation to determine the constituents of combinations of different foods. A point representing the combination of any number of different foods was obtained by taking the centre of gravity of the points representing the respective foods, each weighted in proportion to the calories or standard portions which enter into the combination. Since the resultant point was the centre of gravity, it could be obtained by means of a mechanical method. The cardboard (see Figure 6.2) with the right-angled triangle on which points were located to represent the

Figure 6.2   Mechanical diet indicator

Source: Fisher (1906, p. 430, figure 22).

various foods employed was the essential element of the mechanical indicator. At specific points representing foods eaten, pins with heavy heads were stuck through the cardboard. When the card was placed in a 'basket' and suspended on the standard, one could easily find the centre of gravity (see Figure 6.2).

The making of index numbers

The index-number problem

Fisher's original interest in index numbers arose from the problem of determining the purchasing power of money. The purchasing power of money was defined as the reciprocal of the price level. A core element of Fisher's quantity theory was the equation of exchange:

$$MV = pQ + p'Q' + p''Q'' + \ldots = \Sigma pQ$$

where p represents the individual prices, Q the individual quantities, M is money in circulation and V the velocity of its circulation.

The price level was obtained by the conversion of the right side into the form PT, where P is a weighted average of all the prices, representing the price level, and T the sum of all the Q's, representing the volume of trade. So, the 'principles' determining the purchasing power were represented by the now well-known equation of exchange:

$$MV = PT$$

As a result, the price level had to be consistent with the above equation of exchange. P and T were connected with each other by the relation

$$PT = \Sigma pQ \tag{6.1}$$

In other words, every form of P implied via equation (6.1) a corresponding, or in Fisher's ([1911] 1963: 385) terminology, a 'correlative form' of T and vice versa. To find an adequate formula for P, Fisher suggested starting with T. T was the sum of all the Q's, but the various Q's were measured in different units. Fisher proposed to take as the unit for measuring any goods the amount that constitutes a 'dollar worth' at some particular year called the base year. As a result, T was defined as

$$T = \Sigma p_0 Q$$

where the subscript zero indicates the base year. This definition implied the 'correlative form' of P:

$$P = \frac{\Sigma pQ}{T} = \frac{\Sigma pQ}{\Sigma p_0 Q} = \Sigma w \frac{p}{p_0} \tag{6.2}$$

where $w = \dfrac{p_0 Q}{\Sigma p_0 Q}$. In other words, for the purpose of commensurability, P had to be seen as the weighted average of *price ratios*. Thus in general, Fisher had to consider P not as a price level but as a price index.[8]

The above 'strict algebraic statement' (Fisher [1911] 1963: 24) of the equation of exchange was preceded by an 'arithmetical illustration' and a 'mechanical illustration' (p. 21). The mechanical illustration was a visual representation, a picture of a mechanical balance in equilibrium, the two sides of which symbolised respectively the money side and the goods side of the equation of exchange (see Figure 6.3). The weight at the left, symbolised by a purse, represented the money in circulation; the arm or distance from the fulcrum at which the purse is hung represented the velocity of circulation. In Figure 6.3(a), on the right side of the balance were three weights – bread, coal and cloth, symbolised respectively by a loaf, a coal scuttle and a roll of cloth. The distance of each article from the fulcrum represented its price. Because Fisher was interested in price levels, all the articles (the loaf, the coal scuttle and the roll of cloth) were hung in one basket at a single point on the right-hand side (see Figure 6.3(b)). This meant that the distance from the fulcrum now represented the average price.

According to Ragnar Frisch's (1936: 3) survey article on index numbers, the latter part of the analogy was 'dangerously misleading'. In the mechanical analogy,

(a)

(b)

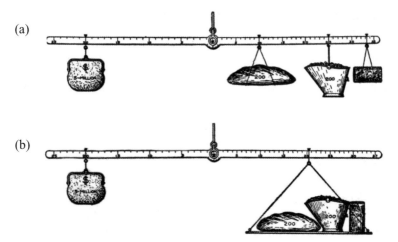

Figure 6.3   Mechanical balance. The diagram shows a mechanical illustration of the
equation of exchange. The left-hand side symbolizes the money side with the
purse representing money in circulation. The distance from the fulcrum to the
purse represents the velocity of circulation. The right-hand side symbolises
the goods side, with loaf, coal scuttle and a roll of cloth representing commodities. In the top illustration, the distance of each article from the fulcrum
represents its price. In the lower illustration, the distance from the fulcrum to
the basket represents average price.

Source: Fisher ([1911] 1963, p. 21, Figure 2; p. 22, Figure 3).

it is only because there is a physical common denominator for all three commodities,
namely their weight, that the average price (distance to the fulcrum) can be
determined. So, he concluded that 'it is precisely the *absence* of this physical
commensurability that constitutes the index-number problem' (p. 3). In other words,
for an index to be defined as a weighted average, the main problem was to determine
the appropriate weighting system. The analogy with a mechanical balance seems
to mask that problem. Frisch was right about the nature of the index-number
problem, but his judgement that Fisher's approach is 'misleading' was wrong.
Fisher was well aware of this commensurability problem, and his engagement in
index numbers stemmed from it. In looking for a common unit, Fisher proposed
to take that amount of a good that constitutes a 'dollars worth'. This change in
unit shifted the meaning of P in the equation of exchange from being the average
price level to the average of price ratios, the price index. As in the case of the
mechanical diet indicator, changing the standard unit made commensurability
possible. The right-hand basket of the mechanical balance was constructed
according to similar principles as the diet indicator.

Tests of the index formulae

The index formula (6.2) was consistent with Fisher's equation of exchange, but Fisher did not stop there. Before he finally decided this index-number formula was the best, he submitted it to several 'tests'. In the appendix to Chapter 10 of his *Purchasing Power of Money* ([1911] 1963), Fisher reviewed eight tests including 'all the tests which have been hitherto applied in the study of index numbers and some others' (p. 400). Each test consisted of a general and a particular version. For the general case the test should be fulfilled for any two years, indicated by the subscripts 1 and 2; for the particular case it should only be fulfilled when one of the years is the base year, indicated by the subscript 0. Thus the particular version was a weaker version of the general one.

1   *Test of proportionality as to prices* (F1). A formula for the price index should be such that the price index will agree with all individual price ratios when these all agree with each other.
    Given $p_1/p_2 = p'_1/p'_2 = \ldots = k$

    General: $P_{0,1}/P_{0,2} = k$
    Particular: $P_{0,1} = k$

2   *Test of proportionality as to trade* (F2). The 'correlative formula' for the trade index should be such that the trade index will agree with all individual trade ratios when these all agree with each other.
    Given $Q_1/Q_2 = Q'_1/Q'_2 = \ldots = k$

    General: $T_1/T_2 = k$
    Particular: $T_1 = k$

Because the trade index and the price index were corresponding indexes ($PT = \Sigma pQ$), this test could also be considered as a test on the price index.

General:
$$\frac{P_{0,1}}{P_{0,2}} = \frac{\Sigma p_1 Q_1}{\Sigma p_2 Q_1} = \frac{\Sigma p_1 Q_2}{\Sigma p_2 Q_2}$$

Particular:
$$P_{0,1} = \frac{\Sigma p_1 Q_1}{\Sigma p_0 Q_1} = \frac{\Sigma p_1 Q_0}{\Sigma p_0 Q_0}$$

3   *Test of determinateness as to prices* (F3). A price index should not be rendered zero, infinity, or indeterminate by an individual price becoming zero.
4   *Test of determinateness as to trade* (F4). The 'correlative trade index' should not be rendered zero, infinity, or indeterminate by an individual quantity becoming zero.

5   *Test of withdrawal or entry as to prices* (F5). A price index should be unaffected by the withdrawal or entry of a price ratio agreeing with the index.
6   *Test of withdrawal or entry as to trade* (F6). The 'correlative trade index' should be unaffected by the withdrawal or entry of a quantity ratio agreeing with the index.
7   *Test by changing base* (F7). The ratios between various price indexes (and therefore those between the 'correlative' trade indexes) should be unaffected by reversing or changing the base (from zero to a so-called year 8).

$$\text{General:} \qquad \frac{P_{0,1}}{P_{0,2}} = \frac{P_{8,1}}{P_{8,2}}$$

This test implies a particular version that, in turn, implies a weaker version. Because both played a more prominent role in Fisher's *The Making of Index Numbers* ([1922] 1967) and the axiomatic index literature that followed from this (see below), they will be labelled by the names that were later given to them.

Particular versions

Circular Test (F7–C): $P_{1,2} \times P_{2,3} = P_{1,3}$
Time Reversal Test (F7–T): $P_{0,1} \times P_{1,0} = 1$

8   *Test by changing unit of measurement* (renamed in Fisher [1922] 1967 as *Commensurability Test* [F8]). The ratios between various price indexes (and therefore those between the correlative trade indexes) should be unaffected by changing any unit of measurement.
Given Q_1 and p_1 changed in inverse ratio

General: $P_{0,1}/P_{0,2}$ unchanged
Particular: $P_{0,1}$ unchanged

These eight tests were not considered to be of equal importance. The Paasche Index, $P_P = \Sigma pQ/\Sigma p_0 Q$ (see formula (6.2)), was Fisher's favourite in his 1911 publication: 'theoretically at least, the best form of *P*' (Fisher [1911] 1963: 201). It represented how prices will change on average in all cases of variation of *M*, *V* and *Q*, except when the *Q*'s vary relatively to each other. This was shown with the aid of the equation of exchange, so that changes in one of the factors and their results can be rendered as follows:

$$\frac{MV}{M_0 V_0} = \frac{PT}{P_0 T_0}$$

Note that $P_0 = 1$.

If Q remains invariable ($Q = Q_0$) and thus $T = T_0$, while M and/or V change, then P_p express how prices will change on average:

$$\frac{MV}{M_0V_0} = \frac{\Sigma\, pQ_0}{\Sigma\, p_0Q_0} = \frac{\Sigma\, pQ}{\Sigma\, p_0Q} = P_p$$

If the Q's all vary in a given ratio ($Q = kQ_0$)

$$P\frac{T}{T_0} = k\frac{\Sigma\, pQ_0}{\Sigma\, p_0Q_0} = k\frac{\Sigma\, pQ}{\Sigma\, p_0Q}$$

This means that if $T/T_0 = k$ (required by Test F2) then P has the form of P_p, and therefore P_p is imposed by Test F2.

Because 'the equation of exchange itself prescribes test No. 2' (p. 404), it was considered by Fisher as 'the most important of all the eight tests for prices' (p. 406). None of the forty-four index numbers passed all eight tests, but if Test F2 was imposed, the Paasche index came out as being the best formula.

Test F2 was also important because 'it is the only test which indicates the kind of *weighting* required' (p. 406). However, Test F2 did not account for the case that the Q's do not vary proportionally.

> When the Q's vary unequally, however, there seems to be *no* perfectly satisfactory formula. Under these circumstances the two systems of weights – one in terms of Q_1's, the other in terms of Q_0's – conflict with each other. But the conflict has been shown by Edgeworth to be slight. In fact, the weights are of much less importance in determining an index number of prices than prices themselves.
>
> (Fisher [1911] 1963: 406)

F.Y. Edgeworth had shown (in the Reports of the British Association for the Advancement of Science for 1887 and 1888) that an 'error' in the *weights* only makes an 'error' one twentieth as great in the resultant index number, while an 'error' in the *prices* themselves makes an 'error' in the resultant index number one-fourth or one-fifth as great. From this result, Fisher concluded that 'considerable variation in weighting is of comparatively little practical importance' (p. 422).

This point was criticised in Keynes' (1911) review of *The Purchasing Power of Money*. In the appendix to Chapter 12, Fisher endeavoured to determine statistically the magnitude of each of terms of the equation of exchange, M, V, P and T. To calculate T, Fisher chose the weights rather arbitrarily. As Fisher stated: 'These weights are, of course, merely matters of opinion, but, as is well known, wide differences in systems of weighting make only slight differences in the final averages' (p. 485).

Keynes considered the chosen weights as 'unscientific guesses of the wildest character' (Keynes 1911: 397). He believed that Fisher had misapprehended Edgeworth's results.

> Professor Fisher's theory, that the weights employed in compiling an index number seldom affect the result, naturally leads him to think that an index number made for one purpose is equally suitable for another, and that the method of compilation can be safely determined by considerations of taste and convenience.
>
> (Keynes 1911: 397–8)

Empirical test of the index numbers

Fisher, as the author of the 1911 publication, can rightly be called an apriorist with respect to index numbers. The best index number form was the one that fulfilled the test prescribed by the equation of exchange (F2). The 'chief object' of his *Purchasing Power of Money* was 'to explain the causes determining the purchasing power of money' (Fisher [1911] 1963: 13). Therefore, he first 'reconstructed' the quantity theory of money into the equation of exchange, and then statistically verified this equation in the second part of his book. For this statistical verification, he needed an index number formula in accordance with the equation of exchange and, as shown above, in dealing with the commensurability problem he arrived at the Paasche index. The evaluation of the forty-three other index formulae on the basis of eight tests was not his primary interest and was relegated to an appendix. But in the years that followed, Fisher became more and more interested in developing the best index formula 'for all purposes'. That is, he treated the best index number problem as an important problem in its own terms and as a problem with a more general application than verifying the quantity theory of money.

Ten years after the publication of his *Purchasing Power of Money*, Fisher presented a paper 'The best form of index number' (1921) at a meeting of the American Statistical Association. The discussion of the best form was not based on any economic-theoretic assumption – in contrast with his *Purchasing Power of Money*. The point of departure was the ratio of money value, in which 'there can be no ambiguity': 'There is only one index number of value – the value itself' (Fisher 1921: 533). The problem was to find how far the ratio of the money value of a certain year to the money value of a base year is a matter of inflated prices and how far it is a matter of increased quantities (volume of trade). In other words, if one tries to split this ratio of money values into two factors, P and Q (where capital Q now indicates the quantity index and lower case q's the individual quantities), that is,

$$P_{0,1}Q_{0,1} = \frac{\sum p_1 q_1}{\sum p_0 q_0} = V_{0,1}$$

then what is the best form for each factor, P and Q?

Instead of the eight tests, Fisher now suggested only two 'supreme' tests. The first was the *Factor Reversal Test* (F9). 'The formula should *work both ways* as to the two factors, prices and quantities' (p. 534). If the quantity index is obtained by interchanging the prices and quantities in the price index formula, then the two indexes multiplied together should give the value ratio.

The second was the *Time Reversal Test* (F7–T):

$$P_{0,1} \times P_{1,0} = 1$$

'The formula should *work both ways* as to time' (p. 534). This test was in fact the weakest version of the 'test by changing base' (F7) of his *Purchasing Power of Money*.

It appeared that the simplest formula conforming to both reversal tests (F9 and F7–T) was the geometric mean of the Paasche and Laspeyres indexes, the so-called 'ideal' index.

The paper itself was not published, though an abstract was printed together with the discussion that took place at the meeting. The most important critiques focused on Fisher's claim that his 'ideal' index was the best form for *all* purposes. In countering these critiques Fisher ended up not with a paper, but with a large book of more than five hundred pages: *The Making of Index Numbers*, published in 1922. The reason for this extension was that Fisher examined more than a hundred formulae, using calculations from actual historical data.

> This book is, therefore, primarily an inductive rather than a deductive study. In this respect it differs from the Appendix to Chapter X of the *Purchasing Power of Money*, in which I sought deductively to compare the merits of 44 different formulae. The present book had its origin in the desire to put these deductive conclusions to an inductive test by means of calculations from actual historical data. But before I had gone far in such testing of my original conclusions, I found, to my great surprise, that the results of actual calculation constantly suggested further deduction until, in the end, I had completely revised both my conclusions and my theoretical foundation. Not that I needed to discard as untrue many of the conclusions reached in the *Purchasing Power of Money*; for the only definite error which I have found among my former conclusions has to do with the so-called 'circular test' which I originally, with other writers accepted as sound, but which, in this book, I reject as theoretically unsound.
>
> (Fisher [1922] 1967: xii–xiii)

The reason to abandon the circular test (F7–C: $P_{1,2} \times P_{2,3} = P_{1,3}$) was that this test is a multiple comparison, and according to Fisher, index numbers were only appropriate for dual comparisons. Note that the Time Reversal Test, being a weaker version of the Circular Test, is not a multiple but a dual comparison.

Fisher assumed that the only formulae that conform to the Circular Test are index numbers that have constant weights, and constant weighting was according to him 'not theoretically correct' (p. 275) because it did not take into account the differences between countries or times.

> Such a formula would prove too much, for it would leave no room for qualitative differences. Index numbers are to some extent empirical, and the supposed inconsistency in the failure of (variably weighted) index numbers to conform to the circular test, is really a bridge to reality.
>
> (Fisher [1922] 1967: 274)

In his book, *The Purchasing Power of Money*, Fisher ([1911] 1963: 406) maintained that, 'the weights are of much less importance in determining an index number of prices than prices themselves'. However, in his book the *Making of Index Numbers*, he took the opposite position in saying that only a formula leaves room for 'qualitative differences' would be 'a bridge to reality'. He shifted from neglecting the importance of the index's sensitivity to variations in the weights, to a position in which he emphasised that index numbers should be susceptible to changes in the weight system. In the axiomatic index literature that evolved from Fisher's work this shift was ignored and the main conclusions of *The Making of Index Numbers* were disregarded. In fact, the Circular Test was treated as inseparable from Fisher's system of tests. And, although Fisher ([1911] 1963: 200) had admitted that 'it seems theoretically impossible to devise an index number, P, which shall satisfy all of the tests we should like to impose', consistency of the tests became one of the central issues in the axiomatic index approach.

The axiomatic versus the instrumental approach

Consistency of Fisher's tests

Ragnar Frisch's (1930) 'Necessary and sufficient conditions regarding the form of an index number which shall meet certain of Fisher's tests' was the first publication to prove the impossibility of maintaining a certain set of tests simultaneously. It was the starting point for a whole series of publications in which the inconsistency of Fisher's tests was discussed.

Frisch's 1930 essay was actually a discussion of seven of Fisher's tests.

1   Identity Test: $P_{t,t} = 1$
2   Time Reversal Test (F7–T)
3   Base Test (F7)
4   Circular Test (F7–C)
5   Commensurability Test (F8)
6   Determinateness Test (F3 and F4)
7   Factor Reversal Test (F9).

Frisch did not discuss or even mention either tests of withdrawal or entry (F5 and F6). Neither did he discuss either of Fisher's tests of proportionality (F1 and F2); he discussed only a weak version, namely the Identity Test mentioned above.

The aim of Frisch's essay was 'to derive the general form which it is necessary and sufficient that an index number shall have in order that certain combinations of the above test [sic] shall be fulfilled' (Frisch 1930: 400). While Fisher's approach was to select index formulae by testing them, Frisch's method was to derive the appropriate form from these tests mathematically. By interpreting the tests as conditions on the functional form of the index number formula, Frisch was able to derive the unique index number formula satisfying the Commensurability Test (F8), the Circular Test (F7–C), and the Factor Reversal Test (F9).

However, Frisch also showed that the Base Test (F7) (or Circular Test, F7–C), the Commensurability Test (F8) and the Determinateness Test (F3 and F4) could not all be fulfilled at the same time – they were 'incompatible'. So, according to Frisch, one has to choose between the tests. Since he favoured a chain index, the Circular Test was not questioned. The choice was then between satisfying the Determinateness Test and the Commensurability Test. Frisch chose the Determinateness Test.

To better understand Frisch's criticism of Fisher's tests, one should first note that Frisch advocated the microeconomic approach, based on individual choice theory.[9] In his survey paper on index numbers, Frisch (1936) developed a theory of price indexes from the viewpoint of utility theory. He proposed that the price index is the ratio of the cost of achieving a given utility level in two situations, which means that the resulting price index is a function of utility level. His very first paper on an economic topic, 'Sur un problème d'économie pure' ([1926] 1971) started with an axiomatic formulation of measurable utility. 'Though this approach is so familiar today, after the work of von Neumann and Morgenstern, Frisch's paper is very possibly the first formulation of its type' (Arrow 1960: 176). It is considered a classic in the theory of consumer behaviour because it, 'apparently' for the first time, introduced the axiomatic approach into the theory of economic choice (Chipman *et al.* 1971: 326).

The main critique on Frisch's paper came from another advocate of the microeconomic approach, Subramanian Swamy. Frisch's conclusion that Fisher's tests are inconsistent was never doubted, but Frisch's proofs were (unjustly) criticised and this created some confusion about Frisch's results. In a debate that took place over many years (Frisch 1934; Swamy 1934, 1940, 1965), both the correctness of Frisch's proofs and the economic interpretation and significance of Fisher's tests were discussed. The inconsistency of the tests called for a selection of the most essential ones. The question of which test needed to be rejected 'must be analysed within the framework of economic analysis' (Swamy 1965: 622). Swamy considered Fisher's approach with its 'mechanical tests' (Samuelson and Swamy 1974: 576) economically unfounded; in particular, both the Determinateness (F4) and the Factor Reversal Test (F9) were considered to be 'suspect'.

Parallel to this debate, Abraham Wald also proved the inconsistency of Fisher's tests, in his 1937 article 'Zur Theorie der Preisindexziffern'. Wald showed that there is no index that fulfills the Proportionality Test (F1 and F2), the Circular

Test (F7–C) and the Factor Reversal Test (F9) at the same time. He saw the Factor Reversal Test as 'economically completely unfounded' [*ökonomisch vollkommen unbegründet*] in that its economic meaning was not apparent (Wald 1937: 183). Wald concluded that the formal mathematical approach was not suitable for solving the index problem. Most of his paper consisted of a discussion of an economic approach to index numbers, based on individual choice theory.

An important reason that economists maintain the Circular Test is that when the test criteria are met an index number is freed from one base year. Another reason, crucial to a microeconomic approach, is that 'so long as we stick to the economic theory of index numbers, the circular test is as required as is the property of transitivity itself' (Samuelson and Swamy 1974: 576). Moreover, the forms of indexes provided by Samuelson and Swamy contradicted Fisher's assertion that only fixed weights can lead to the Circular Test being satisfied.

Wolfgang Eichhorn systematically looked at the inconsistencies between tests (and how to prove such inconsistencies) by means of the so-called Axiomatic Index Theory, which is based on functional equation theory. Functional equation theory is transferred into index theory if the price index is defined as a positive function that satisfies a number of axioms. These axioms do not determine a unique form of the price index function. Several additional tests are needed 'for assessing the quality of a potential price index' (Eichhorn and Voeller 1976: 29). Both axioms and tests are formalised as functional equations. The inconsistency theorems can then be proved by showing that for the relevant combinations of functional equations, the solution space is empty.

The power of this approach was immediately demonstrated in Eichhorn's first publication on index theory, 'Zur axiomatischen Theorie des Preisindex' (1973). The paper discussed five of Fisher's tests:

1   Proportionality Test (F1)
2   Commensurability Test (F8)
3   Circular Test (F7–C)
4   Determinateness Test (F3 and F4)
5   Factor Reversal Test (F9).

Eichhorn obtained the same results as Frisch (1930) – namely, the functional form of an index that fulfilled the Commensurability Test (F8), the Circular Test (F7–C) and the Factor Reversal Test (F9). However, his results were derived from functional equation theory, in particular Josef Aczél's (1966) solution of Cauchy's functional equations. Eichhorn also showed that the derived index fulfills the Determinateness Test (F3 and F4) but not the Proportionality Test (F1).

However, these five tests are inconsistent, which requires that one test be rejected. Because the economic significance of the Factor Reversal Test (F9) was controversial, Eichhorn abandoned this test. He then showed that the other four are independent but still inconsistent. A set of tests is independent when any set minus one can be satisfied by an index that does not fulfill the remaining test.

Eichhorn's paper was written in German and published in a mathematical journal. Three years later these results were published in English in *Econometrica* (Eichhorn 1976), in which a weaker version of Fisher's system of tests was also discussed. However, even this weaker system was inconsistent. Eichhorn again demonstrated that this weaker set of five tests is independent, but if one wants to hold on to five tests, the question is: how much further must the tests be weakened to obtain a consistent set? It appeared that if one weakens only the Circular Test (F7–C), by replacing it by the Time Reversal Test (F7–T), then the system of five tests is consistent. In the end, Fisher's system of tests was proved to be consistent, but Eichhorn made no mention of this.

Eichhorn's axiomatic approach, his 'art of model building' which he not only applied to index numbers but also to production functions, can be summarised as follows:

> He
> – formulated some important properties $(P_1, \ldots , P_k, say)$ of production functions,
> – proved their consistency by presenting a function that has all these properties,
> – showed the independence of the properties ...
> The properties (assumptions, hypotheses, premises, desiderata, axioms) constitute a model.
>
> (Stehling 1993: viii–ix)

Eichhorn's axiomatic method of defining economic models was further developed in his 'economic measurement theory', with its central notion the term of an economic index. According to Eichhorn's definition an

> economic index is an economic measure, i.e. a function $F : D \rightarrow \mathfrak{R}$ which maps, on the one hand, a set D of economically interesting objects into the set $\mathfrak{R}$ of real numbers and which satisfies, on the other hand, a system of economically relevant conditions ... The form of these conditions depends on the economic information which we want to obtain from the particular measure.
>
> (Eichhorn 1978: 3)

This 'economic' measurement theory was based on Pfanzagl's (1968) *Theory of Measurement*, exemplary for the axiomatic approach to measurement in general.

Fisher's instrumental approach to indexes

In the axiomatic index literature, axioms were considered to be prescribed by economic theory and problems caused by inconsistency were solved by omitting those 'tests' that had no, or dubious, economic meaning. Fisher diverged from this approach in two respects. First, he distanced himself from economic theory in assessing index number formulae. Second, he did not believe that inconsistency was a problem. The index number 'should be the "just compromise" among conflicting elements, the "fair average", the "golden mean"' (Fisher [1922] 1967: 10). Fisher compared the construction of an index with that of lenses:

> [A]lthough in the science of optics we learn that a perfect lens is theoretically impossible, nevertheless, for all practical purposes lenses be constructed so nearly perfect that it is well worth while to study and construct them. So, also, while it seems theoretically impossible to devise an index number, *P*, which shall satisfy all of the tests we should like to impose, it is, nevertheless, possible to construct index numbers which satisfy these tests so well for practical purposes that we may profitably devote serious attention to the study and construction of index numbers.
>
> (Fisher [1911] 1963: 200)

The problem of specifying which is the most suitable lens for the purpose boils down to a discussion of the most important defects of a particular lens, namely its aberrations. When the aberrations are identified, means for their control must be found. In the case of a simple lens, control of all the aberrations is sometimes impossible and so a compromise becomes necessary (see quote at the beginning of this chapter). Using multiple lenses in an optical instrument, so that the errors of each lens nullify each other, normally solves this problem.

Fisher's empirical approach comes clearly to the fore in his discussion of the Circular Test (F7–C). Although he could not use this test as an *a priori* condition because it was 'theoretically unsound', he investigated how well the Circular Test could be used as an empirical test. The 'important' question is: '*How near* is the circular test to fulfillment in actual cases? If very near, then practically we may make some use of the circular test as an approximation [to both Reversal Tests (F7–T and F9)] even if it is not strictly valid' (Fisher [1922] 1967: 276). It appeared that for all index numbers that fulfilled both Reversal Tests, the discrepancies between a dual comparison and a multiple comparison were slight. The 'circular gaps' were small and especially so in his 'ideal' index, which fulfilled the Circular Test to within one fourth of one percent (p. 284). Fisher noted that the Circular Test could be considered 'at bottom, to be simply a triangular test' (p. 295), and if one takes a '3-around' comparison, the drawn triangle was almost closed (see Figure 6.4). 'The lines return so nearly to the starting point in each case that the observer has to look [very!] closely to see the gap' (p. 287). So, 'practically, then, the test may be said to be a real test' (pp. 291–2).

It is rather remarkable that Fisher expressly argued against taking the circular test as a theoretical requirement on one hand but on the other hand spent twenty pages using and recommending it as an empirical test for index formulae. Fisher had a very practical reason to do so. Unless one accepts constant weights, index number formulae only allow for dual comparisons. But in practice one would like to make a multiple comparison between countries or times. Using a fixed base system for each comparison between any two years requires calculating a specific

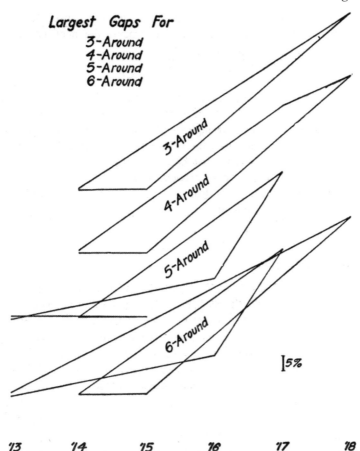

Largest Gaps For

3-Around
4-Around
5-Around
6-Around

3-Around

4-Around

5-Around

6-Around

|5%

'13   '14   '15   '16   '17   '18

CHART 52. The circular test gap (at the left of each of the four circuits), even at its greatest, as here charted for Formula 353, is remarkably small in all cases. It slightly increases as the circuit of year-to-year index numbers becomes more circuitous, reaching over one per cent in the 6-around circuit, 1913–'16–'17–'14–'15–'18–'13.

Figure 6.4 Circular test. 3-around, 4-around, 5-around and 6-around comparisons of Fisher's 'ideal' index show small gaps at the left of each of the four circuits.

Source: Fisher ([1922] 1967, p. 286, chart 52).

index number, which would entail 'very great labor and expense' (p. 299). Using a chain system, it is only necessary to calculate the index numbers of two successive years and then these can be chained for any other comparison. For example, to compare years i and j, one can chain the following index numbers:

$$P_{i,j} = P_{i,i+1} \times P_{i+1,i+2} \times \ldots \times P_{j-1,j}$$

In principle both sides of the equation are inconsistent because '*theoretically* the circular test ought not to be fulfilled', but in practice the inconsistency is 'so slight as *practically* to be negligible' (p. 303).

To understand Fisher's paradoxical stance towards the Circular Test, it is illuminating to compare his ideas with those related to the rise of non-Euclidean geometry. One obvious way to measure the properties of physical space was to determine the sum of the angles of a triangle. There is a close relation between triangles that are not closed and triangles with sums of angles larger or smaller than 180°. As an empirical test rather than a theoretical requirement, the 'triangular test' is analogous to the measurement of the sum of angles to find the properties of a space. It can be used to observe the properties of the index number space. The triangle test showed that Fisher's ideal index is an object of a slightly curved index-number space, but the curvature is so slight that one can practically assume a flat, Euclidean space.

World maps and globes

Fisher was not a supporter of the axiomatic movement nor did he like Hilbert's programme of axiomatisation. Being an inventor, he knew that when designing an instrument one sometimes has to make a compromise between contradictory requirements. Moreover, he believed that the naked eye was a reliable way to assess the best balance. A mathematically impossible object could still be created in practice. This attitude underpinned Fisher's approach to scientific problems throughout his life. It was most apparent in the design of his last but one invention, the icosahedral world map.

Three years before he died in 1947, Fisher, in co-authorship with O.M. Miller, published a book, *World Maps and Globes*, to discuss the qualities desirable in world map projections and the methods by which these qualities can be obtained. The 'map-projection problem' exists because of 'the fact that every map, large or small, must have some distortions and that every *world* map must have interruptions' (Fisher and Miller 1944: 3). To flatten out a globe, one must stretch and/or shrink it in certain directions and tear it at several places. In particular, there is a tension between interruption and distortion: only by increasing the interruptions of the map can we lessen distortion.

In a chapter entitled, 'The four "cardinal virtues"', the problem was stated in terms of objectives:

1   to have *distances* correctly represented;
2   to have *shapes* correctly represented;
3   to have *areas* correctly represented (that is, square mileage);
4   to have great circles represented by *straight lines*.

(Fisher and Miller 1944: 27–8)

It is a geometric impossibility to have all four of these virtues on a flat surface and to have them in every part. So, 'projections are confessedly compromises, being perfect in none of the four ways but balancing the different kinds of errors against one another' (Fisher and Miller 1944: 34).

To find a proper balance between the different kind of errors, Fisher and Miller suggested using a triangular grid for evaluating various map projections. Conventional maps have a grid of latitudes and longitudes. However, the areas bounded by these grid lines are not all the same size on a sphere, and comparisons between different map projections are therefore not easy to visualise (see Figure 6.5). 'The triangular grid (shown on almost all the maps in this book) will be found an easy means of making these comparisons by eye' (pp. 87–8).

Fisher advocated the icosahedral projection as the 'most satisfactory' world map. The icosahedron is the fifth and last platonic body: namely, it is a regular polyhedron having the largest number of faces (twenty) that are equilateral triangles. Because it has the largest number of faces, it has the smallest average distortion of all the regular polyhedrons. It had to be a *regular* polyhedron because 'symmetry plays an important part in conveying to the eye the relation between the flat map and the globe (or its approximations) and this is accomplished only when all the faces are of the same size and shape' (p. 100).

Fisher copyrighted this idea of an icosahedral world map. The map itself, with instructions for folding the map into an icosahedron, was published in *The Geographical Review* in 1943.

Conclusions

There is a tacit but strong belief in economics that axiomatisation leads to better theory. One finds the same kind of conviction in measurement theory. The *Foundations of Measurement* (Krantz *et al.* 1971), a standard work in measurement

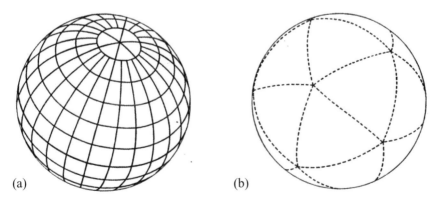

(a)   (b)

Figure 6.5 Triangular grid. Illustration (a) shows conventional grid of latitudes and longitudes. Illustration (b) shows a triangular grid.

Source: Fisher and O.M. Miller (1944, p. 10, Figures 4 and 5).

theory, is an example of that conviction. This view of axiomatics is also dominant in index number theory. However, even the most authoritarian axiomatiser of economics, John von Neumann, warned against too much 'de-empirisation', as he called axiomatisation. He said that, 'at a great distance from its empirical source, or after much "abstract" inbreeding, a mathematical subject is in danger of degeneration' (von Neumann 1961: 9). According to von Neumann, the 'prime' reason why Euclid's fifth postulate was the one questioned was its unempirical character (p. 3). He found it 'hardly possible to believe in the existence of an absolute, immutable concept of mathematical rigor, dissociated from all human experience' (p. 6).

Fisher's instrumental approach to constructing index numbers gives us a good example of how rigour and human experience can work together. Inconsistency between the theoretical requirements does not preclude rigour. As his work on converting the three-dimensional globe into a two-dimensional flat world map illustrated, if the perfect instrument is impossible we still can aim at a well-founded approximation. Fisher's rule of assessment was that an instrument's performance should approximate a standard within acceptable margins. The assessment whether the approximation was acceptable was based on judgments of the naked eye, and not on mathematical considerations of consistency whatsoever. Which standard is appropriate depends on the particular case under consideration. However, the standard should always be set with the aim to provide good fit with the empirical world.

7 Conclusions

It is my view that most individuals underestimate the uncertainty of the world. This is almost a true of economists and other specialists as it is of the lay public. To me our knowledge of the way things work, in society or in nature, comes trailing clouds of vagueness. … Experience during World War II as a weather forecaster added the news that the natural world was also unpredictable. An incident … illustrates both uncertainty and the unwillingness to entertain it. Some of my colleagues had the responsibility of preparing long-range weather forecasts, i.e., for the following month. The statisticians among us subjected these forecasts to verification and found they differed in no way from chance. The forecasters themselves were convinced and requested that the forecasts be discontinued. The reply read approximately like this: 'The Commanding General is well aware that the forecasts are no good. However, he needs them for planning purposes'.

(Arrow 1992: 46–7)

The models discussed in this book are understood as representatives of objects or systems in the world. The key philosophical question regarding the nature of these models is how they function as representations and how reliable the information is that they provide. Margaret Morrison (1999) formulated this problem as follows.

It seems not quite correct to say that models accurately describe physical systems since in many cases they not only embody an element of idealisation or abstraction, but frequently represent the world in ways that bear no similarity to physically realisable objects … Hence, we need a reformulation of the philosophical question; more specifically, since models are sometimes deliberately based on characterisations we know to be false, how can they provide us with information about the world.

(Morrison 1999: 38)

The answer she (and Mary Morgan) gave is quite simple: because models function as instruments of investigation. This answer, however, has far-reaching implications for the way models should be assessed. As we have seen in the preceding chapters, a methodology designed for models considered as instruments differs from a methodology for theories in various directions.

A second feature of the models discussed here and which has implications for any methodology is that they are the instruments of social scientists, in particular economists. And the scientists discussed in this monograph are not found in cut-off laboratories, e.g. the 'closed worlds of our brave new world' where Mirowski (2002) places his subjects; they are more like Humboldtian scientific travellers, carrying with them the latest instruments of measurement. Of course, today the latest instruments are not the ones Humboldt carried with him around 1800: chronometer by Berthoud, demi-chronometer by Seuffert, three-foot achromatic telescope by Dolland, small telescope by Caroché, *lunette d'epreuve* with micrometer by Kohler, ten-inch sextant by Ramsden, two-inch snuff-box sextant by Troughton, etc. (Cannon 1978: 75). Modern scientific travellers today carry with them the latest gadgets which are applications of the latest developments of micro-electronic techniques, mini-computers, because the larger ones are just too heavy. The science practised by these economists can be characterised as Humboldtian science, as described by Susan F. Cannon:

> the accurate, measured study of widespread but interconnected real phenomena in order to find a definite law and a dynamical cause. Compared to this, the study of nature in the laboratory or the perfection of differential equations was old-fashioned, was simple science concerned with easy variable. Insofar as you find scientists studying geographical distribution, terrestrial magnetism, meteorology, hydrology, ocean currents, the structures of mountain-chains and the orientation of strata, solar radiation; insofar as they are playing around with charts, maps, and graphs, hygrometers, dip needles, barometers, maximum and minimum thermometers; insofar as they spend much of their time tinkering with their instruments and worrying about error.
>
> (Cannon 1978: 105)

It should be noted that for a Humboldtian scientist the study of complex phenomena does not exclude the use of simple measuring instruments or the goal of discovering quantitative mathematical connections and interrelationships, on the contrary (p. 77). Maas (forthcoming a) uses this image of a Humboldtian scientist to characterise Jevons's work, but my view is that this image of Humboldtian science is also applicable to the later twentieth-century quantitative empirical tradition that arose from Jevons's work: econometrics, macroeconomics and the combination of both, macroeconometrics.

The instruments used by twentieth-century economists are non-material mathematical models. It has been argued that the mathematical forms and techniques function in the same way as the materials needed to build material instruments. However, some materials are better suited to build a model for a certain purpose than other materials. How do we choose the appropriate mathematical forms and techniques? The problem is that most economic theories do not provide the mathematics needed to represent the phenomena. At the same time, the phenomena themselves are not helpful either, for they also do not prescribe any particular kind of formalism. As we have seen, the choice of the mathematics for constructing a model comes from simple mechanisms that are used as recipes for building new models. These simple mechanisms function as analogies and can in principle be picked up from anywhere, though it seems to be that – at least for the cases discussed in this book – the favourite sources are hydraulics and mechanics. These mechanisms not only contribute to the explanation of the phenomenon but also provide the accompanying tool kit, the mathematical techniques to operate the models. When the construction of a new model succeeds, it can function as recipe for another model needed for similar purposes.

Models built in this way for the purpose of measurement are artifacts as defined by Herbert Simon (1969: 7): the interface between an inner environment, the substance and organisation of the artifact itself, and an outer environment, the surrounding in which it operates. To clarify this idea of artifact, Simon uses the example of a clock. The purpose of a clock is to measure time. The inner environment of the clock is its internal construction. Simon emphasises that whether a clock will in fact tell the time is also dependent on where it is placed. The environment moulds the artifact: a sundial performs as a clock in sunny climates, but to devise a clock that would tell the time on a rolling and pitching ship it has to be endowed with many 'delicate' properties, some of them largely or totally irrelevant to the performance of a 'landlubber's clock'. 'The designer insulates the inner system from the environment, so that an invariant relation is maintained between inner system and goal, independent of variations over a wide range in most parameters that characterize the outer environment' (Simon 1969: 9).

In contrast to physics, in which one is able to create stable environments for measurements, in economics one has often to take measurements in a constantly changing environment. Unable to command the environment, invariance has to be built into the instrument. Simon's example of a clock on a ship is a material instrument within which one can build stabilising mechanisms. But economic models are not material, so that invariance has to be built-in differently, namely by taking care that the model is a representation of a system of relationships that are as autonomous as possible.

The problem is whether and how we can find these autonomous relationships. Because autonomous relationships are crucial for reliable measurement, their discussion is one of the central themes of this book. To summarise (and therefore necessarily simplify) this discussion I will use again the framework that structured the discussions of this theme in the preceding chapters. The reason for doing this is in the first place a personal one: from the beginning of my project on measurement it helped me to shape and develop my own thoughts about measurement. The second reason is that after a closer reading of Haavelmo's Probability (1944) paper, to my surprise, I discovered he was using a similar framework (see Chapter 3).

The framework is:

$$\Delta y = \Delta F(x, OC; \alpha_1, \cdots, \alpha_n) = \frac{\partial F}{\partial x} \Delta x + \frac{\partial F}{\partial OC} \Delta OC \qquad (7.1)$$

where y are the measurement readings, the observations; x is the property of a phenomenon we are measuring; OC is an abbreviation of 'other circumstances' which form the noisy background; F indicates the function that indicates in what way x and the OC influence y; and the a's are the model parameters. In metrology, the partial derivatives, $\partial F/\partial x$ and $\partial F/\partial OC$, are referred to as 'sensitivity coefficients' (see e.g. Taylor and Kuyatt 1994: 8). Within this framework, autonomy is defined as $\partial F/\partial OC \approx 0$ and Δx does not have any effect on the shape of $\partial F/\partial x$. The second term of equation (7.1), $\dfrac{\partial F}{\partial OC} \Delta OC$, is the so-called measurement error. So, within this framework, precision can be defined as the reduction of this error term.

The original Tinbergen and Frisch approach to model business-cycle mechanisms requests the full cooperation of all three main participants for model building: mathematics, (economic) theory and statistics. Mathematics is needed for moulding the model such that it mimics the characteristics of the phenomenon under investigation. It captures both finding to most appropriate shape for F and tuning, i.e. the selection of appropriate parameter values. To clarify how this works, let us assume that the above framework (7.1) is a representation of a dynamical system: $\Delta y = y_t - y_{t-1}$ and $\Delta x = x_t - x_{t-1}$. Then one moulds F in such a way that the assumed time shape of the phenomenon under investigation, x_t, is similar to the one that is generated by the model, y_t. The values of the parameters $\alpha_1, \ldots, \alpha_n$, are chosen so that $\partial F/\partial OC = 0$. Note that for a successful application of this strategy, one should ascertain that the time-shape is stable and not spurious.

Because mathematical moulding perished as a modelling tool halfway through the twentieth century, autonomy became very hard to find. Other means were suggested. Ragnar Frisch, for example, was rather pessimistic whether theory and statistics could handle it alone and proposed localising invariance on the micro level, to be found by the 'interview method':

> It is very seldom indeed that we have a clear case where the statistical data can actually determine numerically an autonomous structural equation. In most cases we only get a covariational equation with a low degree of autonomy. ... We must look for some other means of getting information about the numerical character of our structural equations. The only possible way seems to be to utilize to a much larger extent than we have done so far the interview method, *i.e.*, we must ask persons or groups what they would do under such and such circumstances.
>
> (Frisch 1948: 370)

Generally in macroeconometrics, it is assumed that F is a linear function:

$$\Delta y = \alpha_x \Delta x + \alpha_{OC} \Delta OC \tag{7.2}$$

or

$$y = \alpha_x x + \alpha_{OC} OC \tag{7.3}$$

In other words, $\partial F/\partial x = \alpha_x$ and $\partial F/\partial OC = \alpha_{OC}$. Because $\alpha_{OC} OC$ is the error term, equation (7.3) can be represented as

$$y = \alpha_x x + \varepsilon$$

One can now easily see that autonomy at least means stable parameters.

Lawrence Klein, assuming that the model equations are autonomous (= structural), aimed at precision. His strategy was that each time the equation was not precise enough one should open the 'pound' OC and take out a causal factor to reduce the error term:

$$y = \alpha_1 x_1 + \varepsilon \rightarrow y = \alpha_1 x_1 + \alpha_2 x_2 + \varepsilon'$$

should reduce the error term: $\varepsilon' < \varepsilon$

> In contrast with the parsimonious view of natural simplicity, I believe that economic life is enormously complicated and that the successful model will try to build in as much of the complicated interrelationships as possible. That is why I want to work with large econometric models and a great deal of computer power. Instead of the rule of parsimony, I prefer the following rule: the largest possible system that can be managed and that can explain the main economic magnitudes as well as the parsimonious system is the better system to develop and use.
>
> (Klein 1992: 184)

One of the major efforts of the 1960s in this respect was the Brookings model (Dusenberry *et al.* 1965). This model was a joint effort of many individuals, and at its peak it contained nearly 400 equations. Although much was learned from this exercise, the model never achieved the success that was initially expected, and it was laid to rest around 1972 (Fair 1992: 2). One can only wonder what 'understanding' means in relation to such an enormous model, of which the builders only survey the part they have contributed and of which the overall dynamic behaviour can only be revealed by computer simulations.

The above rule of parsimony, which Klein is arguing against, is to seek a transparent, easily manageable, and elegant model. The smallest or most compact system that is capable of generating results that are of interest is the preferred system. The most explicit spokesman of this rule is, of course, Milton Friedman. His strategy was to start with a simple model ((7.1) or (7.2)) and to investigate for which domain this model is an accurate description. In other words, search for those phenomena for which $\partial F/\partial x \gg \partial F/\partial OC$ or $\alpha_x \gg \alpha_{OC}$.

Another adherent of transparent, easily manageable, and simple models is Robert Lucas. His strategy for accuracy is to calibrate models. In the above framework (7.2), calibration works as follows: use stable facts about the phenomenon to adjust the parameters to get as far as possible preciseness, that is closeness of results. When there are situations in which we expect that x is stable ($\Delta x \approx 0$), then we can adjust the parameter α_{OC} so that Δy is as small as possible:

$$\min_{\alpha_{OC}} \Delta y = \alpha_{OC} \Delta OC$$

All the above strategies with respect to autonomy have in common that their success depends on the existence of invariance anywhere to be found: stable facts about phenomena, stable time shapes, or structural equations. For each strategy there is a danger that these propositions about invariance are more conventional – stylised – than empirical. The more they are conventional the less reliable are the instruments, the more they can lead to spurious results.

Simon's notion of artifacts also justifies simple mechanisms, as long as they accomplish identical goals in similar outer environments. The appeal of simple and elegant models is that they are intelligible, in their simplicity they provide a kind of understanding one at least could communicate to students or colleagues. Lucas (1988: 39) preferred to call them 'mechanics': 'a system of differential equations the solution to which imitates some of the main features of the economic behavior we observe in the world economy'. In my view it would be better to call them 'mechanisms', defined by Machamer *et al.* (2000: 3) as 'entities and activities organized such that they are productive of regular changes from start or set-up to finish or terminate conditions'. The understanding provided by a mechanistic explanation arises not from its correctness, but rather from an elucidative relation between the setup conditions and intermediate entities and activities and the termination condition of the phenomenon to be explained. 'Mechanism descriptions show *how possibly, how plausibly,* or *how actually* things work' (p. 21). A mechanism can be communicated to others without the need to mention or explain matters from outside the mechanism, even more so when they are simple machines that 'can be drawn or reproduced in a picture or recipe book. Such things can be seen or made by everyone and anyone' (Machamer 1998: 70).

To take the title of this book, now put as a question – 'How do economists model the world into numbers?' – my answer is that economists, after a century of mathematical modelling, now prefer very simple mechanisms with the faith that they will be calibrated in the future.

Notes

1 Introduction

1 See Morgan (2002) for a similar account. Considered as a historical claim, this is supported by Morgan's (2003a) characterisation of twentieth-century modern economics as an engineering science and the accompanying observation that 'during the 1930s, mathematics became attached to another tool – namely, "modeling" – to create a new style of scientific argument in economics' (Morgan 2003a: 286); and by Solow's (1997) similar characterisation of late twentieth-century economics not as formalistic, abstract, negligent of the real world, but as a model-building science obsessed with data.

2 It is the aim to understand the practice of economic research, but we are not discussing so-called 'lower-case-m' methodology, that is to say, the study of methods: the practical techniques employed by economists in the execution of their day-to-day professional activities. However, methodology has traditionally been about the appraisal of theories (see Hands 2001: 3). The aim is to redirect the focus of methodology to models.

3 A related account is Chao (2002), which discusses an econometric methodology of models, but from a semantic approach perspective.

4 This requirement of materiality for controllability (in the usual meaning of this term) has been discussed in Boumans and Morgan (2001) and Morgan (2003b). Both essays also treat the kinds of controllability that are possible in the case of quasi-material or non-material experiments.

5 Boumans (1999) provides, in addition to this one, two other exemplary cases of business-cycle modelling.

6 The original Polish text of 1933 is translated and published as 'Essay on the business cycle theory' (Kalecki 1990: 65–108) with only minor editorial corrections.

7 See for example testimonies of Robert Solow (1997: 48) and Robert Lucas (interviewed by Klamer 1984: 30).

8 For much more detail and background of this machine, see Leeson (2000).

9 A similar view is developed by Nancy Cartwright (1983) in her simulacrum account of models, see below.

10 Fleischhacker (1992) uses the term 'quasi-substance' to indicate that mathematical objects are analysable into matter and form. To emphasise their matter-aspect, I prefer the term quasi-matter.

11 E.g. R. Belmann and K. Cooke (1963) *Differential-Difference Equations*. However, the various mathematical aspects of this kind of equation attracted attention in the 1930s. In the first place, there is R. Frisch and H. Holme (1935) 'The characteristic solutions of a mixed difference and differential equation occurring in economic dynamics', which was a discussion of Kalecki's reduced form equation (1.8), but also three papers by R.W. James and M.H. Belz (1936) 'On a mixed difference and differential equation'; (1938a) 'The influence of distributed lags on Kalecki's theory of the trade cycle'; (1938b) 'The significance of the characteristic solutions of mixed difference and differential equations'.

12 As is known, Polya's heuristics functioned also as starting point for Lakatos' (1976) 'logic of mathematical discovery'. Although we share the view to consider mathematical objects as 'quasi-empirical' objects, we arrive at different methodologies.

2 A new practice

1 Qin (1993: 37) dates the 'creation' of this separate entity 'model' in econometrics in the same period. She explains this new creation by the conceptual separation of statistical laws from economic laws and the shift of use from mainly descriptive statistical tools to those of statistical inference. Although we agree on the standpoint that models must be seen as an answer to the difficulties of measuring laws directly, in my view one of the targets of modelling is still the measurement of economic laws. See Chapter 4.

2 In German philosophy, there is a distinction between 'Darstellung' and 'Vorstellung'. While a 'Vorstellung' is a passive mental image of a sense datum, a 'Darstellung' is a consciously constructed scheme for knowing (see Janik and Toulmin 1973: 139–40).

3 The original paper of 1936 is available in English under the title: 'An economic policy for 1936' in (Tinbergen 1959). For a revised version, which concentrates on econometric aspects, see (Tinbergen 1937).

4 Herbert Mehrtens (2004) discusses in detail these three-dimensional mathematical models.

5 The history given below is based on the works of two historians, the Dutch historian of mathematics, Gerard Alberts (1998), and the American historian of physics, Martin J. Klein (1970).

6 It is interesting to note that Morrison, who endorses a closely related model account (see e.g. Morrison 1999), also takes Maxwell's ideas on analogies as a starting point in her various papers (1992a, 1992b, 1995) on the role and function of models in physics.

7 Apart from a difference in materiality, the meaning of 'image' and 'model' in Hertz's *Principles* are so close that Janik and Toulmin (1973: 283 note 45) decided to deviate from the standard English translation and to render the term 'Bild' as 'model' and not as 'image'.

8 Some of the texts discussed in this chapter are written in German or Dutch. When I have translated quotes from these texts, these are indicated by 'trans'. Boltzmann translated and annotated Maxwell's papers of 1855 (1965a) and 1861(1965b) into German.

9 But it was J. Willard Gibbs who gave the name, 'statistical mechanics', to this new science in which the calculus of probabilities was applied to complex mechanical systems.

10 For detailed reconstruction of the arguments, see Klein (1970).

11 Following Pareto, Tinbergen called utility: 'ophelimity'.

12 Boumans (1993) discusses these four schemes in more detail.

13 This explains the name 'quadrature theory'. Quadrature stands for the process of determining the area of a plane geometric figure by dividing it into a collection of shapes of known area (usually rectangles) and then finding the sum of these areas. The integral denotes this process for infinitesimal rectangles.

14 This shipbuilding mechanism is, of course, the one that Kalecki successfully integrated in his macrodynamic model, as discussed in Chapter 1.

15 In his own day, Antoine-Augustin Cournot (1801–77) was better known as a philosopher of probabilities and chance (see Mirowski 1990: 590). In his 1908 paper 'The statistical complement of pure economics', written 'to indicate the manner in which the theory of economics and the science of statistics are being brought together' (p. 2), Moore refers to Cournot as having made 'very great contributions towards the construction of an inductive, statistical science' (p. 3).

16 There is apparently a misprint in the original text (p. 279). Above I have reproduced the corrected version.

17 Memorandum, League of Nations Economic Intelligence Theories of Business-Cycle Services of Mr Tinbergen 1936–7, class. no. 10B, list no. 19, file no. 25920 12653 (1936, Archive of the League of Nations, Palais de Nation, Genève). I would like to thank Pépin Cabo and Neil de Marchi for bringing this memorandum to my attention.

18 Morgan and Boumans (2004) discuss how A.W.H. Phillips built his famous hydraulic machine to get a grip on the macroeconomic thinking of his day, see also Chapter 1. It is an engineering way of understanding, through the 'eyes and fingers', labelled by Eugene Ferguson as understanding through the 'mind's eye', 'the organ in which a lifetime of sensory information – visual, tactile, muscular, visceral, aural, olfactory, and gustatory – is stored, interconnected, and interrelated' (Ferguson 1992: 42).

3 Autonomy

1 The quotation is from (Einstein 1954: 274). Holton corrected one line of mistranslation.

2 See for example the opening sentence of Aldrich's (1989) paper on Autonomy: 'Knowledge of structure is valuable and available – but only to those prepared to use both economic theory and statistical analysis.'

3 This similarity account is closely related to Ronald Giere (1999).

4 This memorandum was only available in mimeo from the University of Oslo, but is now (for the first time) published in Hendry and Morgan (1995). Page numbers refer to this latter published version.

5 This was not Frisch's terminology, nor Haavelmo's, but Koopmans'. Aldrich (1994) gives an account of the development of the identification theory from Frisch to Koopmans by focusing on Haavelmo (1944), including a discussion of the change in terminology.

6 The $i\theta$ range of equation (3.1) is the set $I \times \Theta$, $I \subset N$, and $\Theta \subset Re$; where N is the set of natural numbers and Re the set of real numbers.

7 Boumans (1995), which discusses the more technical details of Frisch's memorandum, also provides the derivation of this rule.

8 The superscript (n) indicates the order of the differential.

9 Without loss of generality, we assume that F is a monotonic non-decreasing function.

10 The Cowles Commission for Research in Economics was set up in 1932 to undertake econometric research. The journal *Econometrica*, in which Haavelmo's paper appeared, was run from the Cowles Commission.

11 Both monographs are considered as containing the main body of the Cowles Commission's theoretical results (see Christ 1994: 32).

12 But, as Christ (1994: 54) noted, the Cowles Commission had no method of testing whether the designation of variables as exogenous had been done correctly or not.

13 For a comprehensive discussion of this debate, see Morgan (1991).

4 Design of experiments

1 To avoid discussions about the correct naming of the techniques and methodology discussed here – the candidates are computer science, computational economics, artificial intelligence, artificial life, sciences of the artificial, etc. – the original name is chosen: Artificial Intelligence. Artificial intelligence can briefly be characterised as the discipline that tries to gain an understanding of systems of such complexity (like the mind) that they are beyond the scope of mathematics alone. In other words, the relevant point is the following: 'Given a certain model with a certain parameterization, can one reason, i.e. without running a simulation, *which* functions of the

parameterization the outcomes are?' (Vriend 1995: 212n). If not, computer simulations are appropriate.

2   It was essentially completed in 1948 but additional computational work was undertaken in 1949, so it actually appeared in 1950 (see Christ 1952: 41).

3   Friedman kept silent about Tinbergen's tests of mathematical significance (see Chapter 2), so his critique was only partly justified.

4   This refers, of course, to the better-known Alfred Marshall (1842–1924).

5   Mäki (1998b) suggests using the term 'realisticness' instead of 'realism' if one argues about a property or a set of properties of theories and their constituent parts. I follow his suggestion.

6   See Hirsch and De Marchi (1990) for an extensive discussion of Friedman's Methodology and its backgrounds.

7   Today, experimental economists (e.g. Smith 1982) have named it the problem of 'parallelism'. See Guala (1999) for a philosophical treatment of this problem of external validity.

8   Analysing matrix P with the slightly deviating P^* is closely related to the so-called 'perturbation theory' in physics. Perturbation theory is based on the idea of studying a system deviating slightly from an ideal system for which the complete solution is known. Perturbation theory for linear operators was created by Raleigh and Schrödinger. Mathematically speaking, the method is equivalent to an approximate solution of the 'eigenvalue' problem for a linear operator, slightly different from a simple operator for which the problem is completely solved.

9   Klein and Goldberger (1955: 70) had used the slower IBM Card Programmed Calculator.

10   For more about IPL-V and about the IBM 650, see a special issue of the *Annals of the History of Computing*, 8, 1986, no. 1, edited by C. Hurd.

11   I.e. that the facts of the world, properly viewed, are susceptible to simple summarisation and interpretation.

12   Or in more general terms, random walks, low-order autoregressive (AR) models, and simple autoregressive moving average (ARMA) models.

13   Neurath's example of a thousand dollar bill swept by the wind on Saint Stephen's Square.

5   Measurement

1   The term derives from the Greek *omo*, 'alike', and *morphosis*, 'to form' or 'to shape'. It denotes that the assignment M preserves the properties of the relational structure R.

2   See Savage and Ehrlich (1992) for a historical survey of measurement theory, and Finkelstein (1975) for a survey of the epistemological and logical foundations of measurement.

3   G.T. Fechner (1858) 'Das psychischen Mass'; (1887) 'Über die psychischen Massprincipien und das Weber'sche Gesetz'. See also Heidelberger (1993).

4   See, for example, Michell (1993) and Savage and Ehrlich (1992).

5   I have replaced the capitals Q and R in the original text by the lower case letters p and q, respectively, to make the discussion of the measurement literature uniform.

6   IVM is an abbreviation of 'International Vocabulary of Basic and General Terms in Metrology', which is an international agreement on terminology, prepared as a collaborative work of experts appointed by BIPM, IEC, IFCC, ISO, IUPA, IUPAC and OIML.

7   Ellis's account of associative measurement is based on Mach's chapter 'Kritik des Temperaturbegriffes' from his book *Die Principien der Wärmelehre* (1896). This chapter was translated into English and added to Ellis's (1968) book as Appendix I.

8   This difference in materiality has consequences for the functioning of the *ceteris paribus* conditions, see Boumans and Morgan (2001). See also Chapter 4.

9   In the case of derived measurement there exist independent measurements of the q^i, but not of p. The discussion below includes this type of measurement, too.

10 The French-German chemist and physicist Henri Victor Regnault (1810–78) was famous for his studies on chlorine compounds and his determinations of the physical properties of gases. He was appointed to the Chair of Experimental Physics in Paris at the Collège de France, where he had at his disposal a well-equipped laboratory to carry out his experiments on gases (see Williams 1982: 438).

11 Along with this definition it is noted that 'accuracy' is a qualitative concept and that the term 'precision' should not be used for 'accuracy' (IVM 1993: 24).

12 These issues are also discussed by Nancy Cartwright (1991) in a comment on Collins (1991), where she uses the term 'replicability' instead of 'repeatability'.

13 Originally the standard of length was a prototype metre held in the Archives de France, and therefore called the 'Mètre des Archives', and constructed in 1889 to be one ten-millionth of the meridian through Paris from pole to equator. Since 1983 the metre is defined as the length of the path travelled by light in vacuum during a time interval of 1/299 792 458 of a second. The standard kilogram is still today equal to a prototype held in the Archives de France, the 'Kilogramme des Archives', since 1889.

14 The mass of the international prototype increases by approximately 1 part in 10^9 per year due to the inevitable accumulation of contaminants on its surface. For this reason, the CIPM declared that, pending further research, the reference mass of the international prototype is that immediately after cleaning and washing by a specified method (BIPM 1998: 140).

15 Of course there are forerunners, but they did not label their method of parameterisation as calibration.

Appendix 1: Output–inflation tradeoffs

1   The proper output–inflation tradeoff is $\pi/(1 - \pi)$, linking output and inflation:

$$y_t = y_{nt} + \frac{\pi}{1-\pi}\left(P_t - \overline{P_t}\right) + \lambda y_{c,t-1}$$

If π increases from zero to 1, $\pi/(1 - \pi)$ will increase from zero to infinity.

2   This shift from testing the model to testing an implication of the model has been critically discussed in Kim, De Marchi and Morgan (1995), see Chapter 4.

3   Froyen and Waud considered the variance of the inflation rate, σ_p^2, instead of the variance of the general price level, σ^2. Because $\sigma_p^2 = 2\sigma^2$, I have replaced σ_p^2 by σ^2 to make the discussion uniform.

4   In the same way that $x + y + z = 0$ only represents a negative correlation between x and y when z is fixed.

Appendix 2: Filters

1   For a historical account of the Kalman filter, see Klein (2001) and Kailath (1974).

2   The Hodrick–Prescott filter was originally introduced in a 1981 working paper. The 1997 paper is 'substantially the same' as their 1981 one.

3   Though a random walk is not a stationary time series, Bell (1984) shows that equation (A2.3) can be applied to a random walk for signal extraction formulae like a Hodrick–Prescott filter.

6   Rigour

1   This account was opposed by Imre Lakatos (1976), which he labelled as 'formalism'. He showed that mathematics grows as an informal, quasi-empirical discipline.
2   See also Roy Weintraub's essay in *The Age of Economic Measurement* (2001) edited by Mary S. Morgan and Judy Klein. There are two other case studies in this volume in which rigour is not equated with axiomatics. These are Flavio Comim's (2001) discussion of Stone's treatment of consistency in the measurement of national accounts and Martin Kohli's (2001) account of the development of Wassily Leontief's input–output tables.
3   Bos (2001) gives a detailed historical account of the arguments of mathematicians concerning the acceptability of mathematical procedures. However, he prefers to call this quality of mathematical procedures that makes them acceptable 'exactness' instead of 'rigorness', because the latter is used in connection with proofs rather than with constructions.
4   Kline (1972) discusses this implication extensively.
5   Manuscripts and Archives, Yale University Library.
6   The hydrostatic mechanism had also actually been constructed twice. Photographs of both these models were reproduced in Fisher ([1892] 1925).
7   Mary Morgan (1999) provides a detailed account of how Fisher, in his *Purchasing Power of Money* ([1911] 1963), learned about the monetary system by building and using models.
8   A price level depends only on prices of a relevant year, whereas in a price index the prices of two years are compared. Although this might seem to be trivial, it is essential. Eichhorn and Voeller (1976: 59) show that 'the version of Fisher's equation of exchange considered in most textbooks is not correct'; namely equation (6.1) does not hold as P is interpreted as a price level instead of a price index.
9   Diewert (1998) distinguishes four main approaches to index number theory: (1) statistical; (2) test or axiomatic; (3) microeconomic, which relies on the assumption of maximising or minimising behaviour; and (4) neostatistical. Note that Diewert equates the test and axiomatic approach, whereas in this chapter they are treated separately.

Bibliography

Aczél, J. (1966) *Lectures on Functional Equations and Their Applications*, New York: Academic Press.

Adelman, I. (1968) 'Simulation: economic processes', in D.L. Sills (ed.) *International Encyclopedia of the Social Sciences*, vol. 14, New York: Macmillan and The Free Press.

Adelman, I. and Adelman, F.L. (1959) 'The dynamic properties of the Klein–Goldberger model', *Econometrica*, 27: 596–625.

Aftalion, A. (1927) 'The theory of economic cycles based on the capitalistic technique of production', *Review of Economic Statistics*, 9: 165–70.

Alberts, G. (1998) *Jaren van berekening, toepassingsgerichte initiatieven in de Nederlandse wiskundebeoefening 1945–1960*, Amsterdam: Amsterdam University Press.

Aldrich, J. (1989) 'Autonomy', in N. de Marchi and C. Gilbert (eds) *History and Methodology of Econometrics*, Oxford: Clarendon Press.

Aldrich, J. (1994) 'Haavelmo's identification theory', *Econometric Theory*, 10: 198–219.

Allais, M. (1968) 'Irving Fisher', in D.L. Sills (ed.) *International Encyclopedia of the Social Sciences*, vol. 5, New York: Macmillan and The Free Press.

Allen, R.L. (1993) *Irving Fisher, A Biography*, Cambridge, MA: Blackwell.

Anderson, T.W. (1950) 'Estimation of the parameters of a single equation by the limited-information maximum-likelihood method', in T.C. Koopmans (ed.) *Statistical Inference in Dynamic Economic Models*, Cowles Commission monograph 10, New York: Wiley.

Anderson, T.W. and Rubin, H. (1949) 'Estimation of the parameter of a single stochastic difference equation in a complete system', *Annals of Mathematical Statistics*, 20: 46–63.

Ando, A. (1963) 'Introduction', in A. Ando, F.M. Fisher and H.A. Simon, *Essays on the Structure of Social Science Models*, Cambridge, MA: MIT Press.

Ando, A. (1979) 'On the contributions of Herbert A. Simon to economics', *Scandinavian Journal of Economics*, 21: 83–93.

Arrow, K.J. (1960) 'The work of Ragnar Frisch, econometrician', *Econometrica*, 28: 175–92.

Arrow, K.J. (1992) 'I know a hawk from a handsaw', in M. Szenberg (ed.) *Eminent Economists: Their Life Philosophies*, Cambridge: Cambridge University Press.

Bell, W. (1984) 'Signal extraction for nonstationary time series', *Annals of Statistics*, 12: 646–64.

Belmann, R. and Cooke, K. (1963) *Differential–Difference Equations*, New York: Academic Press.

188 *Bibliography*

BIPM (1998) *The International System of Units*, 7th edn, Sèvres: Bureau International des Poids et Mesures.

Bogen, J. and Woodward, J. (1988) 'Saving the phenomena', *Philosophical Review*, 97: 303–52.

Boland, L.A. (1979) 'A critique of Friedman's critics', *Journal of Economic Literature*, 17: 503–22.

Boltzmann, L. [1892] 'Über die Methoden der theoretischen Physik', in W. Dyck (ed.) *Katalog Mathematischer und Mathematisch-Physikalischer Modelle, Apparate und Instrumente*, München: Wolf; reprinted as 'On the method of theoretical physics', in B. McGuinness (ed.) (1974) *Theoretical Physics and Philosophical Problems*, Dordrecht: Reidel.

Boltzmann, L. [1899a] 'On the development of the methods of theoretical physics in recent times', in B. McGuinness (ed.) (1974) *Theoretical Physics and Philosophical Problems*, Dordrecht: Reidel.

Boltzmann, L. [1899b] 'On the fundamental principles and equations of mechanics', in B. McGuinness (ed.) (1974) *Theoretical Physics and Philosophical Problems*, Dordrecht: Reidel.

Boltzmann, L. (1902a) 'Model', in *Encyclopaedia Britannica*, 10th edn, vol. 30, London: The Times Printing House; reprinted in B. McGuinness (ed.) (1974) *Theoretical Physics and Philosophical Problems*, Dordrecht: Reidel.

Boltzmann, L. [1902b] 'On the principles of mechanics', in B. McGuinness (ed.) (1974) *Theoretical Physics and Philosophical Problems*, Dordrecht: Reidel.

Boltzmann, L. (1912) 'Anmerkungen', in L. Boltzmann (ed.) *Faradays Kraftlinien von J.C. Maxwell*, Leipzig: Engelmann.

Borel, E. (1915) 'Molecular theories and mathematics', *The Rice Institute Pamphlet*, 1: 163–93.

Bos, H.J.M. (2001) *Redefining Geometrical Exactness: Descartes' Transformation of the Early Modern Concept of Construction*, New York: Springer.

Boulding, K.J. (1948) *Economic Analysis*, revised edn, New York: Harper.

Boumans, M. (1993) 'Paul Ehrenfest and Jan Tinbergen: a case of limited physics transfer', in N. de Marchi (ed.) *Non-Natural Social Science: Reflecting on the Enterprise of More Heat than Light*, Durham: Duke University Press.

Boumans, M. (1995) 'Frisch on testing of business cycle theories', *Journal of Econometrics*, 67: 129–47.

Boumans, M. (1999) 'Built-in justification', in M.S. Morgan and M. Morrison (eds) *Models as Mediators*, Cambridge: Cambridge University Press.

Boumans, M. (2001) 'Fisher's instrumental approach to index numbers', in J.L. Klein and M.S. Morgan (eds) *The Age of Economic Measurement*, Durham: Duke University Press.

Boumans, M. and Morgan, M.S. (2001) '*Ceteris paribus* conditions: materiality and the applications of economic theories', *Journal of Economic Methodology*, 8: 11–26.

Bracey, R.J. (1960) *The Technique of Optical Instrument Design*, London: English University Press.

Bullock, C.J., Persons, W.M. and Crum, W.L. (1927) 'The construction and interpretation of the Harvard index of business conditions', *Review of Economic Statistics*, 9: 74–92.

Bumstead, H.A. [1906] (1961) 'Biographical sketch', in H.A. Bumstead and R. Gibbs Van Name (eds) *The Scientific Papers of J. Willard Gibbs*, New York: Dover.

Burns, A.F. and Mitchell, W.C. (1946) *Measuring Business Cycles*, New York: National Bureau of Economic Research.

Cannon, S.F. (1978) *Science in Culture: The Early Victorian Period*, New York: Dawson and Science History Publications.

Cartwright, N. (1983) *How the Laws of Physics Lie*, Oxford: Clarendon Press.

Cartwright, N. (1991) 'Replicability, reproducibility, and robustness: comments on Harry Collins', *History of Political Economy*, 23: 143–55.

Cartwright, N. (1999) *The Dappled World. A Study of the Boundaries of Science*, Cambridge: Cambridge University Press.

Chang, H. (2001) 'Spirit, air, and quicksilver: the search for the "real" scale of temperature', *Historical Studies in the Physical and Biological Sciences*, 31: 249–84.

Chao, H.-K. (2002) 'Representation and structure: the methodology of econometric models of consumptions', PhD Thesis, University of Amsterdam.

Chipman, J.S., Hurwicz, L., Richter, M.K. and Sonnenschein, H.F. (eds) (1971) *Preferences, Utility, and Demand*, New York: Harcourt Brace Jovanovich.

Christ, C.F. (1951) 'A test of an econometric model for the United States, 1921–1947', in *Conference on Business Cycles*, New York: National Bureau of Economic Research.

Christ, C.F. (1952) 'History of the Cowles Commission 1932–1952', in *Economic Theory and Measurement*, Chicago: Cowles Commission for Research in Economics.

Christ, C.F. (1994) 'The Cowles Commission's contributions to econometrics at Chicago, 1939–1955', *Journal of Economic Literature*, 32: 30–59.

Cogley, T. and Nason, J.M. (1995) 'Effects of the Hodrick–Prescott filter on trend and difference stationary time series: implications for business cycle research', *Journal of Economic Dynamics and Control*, 19: 253–78.

Collins, H.M. (1991) 'The meaning of replication and the science of economics', *History of Political Economy*, 23: 123–42.

Comim, F. (2001) 'Richard Stone and measurement criteria for national accounts', in J.L. Klein and M.S. Morgan (eds) *The Age of Economic Measurement*, Durham: Duke University Press.

Cooley, T.F. and Prescott, E.C. (1995) 'Economic growth and business cycles', in T.F. Cooley (ed.) *Frontiers of Business Cycle Research*, Princeton: Princeton University Press.

Cornwall, J. (1958) 'Economic implications of the Klein and Goldberger model', *Econometrica*, 26: 621.

Cowles Commission (1952) *Economic Theory and Measurement*, Chicago: Cowles Commission for Research in Economics.

Cournot, A.A. [1838] (1971) *Researches into the Mathematical Principles of the Theory of Wealth*, trans. N.T. Bacon, New York: Augustus M. Kelley.

Cukierman, A. and Wachtel, P. (1979) 'Differential inflationary expectations and the variability of the rate of inflation: theory and evidence', *American Economic Review*, 69: 595–609.

Dawkins, C., Srinivasan, T.N. and Whalley, J. (2001) 'Calibration', in J.J. Heckman and E.E. Leamer (eds) *Handbook of Econometrics*, vol. 5, Amsterdam: Elsevier.

Dawson, R.E. (1962) 'Simulation in the social sciences', in H. Guetzkow (ed.) *Simulation in Social Science: Readings*, Englewood Cliffs, NJ: Prentice Hall.

De Marchi, N. and Gilbert, C. (1989) 'Introduction', in N. de Marchi and C. Gilbert (eds) *History and Methodology of Econometrics*, Oxford: Clarendon Press.

De Regt, H.W. (1999) 'Ludwig Boltzmann's *Bildtheorie* and scientific understanding', *Synthese*, 119: 113–34.

Diewert, W.E. (1998) 'Index numbers', in J. Eatwell, M. Milgate and P. Newman (eds) *The New Palgrave: A Dictionary of Economics*, London: Macmillan.

Duhem, P. (1954) *The Aim and Structure of Physical Theory*, trans. P.P. Wiener, Princeton: Princeton University Press.

Dusenberry, J.S., Fromm, G., Klein, L.R. and Kuh, E. (eds) (1965) *The Brookings Quarterly Econometric Model of the United States*, Chicago: Rand McNally.

Edgeworth, F.Y. (1887, 1888) 'Report on the best methods of ascertaining and measuring variations in the value of the monetary standard', *Report of the British Association for the Advancement of Science*, 1887: 247–301, 1888: 181–209.

Ehrenfest, P. and Ehrenfest, T. (1912) 'Begriffliche Grundlagen der statistischen Auffassung in der Mechanik', in F. Klein and C. Müller (eds) *Encyklopädie der Mathematischen Wissenschaften*, vol. 4:2:2 no. 6, Leipzig: Teubner; reprinted in *The Conceptual Foundations of the Statistical Approach in Mechanics* (1990), trans. M.J. Moravcsik, New York: Dover.

Eichhorn, W. (1973) 'Zur axiomatischen Theorie des Preisindex', *Demonstratio Mathematica*, 6: 561–73.

Eichhorn, W. (1976) 'Fisher's tests revisited', *Econometrica*, 44: 247–55.

Eichhorn, W. (1978) 'What is an economic index? An attempt of an answer', in W. Eichhorn, R. Henn, O. Opitz and R.W. Shephard (eds) *Theory and Applications of Economic Indices*, Würzburg: Physica-Verlag.

Eichhorn, W. and Voeller, J. (1976) *Theory of the Price Index*, Berlin: Springer-Verlag.

Einstein, A. (1954) 'On the method of theoretical physics', in *Ideas and Opinions*, New York: Crown Trade Paperbacks.

Ellis, B. (1968) *Basic Concepts of Measurement*, Cambridge: Cambridge University Press.

Elzas, M.S. (1984) 'System paradigms as reality mappings', in T.I. Ören, B.P. Zeigler and M.S. Elzas (eds) *Simulation and Model-Based Methodologies: An Integrative View*, Berlin: Springer-Verlag.

Fair, R.C. (1992) 'The Cowles Commission approach, real business cycle theories, and New Keynesian economics', Working Paper 3990, Cambridge: National Bureau of Economic Research.

Fechner, G.T. (1858) 'Das psychischen Mass', *Zeitschrift für Philosophie und philosophische Kritik*, 32: 1–24.

Fechner, G.T. (1887) 'Über die psychischen Massprincipien und das Weber'sche Gesetz', *Philosophische Studien*, 4: 161–230.

Ferguson, E.S. (1992) *Engineering and the Mind's Eye*, Cambridge, MA: MIT Press.

Finkelstein, L. (1975) 'Fundamental concepts of measurement: definition and scales', *Measurement and Control*, 8: 105–10.

Finkelstein, L. (1982) 'Theory and philosophy of measurement', in P.H. Sydenham (ed.) *Handbook of Measurement Science, Volume 1: Theoretical Fundamentals*, Chichester: Wiley.

Fisher, I. (1890) 'Mathematical contribution to philosophy; attacking Kant's theory of geometrical axioms', unpublished manuscript, Fisher's Archives, Yale University.

Fisher, I. (1903) 'A new tent for the treatment of tuberculosis', *Journal of the American Medical Association*, 26: 1576–7.

Fisher, I. (1906) 'A new method for indicating food values', *American Journal of Physiology*, 15: 417–32.

Fisher, I. (1917) 'The "ratio" chart, for plotting statistics', *Quarterly Publications of the American Statistical Association*, 15: 577–601.

Fisher, I. (1921) 'The best form of index number', *Quarterly Publication of the American Statistical Association*, 17: 533–7.

Fisher, I. [1892] (1925) *Mathematical Investigations in the Theory of Value and Prices*, New Haven: Yale University Press.

Fisher, I. (1930) 'The application of mathematics to the social sciences', *Journal of the American Statistical Association*, 36: 225–43.

Fisher, I. (1939) 'A three-dimensional representation of the factors of production and their remuneration, marginally and residually', *Econometrica*, 7: 304–11.

Fisher, I. (1943) 'A world map on a regular icosahedron by gnomonic projection', *Geographical Review*, 33: 605–19.

Fisher, I. [1911] (1963) *The Purchasing Power of Money: its determination and relation to Credit, Interest and Crises*, 2nd rev. edn, New York: Kelley.

Fisher, I. [1922] (1967) *The Making of Index Numbers: A Study of Their Varieties, Tests, and Reliability*, 3rd rev. edn, New York: Kelley.

Fisher, I. (1997) *The Works of Irving Fisher*, vol. 13, W.J. Barber (ed.), London: Pickering and Chatto.

Fisher, I. and Miller, O.M. (1944) *World Maps and Globes*, New York: Essential Books.

Fleischhacker, L. (1992) 'Mathematical abstraction, idealisation and intelligibility in science', in C. Dilworth (ed.) *Idealization IV: Intelligibility in Science*, Amsterdam and Atlanta, GA: Rodopi.

Franklin, A. (1986) *The Neglect of Experiment*, Cambridge: Cambridge University Press.

Franklin, A. (1997) 'Calibration', *Perspectives on Science*, 5: 31–80.

Friedman, M. (1940) 'Business cycles in the United States of America, 1919–1932. By Jan Tinbergen. Vol. II', *American Economic Review*, 30: 657–60.

Friedman, M. (1949) 'The Marshallian demand curve', *Journal of Political Economy*, 57: 463–95.

Friedman, M. (1951) 'Comment', in *Conference on Business Cycles*, New York: National Bureau of Economic Research.

Friedman, M. (1953) 'The methodology of positive economics', in *Essays in Positive Economics*, Chicago and London: University of Chicago Press.

Friedman, M. and Schwartz, A.J. (1963) *A Monetary History of the United States, 1867–1960*, New York: Princeton University Press.

Frisch, R. (1930) 'Necessary and sufficient conditions regarding the form of an index number which shall meet certain of Fisher's tests', *Journal of the American Statistical Association*, 25: 397–406.

Frisch, R. (1933a) 'Editorial', *Econometrica*, 1: 1–4.

Frisch, R. (1933b) 'Propagation problems and impulse problems in dynamic economics', in *Economic Essays in Honour of Gustav Cassel*, London: Allen and Unwin.

Frisch, R. (1934) 'Reply to Mr. Subramanian's note', *Journal of the American Statistical Association*, 29: 317.

Frisch, R. (1936) 'Annual survey of general economic theory: the problem of index numbers', *Econometrica*, 4: 1–38.

Frisch, R. (1948) 'Repercussion studies at Oslo', *American Economic Review*, 38: 367–72.

Frisch, R. [1926] (1971) 'On a problem in pure economics', in J.S. Chipman, L. Hurwicz, M.K. Richter and H.F. Sonnenschein (eds) *Preferences, Utility, and Demand*, New York: Harcourt Brace Jovanovich.

Frisch, R. [1938] (1995) 'Statistical versus theoretical relations in economic macro-dynamics', in D.F. Hendry and M.S. Morgan (eds) *The Foundations of Econometric Analysis*, Cambridge: Cambridge University Press.

Frisch, R. and Holme, H. (1935) 'The characteristic solutions of a mixed difference and differential equation occurring in economic dynamics', *Econometrica*, 3: 225–39.

Froyen, R.T. and Waud, R.N. (1980) 'Further international evidence on output–inflation tradeoffs', *American Economic Review*, 70: 409–21.

Gibbs, J.W. [1902] (1960) *Elementary Principles in Statistical Mechanics, Developed with Special Reference to the Rational Foundation of Thermodynamics*, New York: Dover.

Gibbs, J.W. [1873] (1961) *The Scientific Papers of J. Willard Gibbs*, H.A. Bumstead and R. Gibbs Van Name (eds), New York: Dover.

Giere, R.N. (1999) 'Using models to represent reality', in L. Magnani, N.J. Nersessian and P. Thagard (eds) *Model-Based Reasoning in Scientific Discovery*, New York: Kluwer Academic/Plenum.

Girshick, M.A. and Haavelmo, T. (1953) 'Statistical analysis of the demand for food: examples of simultaneous estimation of structural equations', in W.C. Hood and T.C. Koopmans (eds) *Studies in Econometric Method*, Cowles Commission monograph 14, New York: Wiley.

Goldberger, A.S. (1958) 'Properties of an econometric model of the United States', *Econometrica*, 26: 620.

Goodwin, R. (1948) 'Secular and cyclical aspects of the multiplier and the accelerator', in L.A. Metzler (ed.) *Income, Employment and Public Policy: Essays in Honor of Alvin H. Hansen*, New York: Norton.

Gouriéroux, C. and Monfort, A. (1996) *Simulation-Based Econometric Methods*, Oxford: Oxford University Press.

Granger, C.W.J. (1999) *Empirical Modeling in Economics: Specification and Evaluation*, Cambridge: Cambridge University Press.

Gregory, A.W. and Smith, G.W. (1990) 'Calibration as estimation', *Econometric Reviews*, 9: 57–89.

Gregory, A.W. and Smith, G.W. (1991) 'Calibration as testing: inference in simulated macroeconomic models', *Journal of Business and Economic Statistics*, 9: 297–303.

Gregory, A.W. and Smith, G.W. (1993) 'Statistical aspects of calibration in macro-economics', in G.S. Maddala, C.R. Rao and H.D. Vinod (eds) *Handbook of Statistics*, vol. 11, Amsterdam: North-Holland.

Guala, F. (1999) 'The problem of external validity (or "parallelism") in experimental economics', *Social Science Information*, 38: 555–73.

Haavelmo, T. (1940) 'The inadequacy of testing dynamic theory by comparing theoretical solutions and observed cycles', *Econometrica*, 8: 312–21.

Haavelmo, T. (1944) 'The probability approach in econometrics', supplement to *Econometrica*, 12.

Haavelmo, T. (1950) 'Remarks on Frisch's confluence analysis and its use in econometrics', in T.C. Koopmans (ed.) *Statistical Inference in Dynamic Economic Models*, Cowles Commission monograph 10, New York: Wiley.

Hacche, G. (1979) *The Theory of Economic Growth: An Introduction*, London: Macmillan Press.

Hammond, J.D. (1991) 'Alfred Marshall's methodology', *Methodus*, 3: 95–101.

Hanau, A. (1928) *Die Prognose der Schweinepreise*, Vierteljahrshefte zur Konjunktur-forschung, Sonderheft 7.

Hanau, A. (1930) *Die Prognose der Schweinepreise*, Vierteljahrshefte zur Konjunktur-forschung, Sonderheft 18.

Hands, D.W. (2001) *Reflection without Rules: Economic Methodology and Contemporary Science Theory*, Cambridge: Cambridge University Press.

Hansen, L.P. and Heckman, J.J. (1996) 'The empirical foundations of calibration', *Journal of Economic Perspectives*, 10: 87–104.

Harvey, A.C. and Jaeger, A. (1993) 'Detrending, stylized facts and the business cycle', *Journal of Applied Econometrics*, 8: 231–47.

Harvey, C.R. (1991) 'The term structure and world economic growth', *Journal of Fixed Income*, 1: 7–19.

Hausman, D.M. (1992) *The Inexact and Separate Science of Economics*, Cambridge: Cambridge University Press.

Heath, T.L. (1956) *The Thirteen Books of Euclid's Elements*, vol. 1, New York: Dover.

Heidelberger, M. (1993) 'Fechner's impact for measurement theory', *Behavioral and Brain Sciences*, 16: 146–8.

Heidelberger, M. (1994a) 'Alternative Interpretationen der Repräsentationstheorie der Messung', in G. Meggle and U. Wessels (eds) *Proceedings of the 1st Conference 'Perspectives in Analytical Philosophy'*, Berlin and New York: Walter de Gruyter.

Heidelberger, M. (1994b) 'Three strands in the history of the representational theory of measurement', unpublished paper, Humboldt University, Berlin.

Helmholtz, H. von (1876, 1878) 'The origin and meaning of geometrical axioms', *Mind*, 1: 301–21, 3: 212–25.

Helmholtz, H. von (1887) 'Zählen und Messen, erkenntnis-theoretisch betrachtet', *Philosophische Aufsätze: Eduard Zeller zu seinem fünfzig jährigen Doctor-Jubiläum gewidmet*, Leipzig: Fues.

Hendry, D.F. and Morgan, M.S. (eds) (1995) *The Foundations of Econometric Analysis*, Cambridge: Cambridge University Press.

Hertz, H. [1899] (1956) *The Principles of Mechanics Presented in a New Form*, New York: Dover.

Hertz, H. [1893] (1962) *Electric Waves*, New York: Dover.

Hilbert, D. (1902) 'Mathematical problems, lecture delivered before the international congress of mathematicians at Paris in 1900', trans. M. Winston Newson, *Bulletin of the American Mathematical Society*, 8: 437–79.

Hirsch, A. and De Marchi, N. (1990) *Milton Friedman: Economics in Theory and Practice*, Ann Arbor: University of Michigan Press.

Hodrick, R.J. and Prescott, E.C. (1997) 'Postwar U.S. business cycles: an empirical investigation', *Journal of Money, Credit, and Banking*, 29: 1–16.

Holton, G. (1973) *Thematic Origins of Scientific Thought: Kepler to Einstein*, Cambridge, MA: Harvard University Press.

Hood, W.C. and Koopmans, T.C. (eds) (1953) *Studies in Econometric Method*, Cowles Commission monograph 14, New York: Wiley.

Hoover, K.D. (1988) *The New Classical Macroeconomics: A Sceptical Inquiry*, Oxford: Basil Blackwell.

Hoover, K.D. (1994) 'Econometrics as observation: the Lucas critique and the nature of econometric inference', *Journal of Economic Methodology*, 1: 65–80.

Hoover, K.D. (1995a) 'The problem of macroeconometrics', in K.D. Hoover (ed.) *Macroeconometrics: Developments, Tensions and Prospects*, Boston: Kluwer.

Hoover, K.D. (1995b) 'Facts and artifacts: calibration and the empirical assessment of real-business-cycle models', *Oxford Economic Papers*, 47: 24–44.

Hoover, K.D. (2001) *Causality in Macroeconomics*, Cambridge: Cambridge University Press.

Hoover, K.D. (2002) 'Econometrics and reality', in U. Mäki (ed.) *Fact and Fiction in Economics: Models, Realism and Social Construction*, Cambridge: Cambridge University Press.

Hurd, C.C. (ed.) (1986) *Annals of the History of Computing* 8.1, special issue: IBM 650.

Israel, G. (1981) ' "Rigor" and "axiomatics" in modern mathematics', *Fundamenta Scientiae*, 2: 205–19.

IVM (1993) *International Vocabulary of Basic and General Terms in Metrology*, 2nd edn, Geneva: International Organization for Standardization.

Jaeger, A. (1994) 'Mechanical detrending by Hodrick–Prescott filtering: a note', *Empirical Economics*, 19: 493–500.

James, R.W. and Belz, M.H. (1936) 'On a mixed difference and differential equation', *Econometrica*, 4: 157–60.

James, R.W. and Belz, M.H. (1938a) 'The influence of distributed lags on Kalecki's theory of the trade cycle', *Econometrica*, 6: 159–62.

James, R.W. and Belz, M.H. (1938b) 'The significance of the characteristic solutions of mixed difference and differential equations', *Econometrica*, 6: 326–43.

Janik, A. and Toulmin, S. (1973) *Wittgenstein's Vienna*, New York: Simon and Schuster.

Jeffreys, H. (1948) *Theory of Probability*, 2nd edn, Oxford: Clarendon Press.

Jourdain, P.E.B. [1912] (1988) 'The nature of mathematics', in J.R. Newman (ed.) *The World of Mathematics*, vol. 1, Redmond: Tempus Books.

Kailath, T. (1974) 'A view of three decades of linear filtering theory', *IEEE Transactions on Information Theory*, IT-20: 146–81.

Kaldor, N. [1958] (1978) 'Capital accumulation and economic growth', in *Further Essays on Economic Theory*, London: Duckworth.

Kalecki, M. (1935) 'A macrodynamic theory of business cycles', *Econometrica*, 3: 327–44.

Kalecki, M. (1990) 'Essay on the business cycle theory', in J. Osiatynski (ed.) *Collected Works of Michal Kalecki, Volume I: Capitalism, Business Cycles and Full Employment*, Oxford: Clarendon.

Kalman, R.E. (1960) 'A new approach to linear filtering and prediction problems', *Journal of Basic Engineering. Transactions of the ASME*, 82: 35–45.

Karsten, K.G. (1924) 'The theory of quadrature in economics', *Journal of the American Statistical Association*, 19: 14–27.

Karsten, K.G. (1926) 'The Harvard business indexes – a new interpretation', *Journal of the American Statistical Association*, 21: 399–418.

Kendall, M.G. and Buckland, W.R. (1960) *A Dictionary of Statistical Terms*, Edinburgh and London: Oliver and Boyd.

Kendall, M.G. and Stuart, A. (1966) *The Advanced Theory of Statistics, Volume 3: Design and Analysis, and Time-Series*, London: Charles Griffin.

Keynes, J.M. (1911) 'Review of "The Purchasing Power of Money"', *Economic Journal*, 21: 393–8.

Keynes, J.M. (1936) *The General Theory of Employment, Interest and Money*, London: Macmillan.

Keynes, J.M. (1939) 'Professor Tinbergen's method', *Economic Journal*, 49: 558–68.

Kim, J., De Marchi, N. and Morgan, M.S. (1995) 'Empirical model particularities and belief in the natural rate hypothesis', *Journal of Econometrics*, 67: 81–102.

Kim, K. and Pagan, A.R. (1995) 'The econometric analysis of calibrated macroeconomic models', in M.H. Pesaran and M.R. Wickens (eds) *Handbook of Applied Econometrics*, Oxford: Blackwell.

King, R.G. and Rebelo, S.T. (1993) 'Low frequency filtering and real business cycles', *Journal of Economic Dynamics and Control*, 17: 207–31.

Klamer, A. (1984) *The New Classical Macroeconomics: Conservations with the new Classical Economists and their Opponents*, Brighton: Harvester Press.

Klein, J.L. (2001) 'Optimization and recursive residuals in the space age: Sputnik and the Kalman filter', unpublished paper, Mary Baldwin College.

Klein, J.L. (forthcoming) *Engineering the Imperative Mood: The Wartime Nexus of Economics, Statistics, and Control Engineering*.

Klein, L.R. (1950) *Economic Fluctuations in the United States, 1921–1941*. Cowles Commission monograph 11, New York: Wiley.

Klein, L.R. (1992) 'My professional life philosophy', in M. Szenberg (ed.) *Eminent Economists: Their Life Philosophies*, Cambridge: Cambridge University Press.

Klein, L.R. and Goldberger, A.S. (1955) *An Econometric Model of the United States, 1929–1952*, Amsterdam: North-Holland.

Klein, M.J. (1970) *Paul Ehrenfest. Volume 1: The Making of a Theoretical Physicist*, Amsterdam: North-Holland.

Kline, M. (1972) *Mathematical Thought from Ancient to Modern Times*, New York: Oxford University Press.

Kohli, M.C. (2001) 'Leontief and the U.S. Bureau of Labor Statistics, 1941–54: developing a framework for measurement', in J.L. Klein and M.S. Morgan (eds) *The Age of Economic Measurement*, Durham: Duke University Press.

Koopmans, T.C. (1950) 'When is an equation system complete for statistical purposes?', in T.C. Koopmans (ed.) *Statistical Inference in Dynamic Economic Models*, Cowles Commission monograph 10, New York: Wiley.

Koopmans, T.C. and Hood, W.C. (1953) 'The estimation of simultaneous linear economic relationships', in W.C. Hood and T.C. Koopmans (eds) *Studies in Econometric Method*, Cowles Commission monograph 14, New York: Wiley.

Koopmans, T.C., Rubin, H. and Leipnik, R.B. (1950) 'Measuring the equation systems of dynamic economics', in T.C. Koopmans (ed.) *Statistical Inference in Dynamic Economic Models*, Cowles Commission monograph 10, New York: Wiley.

Krantz, D.H., Luce, R.D., Suppes, P. and Tversky, A. (1971) *Foundations of Measurement, Volume 1: Additive and Polynomial Representations*, New York: Academic Press.

Kydland, F.E. and Prescott, E.C. (1982) 'Time to build and aggregate fluctuations', *Econometrica*, 50: 1345–70.

Kydland, F.E. and Prescott, E.C. (1990) 'Business cycles: real facts and a monetary myth', *Federal Reserve Bank of Minneapolis Quarterly Review*, 14: 3–18.

Kydland, F.E. and Prescott, E.C. (1991) 'The econometrics of the general equilibrium approach to business cycles', *Scandinavian Journal of Economics*, 93: 161–78.

Kydland, F.E. and Prescott, E.C. (1996) 'The computational experiment: an econometric tool', *Journal of Economic Perspectives*, 10: 69–85.

Lakatos, I. (1976) *Proofs and Refutations: The Logic of Mathematical Discovery*, in J. Worrall and E. Zahar (eds), Cambridge: Cambridge University Press.

Lane, D.A. (1993) 'Artificial worlds and economics', *Journal of Evolutionary Economics*, 3: 89–107, 177–97.

Latour, B. (1986) 'Visualization and cognition: thinking with eyes and hands', *Knowledge and Society*, 6: 1–40.

Leeson, R. (ed.) (2000) *A.W.H. Phillips: Collected Works in Contemporary Perspective*, Cambridge: Cambridge University Press.

Littauer, S.B. (1950) 'Report of the New York meeting of the Institute', *Annals of Mathematical Statistics*, 21: 151–5.

Lucas, R.E. (1972) 'Econometric testing of the natural rate hypothesis', in O. Eckstein (ed.) *The Econometrics of Price Determination*, Washington, DC: Board of Governors of the Federal Reserve System.

Lucas, R.E. (1973) 'Some international evidence on output–inflation tradeoffs', *American Economic Review*, 63: 326–34.

Lucas, R.E. (1976) 'Econometric policy evaluation: a critique', in K. Brunner and A.H. Meltzer (eds) *The Phillips Curve and Labor Markets*, Amsterdam: North-Holland.

Lucas, R.E. (1977) 'Understanding business cycles', in K. Brunner and A.H. Meltzer (eds) *Stabilization of the Domestic and International Economy*, Amsterdam: North-Holland.

Lucas, R.E. (1980) 'Methods and problems in business cycle theory', *Journal of Money, Credit, and Banking*, 12: 696–715.

Lucas, R.E. (1981) *Studies in Business-Cycle Theory*, Oxford: Basil Blackwell.

Lucas, R.E. (1987a) *Models of Business Cycles*, Oxford: Basil Blackwell.

Lucas, R.E. (1987b) 'Adaptive behavior and economic theory', in R.M. Hogarth and M.W. Reder (eds) *Rational Choice: The Contrast between Economics and Psychology*, Chicago: University of Chicago Press.

Lucas, R.E. (1988) 'On the mechanics of economic development', *Journal of Monetary Economics*, 22: 3–42.

Maas, H. (2001) 'An instrument can make a science: Jevons's balancing acts in economics', in M.S. Morgan and J. Klein (eds) *The Age of Economic Measurement*, Durham: Duke University Press.

Maas, H. (forthcoming a) 'Jevons, William Stanley', in K. Kempf-Leonard (ed.) *Encyclopedia of Social Measurement*, New York: Academic Press.

Maas, H. (forthcoming b) *William Stanley Jevons and the Making of Modern Economics*, Cambridge: Cambridge University Press.

Mach, E. (1896) *Die Principien der Wärmelehre*, Leipzig: Johan Ambrosius Barth.

Mach, E. [1896] (1966) 'Critique of the concept of temperature', in B. Ellis (1966) *Basic Concepts of Measurement*, trans. M.J. Scott-Taggart and B. Ellis, Cambridge: Cambridge University Press.

Machamer, P. (1998) 'Galileo's machines, his mathematics, and his experiments', in P. Machamer (ed.), *The Cambridge Companion to Galileo*, Cambridge: Cambridge University Press.

Machamer, P., Darden, L. and Craver, C.F. (2000) 'Thinking about mechanisms', *Philosophy of Science*, 67: 1–25.

Magnus, J.R. and Morgan, M.S. (1987) 'The ET interview: Professor J. Tinbergen', *Econometric Theory*, 3: 117–42.

Mäki, U. (1998a) 'Ceteris Paribus', in J.B. Davis, D.W. Hands and U. Mäki (eds) *The Handbook of Economic Methodology*, Cheltenham: Edward Elgar.

Mäki, U. (1998b) 'Realisticness', in J.B. Davis, D.W. Hands and U. Mäki (eds) *The Handbook of Economic Methodology*, Cheltenham: Edward Elgar.

Malinvaud, E. (1966) *Statistical Methods of Econometrics*, Amsterdam: North-Holland.

Marschak, J. (1934) 'The meeting of the Econometric Society in Leyden, September–October, 1933', *Econometrica*, 2: 187–203.

Marshall, A. (1920) *Principles of Economics*, 8th edn, London: Macmillan.

Marshall, A. [1898] (1925) 'Mechanical and biological analogies in economics', in A.C. Pigou (ed.) *Memorials of Alfred Marshall*, London: Macmillan.

Marshall, A.W. (1950a) 'A test of Klein's model III for changes of structure', *Annals of Mathematical Statistics*, 21: 141.

Marshall, A.W. (1950b) 'A test of Klein's model III for changes of structure', *Econometrica*, 18: 291.

Maxwell, J.C. [1855] (1965a) 'On Faraday's lines of force', in W.D. Niven (ed.) *The Scientific Papers of James Clerk Maxwell*, vol. I, New York: Dover.

Maxwell, J.C. [1861] (1965b) 'On physical lines of force', in W.D. Niven (ed.) *The Scientific Papers of James Clerk Maxwell*, vol. I, New York: Dover.

Maxwell, J.C. [1865] (1965c) 'A dynamical theory of the electromagnetic field', in W.D. Niven (ed.) *The Scientific Papers of James Clerk Maxwell*, vol. I, New York: Dover.

Maxwell, J.C. [1871] (1965d) 'On the mathematical classification of physical quantities', in W.D. Niven (ed.) *The Scientific Papers of James Clerk Maxwell*, vol. II, New York: Dover.

Maxwell, J.C. [1857] (1990) 'On the measurement of quantities', in P.M. Harman (ed.) *The Scientific Letters and Papers of James Clerk Maxwell*, vol. I, Cambridge: Cambridge University Press.

Mehrtens, H. (2004) 'Mathematical models', in S. de Chadarevian and N. Hopwood (eds) *Models: The Third Dimension of Science*, Stanford: Stanford University Press.

Michell, J. (1993) 'The origins of the representational theory of measurement: Helmholtz, Hölder, and Russell', *Studies in History and Philosophy of Science*, 24: 185–206.

Mirowski, P. (1990) 'Problems in the paternity of econometrics: Henry Ludwell Moore', *History of Political Economy*, 22: 587–609.

Mirowski, P. (2002) *Machine Dreams: Economics Becomes a Cyborg Science*, Cambridge: Cambridge University Press.

Mitchell, W.C. (1927) *Business Cycles. The Problem and its Setting*, New York: National Bureau of Economic Research.

Mitchell, W.C. (1951) *What Happens During Business Cycles*, New York: National Bureau of Economic Research.

Moore, H.L. (1908) 'The statistical complement of pure economics', *Quarterly Journal of Economics*, 23: 1–33.

Moore, H.L. (1929) *Synthetic Economics*, New York: Macmillan.

Morgan, M.S. (1988) 'Finding a satisfactory empirical model', in N. de Marchi (ed.) *The Popperian Legacy in Economics*, Cambridge: Cambridge University Press.

Morgan, M.S. (1990) *The History of Econometric Ideas*, Cambridge: Cambridge University Press.

Morgan, M.S. (1991) 'The stamping out of process analysis in econometrics', in N. de Marchi and M. Blaug (eds) *Appraising Economic Theories: Studies in the Methodology of Research Programs*, Aldershot: Edward Elgar.

Morgan, M.S. (1999) 'Learning from models', in M.S. Morgan and M. Morrison (eds) *Models as Mediators*, Cambridge: Cambridge University Press.

Morgan, M.S. (2002) 'Seeing the world in models', unpublished working paper, University of Amsterdam and London School of Economics.

Morgan, M.S. (2003a) 'Economics', in T.M. Porter and D. Ross (eds) *The Cambridge History of Science, Vol. 7 The Modern Social Sciences*, Cambridge: Cambridge University Press.

Morgan, M.S. (2003b) 'Experiments without material intervention: model experiments, virtual experiments and virtually experiments', in H. Radder (ed.) *The Philosophy of Scientific Experimentation*, Pittsburgh: Pittsburgh University Press.

Morgan, M.S. and Boumans, M. (2004) 'Secrets hidden by two-dimensionality: the economy as a hydraulic machine', in S. de Chadarevian and N. Hopwood (eds) *Models: The Third Dimension of Science*, Stanford: Stanford University Press.

Morrison, M. (1992a) 'Some complexities of experimental evidence', in D. Hull and M. Forbes (eds) *Philosophy of Science Association Proceedings*, vol. 1: 49–62.

Morrison, M. (1992b) 'A study in theory unification: the case of Maxwell's electromagnetic theory', *Studies in History and Philosophy of Science*, 23: 103–45.

Morrison, M. (1995) 'Scientific conclusions and philosophical arguments: an inessential tension', in J.Z. Buchwald (ed.) *Scientific Practice: Theories and Stories of Doing Physics*, Chicago: University of Chicago Press.

Morrison, M. (1999) 'Models as autonomous agents', in M.S. Morgan and M. Morrison (eds) *Models as Mediators*, Cambridge: Cambridge University Press.

Morrison, M. and Morgan, M.S. (1999) 'Models as mediating instruments', in M.S. Morgan and M. Morrison (eds) *Models as Mediators*, Cambridge: Cambridge University Press.

Musgrave, A. (1981) ' "Unreal assumptions" in economic theory: the F-twist untwisted', *Kyklos*, 34: 377–87.

Nagel, E. (1961) *The Structure of Science: Problems in the Logic of Scientific Explanation*, London: Routledge and Kegan Paul.

Osiatynski, J. (ed.) (1990) *Collected Works of Michal Kalecki, Volume I: Capitalism, Business Cycles and Full Employment*, Oxford: Clarendon Press.

OED (1933) *Oxford English Dictionary*, Oxford: Clarendon Press.

Pagan, A. (1994) 'Introduction calibration and econometric research: an overview', *Journal of Applied Econometrics*, 9: S1–S10.

Persons, W.M. (1919) 'An index of general business conditions', *Review of Economic Statistics*, 1: 111–205.

Pfanzagl, J. (1968) *Theory of Measurement*, Würzburg: Physica-Verlag.

Phillips, A.W. and Fisher, I. (1896) *Elements of Geometry*, New York: American Book Company.

Polya, G. (1957) *How To Solve It: A New Aspect of Mathematical Method*, Princeton: Princeton University Press.

Popper, K.R. (1968) 'Epistemology without a knowing subject', in B. van Rootselaar and J.F. Staal (eds) *Logic, Methodology and Philosophy of Science III*, Amsterdam: North-Holland.

Prescott, E.C. (1986) 'Theory ahead of business cycle measurement', *Federal Reserve Bank of Minneapolis Quarterly Review*, 10: 9–22.

Prescott, E.C. (1998) 'Business cycle research: methods and problems', working paper, Federal Reserve Bank of Minneapolis.

Qin, D. (1993) *The Formation of Econometrics: A Historical Perspective*, Oxford: Clarendon Press.

Quah, D.T. (1995) 'Controversy; business cycle empirics: calibration and estimation', *Economic Journal*, 105: 1594–6.

'Report of the New York meeting December 27–30, 1949' (1950) *Econometrica*, 18: 264–7.

Riemann, B. (1882) 'On the hypotheses which lie at the bases of geometry', trans. W.K. Clifford, in W.K. Clifford, *Mathematical Papers*, R. Tucker (ed.), London: Macmillan.

Roos, C.F. (1930) 'A mathematical theory of price and production fluctuations and economic crises', *Journal of Political Economy*, 38: 501–22.

Samuelson, P.A. (1952) 'Economic theory and mathematics – an appraisal', *American Economic Review, Papers and Proceedings*, 42: 56–66.

Samuelson, P.A. and Swamy, S. (1974) 'Invariant economic index numbers and canonical duality: survey and synthesis', *American Economic Review*, 64: 566–93.

Savage, C.W. and Ehrlich, P. (1992) 'A brief introduction to measurement theory and to the essays', in C.W. Savage and P. Ehrlich (eds) *Philosophical and Foundational Issues in Measurement Theory*, Hillsdale, NJ: Lawrence Erlbaum Associates.

Simon, H.A. (1951) 'Theory of automata', *Econometrica*, 19: 72.

Simon, H.A. (1953) 'Causal ordering and identifiability', in W.C. Hood and T.C. Koopmans (eds) *Studies in Econometric Method*, Cowles Commission monograph 14, New York: Wiley.

Simon, H.A. (1962) 'The architecture of complexity', *Proceedings of the American Philosophical Society*, 106: 467–82.

Simon, H.A. (1968) 'On judging the plausibility of theories', in B. van Rootselaar and J.F. Staal (eds) *Logic, Methodology and Philosophy of Science III*, Amsterdam: North-Holland.

Simon, H.A. (1969) *The Sciences of the Artificial*, Cambridge, MA: MIT Press.

Simon, H.A. (1977) *Models of Discovery*, Dordrecht: Reidel.

Simon, H.A. (1984) 'On the behavioral and rational foundations of economic dynamics', *Journal of Economic Behavior and Organizations*, 5: 35–55.

Simon, H.A. and Ando, A. (1961) 'Aggregation of variables in dynamic systems', *Econometrica*, 29: 111–38.

Simon, H.A. and Iwasaki, Y. (1988) 'Causal ordering, comparative statics, near decomposability', *Journal of Econometrics*, 39: 149–73.

Slutzky, E. (1937) 'The summation of random causes as the source of cyclic processes', *Econometrica*, 5: 105–46.

Smith, V.L. (1982) 'Microeconomic systems as an experimental science', *American Economic Review*, 72: 923–55.

Snowdon, B., Vane, H. and Wynarczyk, P. (1994) *A Modern Guide to Macroeconomics: An Introduction to Competing Schools of Thought*, Cheltenham: Edward Elgar.

Solow, R.M. (1970) *Growth Theory: An Exposition*, Oxford: Clarendon Press.

Solow, R.M. (1997) 'How did economics get that way and what way did it get?', *Dædalus*, 126: 39–58.

Staehle, H. (1933) 'La réunion de la société d'econometrie, Lausanne, Septembre, 1931', *Econometrica*, 1: 73–86.

Staehle, H. (1937) 'Report of the fifth European meeting of the Econometric Society', *Econometrica*, 5: 87–102.

Stehling, F. (1993) 'Wolfgang Eichhorn and the art of model building', in W.E. Diewert, K. Spremann and F. Stehling (eds) *Mathematical Modelling in Economics: Essays in Honor of Wolfgang Eichhorn*, Berlin: Springer-Verlag.

Stevens, S.S. (1959) 'Measurement, psychophysics, and utility', in C.W. Churchman and P. Ratoosh (eds) *Measurement: Definitions and Theories*, New York: Wiley.

Swamy, S. (1934) 'On a certain conclusion of Frisch's', *Journal of the American Statistical Association*, 29: 316–7.

Swamy, S. (1940) 'Compatibility of Fisher's tests for index number formulae', *Mathematics Student*, 8: 124–7.

Swamy, S. (1965) 'Consistency of Fisher's tests', *Econometrica*, 33: 619–23.

Sydenham, P.H. (1979) *Measuring Instruments: Tools of Knowledge and Control*, London: Peter Peregrinus.

Sydenham, P.H. (1982) 'Measurements, models, and systems', in P.H. Sydenham (ed.) *Handbook of Measurement Science, Volume 1: Theoretical Fundamentals*, Chichester: Wiley.

Taylor, B.N. and Kuyatt, C.E. (1994) *Guidelines for Evaluating and Expressing the Uncertainty of NIST Measurement Results*, NIST Technical Note 1297, Gaithersburg: Physics Laboratory, National Institute of Standards and Technology.

Thomson, W. [1884] (1987) 'Notes of lectures on molecular dynamics and the wave theory of light', in R. Kargon and P. Achinstein (eds) *Kelvin's Baltimore Lectures and Modern Theoretical Physics*, Cambridge, MA: MIT Press.

Tinbergen, J. (1927) 'Over de mathematies-statistiese methoden voor konjunktuuronderzoek', *De Economist*, 11: 711–23.

Tinbergen, J. (1928) 'Opmerkingen over ruilteorie', *Socialistische Gids*, 13: 431–45, 539–48.

Tinbergen, J. (1929a) *Minimumproblemen in de Natuurkunde en de Ekonomie*, Amsterdam: Paris.

Tinbergen, J. (1929b) 'Konjunkturforschung und Variationsrechnung', *Archiv für Sozialwissenschaft und Sozialpolitik*, 61: 533–41.

Tinbergen, J. (1930) 'Bestimmung und Deutung von Angebotskurven. Ein Beispiel', *Zeitschrift für Nationalökonomie*, 1: 669–79.

Tinbergen, J. (1931) 'Ein Schiffbauzyklus?', *Weltwirtschaftliches Archiv*, 34: 152–64.

Tinbergen, J. (1932) 'Ein Problem der Dynamik', *Zeitschrift für Nationalökonomie*, 3: 169–84.

Tinbergen, J. (1933a) 'Het waarnemen van maatschappelijke verschijnselen', in *De Uitdrukkingswijze der Wetenschap*, Groningen: Noordhoff.

Tinbergen, J. (1933b) 'The notions of horizon and expectancy in dynamic economics', *Econometrica*, 1: 247–64.

Tinbergen, J. (1933c) 'L'utilisation des équations fonctionnelles et des nombres complexes dans les recherches économiques, *Econometrica*, 1: 36–51.

Tinbergen, J. (1933d) *Statistiek en Wiskunde in Dienst van het Konjunktuuronderzoek*, Amsterdam: Arbeiderspers.

Tinbergen, J. (1935a) 'Quantitative Fragen der Konjunkturpolitik', *Weltwirtschaftliches Archiv*, 42: 366–99.

Tinbergen, J. (1935b) 'Annual survey: suggestions on quantitative business cycle theory', *Econometrica*, 3: 241–308.

Tinbergen, J. (1936a) 'Kan hier te lande, al dan niet na overheidsingrijpen, een verbetering van de binnenlandse conjunctuur intreden, ook zonder verbetering van onze exportpositie?' in *Prae-adviezen voor de Vereeniging voor de Staathuishoudkunde en de Statistiek*, The Hague: Nijhoff.

Tinbergen, J. (1936b) 'Memorandum on the continuation of the League's business cycle research in a statistical direction', unpublished memorandum, Archive of the League of Nations, Geneva.

Tinbergen, J. (1937) *An Econometric Approach to Business Cycle Problems*, Paris: Hermann.

Tinbergen, J. (1939a) *Statistical Testing of Business-Cycle Theories I: A Method and its Application to Investment Activity*, Geneva: League of Nations.

Tinbergen, J. (1939b) *Statistical Testing of Business-Cycle Theories II:P Business Cycles in the United States of America*, Geneva: League of Nations.

Tinbergen, J. [1936] (1959) 'An economic policy for 1936', in L.H. Klaassen, L.M. Koyck and H.J. Witteveen (eds) *Jan Tinbergen – Selected Papers*, Amsterdam: North-Holland.

Tinbergen, J. (1988) 'Recollections of professional experiences', in J.A. Kregel (ed.) *Recollections of Eminent Economists*, vol. 1, Basingstoke: Macmillan.

Tinbergen, J. and Van Luytelaer, T. (1932) 'De koffievalorisaties: geschiedenis en resultaten', *De Economist*, 7/8: 517–38.

Tobin, J. (1987) 'Irving Fisher', in J. Eatwell, M. Milgate and P. Newman (eds) *The New Palgrave: A Dictionary of Economics*, London: Macmillan.

Turing, A.M. (1950) 'Computing machinery and intelligence', *Mind*, 59: 433–60.

Vinci, F. (1934) 'Significant developments in business cycle theory', *Econometrica*, 2: 125–39.

Vining, D.R. and Elwertowski, T.C. (1976) 'The relationship between relative prices and the general price level', *American Economic Review*, 66: 699–708.

Vogt, A. and Barta, J. (1997) *The Making of Tests for Index Numbers: Mathematical Methods of Descriptive Statistics*, Heidelberg: Physica-Verlag.

von Neumann, J. (1961) 'The mathematician', in A.H. Taub (ed.) *John von Neumann. Collected works*, vol. 1, Oxford: Pergamon Press.

von Neumann, J. [1951] (1963) 'The general and logical theory of automata', in A.H. Taub (ed.) *John von Neumann. Collected works*, vol. 5, Oxford: Pergamon Press.

Vriend, N.J. (1995) 'Self-organization of markets: an example of a computational approach', *Computational Economics*, 8: 205–31.

Wald, A. (1937) 'Zur Theorie der Preisindexziffern', *Zeitschrift für Nationalökonomie*, 8: 179–219.

Watson, M.W. (1993) 'Measures of fit for calibrated models', *Journal of Political Economy*, 101: 1011–41.

Weintraub, E.R. (1998) 'From rigor to axiomatics: the marginalization of Griffith C. Evans', in M.S. Morgan and M. Rutherford (eds) *From Interwar Pluralism to Postwar Neoclassicim*, Durham: Duke University Press.

Weintraub, E.R. (2001) 'Measurement, and changing images of mathematical knowledge', in J.L. Klein and M.S. Morgan (eds) *The Age of Economic Measurement*, Durham: Duke University Press.

Weintraub, E.R. (2002) *How Economics Became a Mathematical Science*, Durham: Duke University Press.

Williams, T.I. (1982) *A Biographical Dictionary of Scientists*, London: Black.

Woodward, J. (1989) 'Data and phenomena', *Synthese*, 79: 393–472.

Woodward, J. (2000) 'Explanation and invariance in the special sciences', *British Journal for the Philosophy of Science*, 51: 197–254.

Zambelli, S. (1992) 'The wooden horse that wouldn't rock: reconsidering Frisch', in K. Velupillai (ed.) *Nonlinearities, Disequilibria and Simulation*, Basingstoke: Macmillan.

Zellner, A. (1979) 'Statistical analysis of econometric models', *Journal of the American Statistical Association*, 74: 628–43.

Zellner, A. (1988) 'Causality and causal laws in economics', *Journal of Econometrics*, 39: 7–21.

Zellner, A. (1994) 'Time-series analysis, forecasting and econometric modelling: the structural econometric modelling, time-series analysis (SEMTSA) approach', *Journal of Forecasting*, 13: 215–33.

Zellner, A. (2001) 'Keep it sophisticatedly simple', in A. Zellner, H.A. Keuzenkamp and M. McAleer (eds) *Simplicity, Inference and Modelling*, Cambridge: Cambridge University Press.

Index